# FRANCIS WARNER AND TRADITION

# FRANCIS WARNER

# AND

# TRADITION

## An introduction to the plays

### Glyn Pursglove

COLIN SMYTHE
Gerrards Cross, Bucks

HUMANITIES PRESS
Atlantic Highlands, N.J.

Copyright © 1981 Glyn Pursglove

First published in 1981 by Colin Smythe Limited
Gerrards Cross, Buckinghamshire


**British Library Cataloguing in Publication Data**

Pursglove, Glyn
   Francis Warner and tradition.
   1. Warner, Francis — Criticism and
   interpretation
   I. Title
   822'.914        PR6073.A7238Z/

   ISBN 0—86140—083—6

First published in North America by
Humanities Press Inc. 171 First Avenue
Atlantic Highlands, N.J. 07716
ISBN 0-391-02394-2




Produced in Great Britain

Set by Janice Buchanan
and printed and bound by Billing & Sons Limited
Guildford, London, Worcester, Oxford

# Contents

v

# Illustrations

# Acknowledgements

I should like to thank Miss Rosalind Jeffrey for her kindness in allowing me to read and benefit from her *Chess in the Mirror: A Study of Theatrical Cubism in Francis Warner's Requiem and its Maquettes*, prior to its recent publication. I am grateful to Miss Khairat Al-Saleh for her assistance. Martin Woodhead has read some parts of this study, and I have gained much from his knowledge and perception. Parts of Chapters I and VIII were first published in the collection of essays *Francis Warner: Poet and Dramatist*, edited by Tim Prentki and published by Sceptre Press in 1977.

My title acknowledges a debt to F. A. C. Wilson's work on Yeats — a debt owed by both author and subject of this study.

I am most grateful to A. H. Buck, Sarah Horne and John Havelda for their meticulous reading of the book in proof. The errors which remain are my own.

I am indebted to the Musée d' Art moderne de la Ville de Paris for permission to reproduce Picasso's "Le pigeon aux petits pois".

# Abbreviations used in referring to the works of Francis Warner

| | |
|---|---|
| CL | *A Conception of Love* (1978) |
| EP | *Early Poems* (1964) |
| ES | *Experimental Sonnets* (1965) |
| KT | *Killing Time* (1976) |
| LF | *Lying Figures* (1972) |
| LS | *Light Shadows* (1980) |
| M | *Maquettes* (1972) |
| Mad | *Madrigals* (1967) |
| ME | *Meeting Ends* (1974) |
| P | *Perennia* (1962) |
| PFW | *The Poetry of Francis Warner* (1970) |
| R | *Requiem* (1980) |

Above dates are those of first publication, and page references are in all cases made to editions of those dates.

# I

# Introduction: Erected Wit and Infected Will

Francis Warner's work as a dramatist began with the trilogy of one act plays *Maquettes*. These were in the nature of studies for the larger *Requiem* trilogy which was to follow. *Maquettes* was first performed in July 1970. Prior to that, Warner's reputation was as a poet. At first sight there appears to be little or no continuity between poems and plays. The poetry is largely, though not exclusively, pastoral in character, and many of the best poems have a clarity and lucidity of manner and meaning quite different from the surrealistic complexity of the plays. Yet there is a continuity between Warner's use of the two forms of expression. As with all worthwhile artists there exists a unity of thought and imaginative coherence underlying all superficial differences.

One aspect of that continuity is merely external. Several of the lyrics in the plays were not written at the same time as the rest of the play in which they are 'set'. Rather the lyrics are taken from the earlier volumes of poetry and are re-used in the plays as part of a larger, more diverse, vision of things. So, for example, 'Aubade' published in the volume *Madrigals* of 1967 is incorporated in *Lying Figures*, as the opening of Act Four. Several small alterations of text are made, but the poem is substantially unchanged, and its division between two speakers (Laz and Sapphira) merely makes literal something which was already implied typographically in the original. The poem which succeeds 'Aubade' in *Madrigals* is 'Bright Apricot'. This too is pressed into dramatic service, this time in *Lumen*. Only one small change of punctuation is made, but the poem's significance is radically altered by the theatrical comment provided after its closing lines. The poem talks of those "secrecies" which

1

make night fall
And our soft bird his breathing song of bridal call.

In *Lumen* that exquisite closing line is immediately followed by a stage-direction:

*Lights down as cuckoo calls, twice.*   (*M*, 46; *R*, 66)

One other poem from *Madrigals* is put to later use in the plays. The lyric 'Close, close tight buds' is spoken by Kuru as the conclusion of Act One of *Killing Time*. Indeed, even after the *Requiem* plays Warner continues to make use of his earlier poems. 'There is no splendour in the sun' from *Early Poems* of 1964 becomes a love lyric for Gan in *A Conception of Love* (*CL*, 71). That such poems, written a number of years before the plays, should fit so neatly into the later and larger works is, of itself, evidence of a coherency of vision underlying poems and plays.

Even in Warner's earliest poems there are clear statements of some of the themes which were to be central in the plays. His earliest published volume was *Perennia*, an epyllion in Spenserian stanzas, first published by Raymond Lister's Golden Head Press at Cambridge in 1962. *Perennia* sets up a duality which was to play an important part in the later plays. Perennia is a Psyche figure:

And then more lovely than a well-played lute
The voice of Eros spoke beside her ear
Telling her to go in and eat the fruit
That lay upon the table, and to cheer
Herself with honey-mead, the country beer;
And tell him all that she had felt that day;
To lie down on the bed of maiden-hair
And spend the hours in happiness and play
Of childish innocence while he beside her lay.   (*P*, 16)

The idyll is soon to be fractured by "Salt Salacia/Her elder sister" (*P*, 16). Salacia's jealousy takes a particularly insidious form. Lacking any faith in the beyond, she tempts Perennia in a speech which adroitly inverts the languages of love and lust:

'Sweet sister,' then she smiled, 'this luxury
Of animals and birds for retinue
May fascinate; but can your Eros be
So radiant that he must hide from you

In stealthy midnight visitings his true
Form? Can he be a pure, immortal child
Such as you say? If he is fine to view,
Why does he hide a body that is mild
And harmless? He may be a beast, gross and defiled,

'For many a satyr has an easy charm
And glowing look, insinuating trust
That merely leads us on to our own harm
Till we are prostituted to its lust
And every passionate and goatish gust
That shudders through its body. Though he fawns
And flatters you with presents, yet you must
Fly from this place before full morning dawns
And listen to the loving voice of one who warns. (*P*, 17)

The ironies are delightful. Salacia can see the birds only in terms of luxury. Her choice of noun tells us much about her. In stanza XXI the 'retinue' had been presented to us in a catalogue of birds directly in the tradition of Guillaume de Lorris and Alanus de Insulis. Chalone's words at the end of *Killing Time* come to mind: "Birds are divine remembrancers" (*KT*, 70; *R*, 194). The single word "luxury" fills out our own understanding of Salacia's character (Latin *salax* bears the senses both of 'lustful' and of 'that which provokes to lust'). The contrast between Salacia and Perennia, embodied in their contrasted attitudes (and, indeed, in their names) is a contrast which evolves as a central theme in the plays. In Warner's plays, most of the characters are spiritually blind, their energies absorbed in the palpable. Some few individuals, however, do "look towards the beyond" (to borrow the words of Professor Wind, which make up the epigraph to *Perennia*) as the beginning of an attempt to "become balanced in the present".[1]

Another early poem, 'For a Child', appropriately presents matters in the very simplest of terms:

If you cultivate your shell
And starve the kernel in its cell,
When the earth gives you her bed,
Your true part is maggoted.

You are sleeping in this life
In a shadow world of strife;
Yet when the dream grows old and lame
You will wake to life again. (*EP*, 23)

The "shadow world of strife" would be a very fair description of much
that we see in the plays, most notably the *Requiem* plays and *Light
Shadows*. The shadow itself, as my second chapter seeks to demonstrate,
is a potent symbol in Warner's theatre. In *Killing Time* — "a shadow
world of strife" if ever there was one — Kuru and Quark approach, but
fail to achieve, a degree of understanding akin to that expressed so
transparently in 'For a Child'. They fail because, like Salacia, they are
unable to distinguish between desire and love:

| | |
|---|---|
| QUARK | Perhaps when they're that old the fire dies and desires decay. |
| KURU | But love is life's reason! |
| QUARK | Then that's how nature prepares us for death. |
| KURU | I was prepared for life by travelling on a football train. I was sitting in a compartment and in came six hooting fans. They mucked about, and I laughed with them, until they held me across their knees and played around till my bra was off. Then each had a feel with the blinds down. I didn't see a thing — could hardly breathe. Oh, they had a good look. And I was so scared I just giggled all the time. What a nit I was! I'd charge them now. |

(*KT*, 24; *R*, 148)

Kuru's narrative illustrates to perfection the darkened world of the
sensualist:

> each had a feel with the blinds down. I didn't see a
> thing.

and the consequent suffocation of real human vitality:

> [I] could hardly breathe.

This contrast between 'love' and 'desire' is part of the larger contrast
between those who look to this world as the source of their ecstasy,
and those able, or at any rate eager, to look beyond it. It is a contrast
expressed within the *Requiem* plays by an antithesis between love and
marriage. The nearest approaches to love in the trilogy (e.g. Ensoff and
Agappy, Ensoff and Callisterne, Quark and Kuru — as mother and
daughter) are all of them relationships which are specifically non-
marital. The comic vision of *A Conception of Love* in part resides in
the fact that it, on the other hand, sees love and marriage as compatible.
At least one early poem expresses precisely the antithesis that we see
in the *Requiem* plays:

When the wild
Rose is snapped,
And the child
Caught and trapped,
When the hare
Is crushed in the road,
A mental snare
Starts to corrode.

Love is beyond
The worldly man.
Marriage bond
Of Pot and Pan
Is a pale
Mockery;
Lifelong stale
Lechery.

Death's a brave
Ranting shout
In an empty cave;
Life gutters out.
Limbs of an antelope
Stretched in the grass
Make us grope
For the mountain pass.

When the slender
Primrose shoot
Pushing tender
Underfoot
Makes the child
Leap in the womb;
Then undefiled
Will the wild rose bloom.   (*EP*, 10)

In terms of both image and theme there is much here that will be
developed in the dramatic works. Even such details as "the slender/
Primrose shoot/Pushing tender/Underfoot" and the candle of human
life which "gutters out" will recur later. The second stanza is a relatively
straightforward statement of a motif explored in greater detail in the
*Maquettes* and the *Requiem* plays. The poems differ from the plays,
above all, with regard to questions of balance and emphasis. Many of

the best poems celebrate the rare moments of perfected meaning discovered and experienced. Two poems from *Madrigals* will make the
point clearly:

> Love is imaginative sympathy
> Pure in unlimited intensity
> And constant love the truest chastity —
>   So, even such,
>   Your touch.   (*Mad*, 8)

> Your love, perfection's crown, to me is strength,
> Harbour and sanctuary after storm;
> My only-wished renown; the breadth and length
> Of all ideals, and their shaping form.
> I know this is not new, a thousand men
> Have made their loves immortal in a song,
> Paid court and flattered, wooed in verse, and then
> Sewn up unbounded passion with a thong;
> And yet, and yet . . . Why is it each believes
> His is the incontestable delight?
> We cannot measure how another grieves —
> How then reflect our universe of light?
>   Yet, knowing this, I say in spite of all
>   That no man's heart was ever half so full.   (*Mad*, 9)

Poetry's purpose here is to celebrate the moments lived in the "universe
of light". The sense increases, however, that this is too limited and too
limiting a conception. *Experimental Sonnets* contains a number of
poems which confront a range of experiences falling well outside that
"universe of light". The very first sonnet poses the problem:

> In order that some splinter may remain
> Of all that glory, here, in my poor verse,
> Let me evoke the strained, satanic pain
> Of vivisecting parting, and rehearse
> Those moments of brief immortality
> Lying oblivious and locked in one.   (*ES*, 7)

Elsewhere the poet feels himself "one little fragment of the night"
(*ES*, 8) and shows himself well aware of the "splendour of man's
insignificance" (*ES*, 11). Mortality is now a more demanding presence:

Is the high lark, dawn's song-drenched accolade,
Only a small grey hopper round a spade?     (*ES*, 21)

It is the presence of love which makes the world anything more than a
place of "the sodden shroud", "the white, gorged worm" and "inevitable
dark" (*ES*, 22). Life may be no more than a "pantomime" (*ES*, 30),
but perhaps there is greater darkness to fear. Sonnet XXII confronts the
possibility, and does so in a fashion which points forward directly to
the 'Requiem' plays:

> Should we preserve intensity alone?
> The string vibrating at the 'cello's bridge?
> Or stretch to nerve the fingerboard's full range
> In orchestrating waste's cacophonics?
> Is poignancy of beauty's transience
> As time runs over an apple in the stream —
> The hesitancy of a summer's dusk
> When night-stock stuns with scent — ours to forego?
> Must we desert court-ladies on the grass
> Their sunlit dappled breasts and lovers' lutes?
> The skill of craftsman-wrought, firm, rounded themes;
> The guests of Mozart, Purcell and Watteau?
>     Bear with me if I leave such scenes behind:
>     The dark offstage preoccupies my mind.(*ES*, 28)

The first two lines pose as a possibility the continuation of the kind of
poetic conception we have just traced; poems of the "unlimited inten-
sity" achieved in that love which is "imaginative sympathy" (*Mad*, 8);
the second two lines pose a very different possibility — the possibility
realised in the plays. "Waste's cacaphonics" are there explored, and the
fingerboard's full range is certainly exploited as Warner fuses dramatic
resources and methods from a number of different traditions. The
perfectly-formed lucidity of the lyrics, with their "craftsman-wrought,
firm, rounded themes" is left behind, and the dark is confronted more
directly. That the theatrical metaphor dominates the final couplet is
perhaps an indication of Warner's own awareness of the direction that
his writing was to take.

In confronting the darkness, Warner presents an image of it which is
by no means drawn merely from observation of the modern world. It
is an analysis of more than contemporary difficulties, and the plays
stand outside the mainstream of contemporary English drama in
offering no political comment. Warner's vision seems rather to take

sustenance from older and more enduring traditions. It is much influenced, for example, by the tradition of Hermeticism. Beyond matters of detail, we might observe that Warner's dramatic world has much in common with the bleaker passages in the texts of Hermes Trismegistus. One such famous passage is quoted by F. A. C. Wilson — with whose work on Yeats Warner was intimately involved[2] — and will serve to demonstrate the affinity. The passage describes the state of things at the end of a historical cycle:

No-one shall look up to heaven. The religious man shall be accounted insane, the irreligious shall be thought wise, the furious brave, and the worst of men shall be considered a good man. For the soul and all things about it, by which it is either naturally immortal, or conceives that it shall attain to immortality, conformably to what I have explained to you, shall not only be the subject of laughter, but shall be considered as vanity. Believe me likewise, that a capital punishment shall be appointed for him who applies himself to the religion of intellect. New statutes and new laws shall be established, and nothing religious or which is worthy of heaven, or celestial concerns, shall be heard, or believed by the mind. There shall be a lamentable departure of the Gods from men, evil daemons will alone remain, who being mingled with human nature will violently impel the miserable men of that time to war, to rapine, to fraud, and to every thing contrary to the nature of the soul. Every divine voice shall be dumb by a necessary silence.

God's vengeance will necessarily follow. God

washing away all malignity by a deluge, or consuming it by fire, or bringing it to an end by disease and pestilence dispersed in different planes, will restore the world to its ancient form.[3]

Ensoff's punishment is not, in this text's sense, capital, but the evil daemons certainly abound. War, rapine and fraud are not far to seek in the *Requiem* plays or in *Light Shadows*. The divine voices are not, however, silenced absolutely. Chalone may tell us that

if humanity is a race then the game is lost, the future has run out.

(*KT*, 1; *R*, 125)

but he can also remind us that

In the kingdom of light are many rivers. While we linger and tarry on earth the hour of our going, whether it is at midnight or in the morning, is of no moment in the dazzling eyes of God. (*KT*, 45; *R*, 169)

Even in the comedy, *A Conception of Love*, we encounter Fashshar's assertion that the end of the cycle has indeed arrived:

> living as we are at the end of time, our obsession with sex is like a dying man's erection, a final fierce reassertion of Nature against the inevitable. (*CL*, 15)

That, however, is a thesis to which none of the plays can be said to subscribe unreservedly.

Warner's early plays display a profound sense of original sin and of the limitations of the human body — a sense which gives to the nudity in these plays a peculiarly disturbing quality. Nowhere is the vision given more concise expression than in an exchange between Gonad and Guppy in *Lying Figures*:

GONAD     Conceived in sin.
GUPPY     Born in pain.
GONAD     A life of toil.
GUPPY     Inevitable death. (*LF*, 32; *R*, 106)

The clipped phrases create a dialogue rhythm which has its own inevitability about it. In fact Gonad and Guppy share a line and a half translated from the epitaph written for himself by Adam of St. Victor.[4] The poem from which the phrases are taken is a forceful work in the tradition of the *contemptus mundi*, modulating into prayer at its close:

> Haeres peccati, natura filius irae,
>     Exsiliique reus nascitur omnis homo.
>
> Unde superbit homo, cujus conceptio culpa,
>     Nasci poena, labor vita, necesse mori?
>
> Vana salus hominis, vanus decor, omnia vana;
>     Inter vana, nihil vanius est homine.
>
> Dum magis alludent praesentis gaudia vitae,
>     Praeterit, imo fugit; non fugit, imo perit.
>
> Post hominem vermis, post vermem fit cinis, heu! heu!
>     Sic redit ad cinerem gloria nostra suum.
>
> Hic ego qui jaceo miser et miserabilis Adam,
>     Unam pro summo munere posco precem:

Peccavi, fateor, veniam peto, parce fatenti;
Parce, pater, fratres, parcite, parce Deus.[5]

The movement is closely akin to that of the *Requiem*. Yet there is an important difference. Though Warner's plays have much of Adam's *contemptus*, much of his bleakness, they also have a quality of humour and, not so paradoxically as might at first appear, a heightened perception of the beauty of that very world which is elsewhere held in contempt. The plays hold in poise the two attitudes — one might, indeed, suggest that one of the burdens of these plays is the notion that for those who look deepest the two attitudes are ultimately inseparable. The closing pages of *Lying Figures* perhaps offer the most vivid statement, in microcosm, of this realisation:

| | |
|---|---|
| LAZ | So with joy, tenderness and delight we transform ourselves into beasts. |
| SAPPH | What a wonderful and tiny thing a newborn baby is! |
| LAZ | Look to the mother and antisepticize your dugs. |
| SAPPH | She's like a snail that's melting. (*Calling out*) Go on, dear, give her a wide berth! (*Pause*) Today we are all voyeurs, watching ourselves watch ourselves create. |
| LAZ | Off with your grass skirt of flesh. It's only real. (*Pause. With dignity*) We are privileged to watch the suicide of a world. |
| SAPPH | Our future is the art of peace. |
| LAZ | It was one of those beautiful summer days by the river. Sun through morning mist, cornfields copper with scythe and combine, a thrush, distant sunlight shimmering on the hills . . . |
| SAPPH | High wispy clouds, autumn blaze of splendour, the October leaves, green, then lemon-yellow deepening to brown, fully biscuit and off they fall! |
| LAZ | Acres, no, an Eden of beheaded blooms. |
| SAPPH | The brevity of happiness makes it so achingly precious. |
| LAZ | God is ruthless. |
| SAPPH | Ruthless? Don't you mean pitiful? |
| LAZ | Exactly. |
| SAPPH | We see enough to see how little we can see. |

(*LF*, 45; *R*, 119)

Warner's plays are an examination of the image of man as seen simultaneously from these two very different points of view. Their themes are, centrally, the perennial ones of love and death. They are concerned to examine the relationship between love and violence, between love and sexuality, between the spiritual and the sensual. All of them are pervaded by a pressing sense of human mortality, and of the kinds of fear and wisdom that go with that sense. They consider the possibility of happiness in a society

> Where the soul that should be shrined in heaven
> Solely delights in interdicted things,
> Still wandring in the thorny passages
> That intercept itself of happiness.[6]

How far is humanity trapped by its own fantasies, but capable of salvation through imagination properly used? Is marriage merely an attempt on society's part to channel disruptive energies, an attempt which makes "a life of deception absolutely necessary for both parties"[7] — charming or otherwise? The plays seek to consider such problems in the juxtaposition of human behaviour with the moral and theological principles of the Old, and then the New, Testament. The examination is conducted by means of a great variety of dramatic resources. When the light is most wholeheartedly affirmed, in *A Conception of Love*, Warner employs profoundly traditional comic form. In *Light Shadows* and the *Requiem* plays there are less simple, more eclectic relations with the dramatic tradition.

On first encounter Warner's plays might appear to stand quite outside the main lines of dramatic development. Certainly they are very original in conception. Closer examination suggests, however, that, as so often is the case, an original form of expression has been achieved, not by abandoning the traditional, but by a new disposition of traditional elements, by a shifting of previous patterns of emphasis. One obvious relationship is with the plays of Yeats. Warner has worked and lectured extensively on Yeats, and it would have been surprising if there had been no traces of this influence in his plays. Warner, like Yeats, rejects realism:

> If the real world is not altogether rejected it is but touched here and there, and into the places we have left empty we summon rhythm, balance, pattern, images that remind us of vast passions . . . all the chimeras that haunt the edge of trance.[8]

As Yeats developed his dramatic forms, most notably under the influence of his acquaintance with the Noh drama of Japan, he came increasingly to work within an aesthetic which placed great value upon the use of allusion. Wilson describes the appeal of this method for Yeats:

Yeats knew that the Noh is extremely allusive, 'self-conscious and reminiscent' as he calls it, and he knew also that the 'few cultivated people' who made up the audience could be expected to understand the 'literary and mythological allusions and the ancient lyrics quoted'. Accordingly, he proposes to adopt a similar principle in his own work: to make his own drama very highly allusive also, and to give his allusions a consistent direction by referring them to subjective convention and to archetypal myth. He would not have done so without precedent, for he had at all costs to preserve the dynamic impact of his form: but the Noh taught him that he could make the attempt without being undramatic. Its eclecticism had, in fact, a curiously haunting effect, 'always reminding those who understand it of dearly loved things'; it led to a style opaque and secret, 'like a memory or a prophecy'.[9]

Warner carries to a further extreme this Yeatsian allusiveness — my later studies of individual plays seek to show some of the ways in which these allusions function, but many remain undiscussed, and there are doubtless many more to which I have failed to respond. Biblical allusions predominate, but classical sources (e.g. Aeschylus, Plato) and English writers (e.g. Shakespeare, Sidney and Browning) are all pressed into service.[10] Nor are the realms of literature and philosophy the only ones to be brought within the plays' allusive circle. Allusions to the visual arts are also frequent. Photographs printed in the first editions of *Lying Figures* and *A Conception of Love* emphasise specific debts to the works of Paul Delvaux. The later play actually invokes Delvaux explicitly, perhaps as a gloss upon its vision of "men as trees, walking" (*Mark* 8:24), when Griot invites Fashshar to:

Come and see my new Paul Delvaux lithograph over a drink.(*CL*, 26)

In *Meeting Ends*, Act One Scene Five betrays a very evident debt to Kandinsky's *Painting with Red Spot* (1914). My Chapter VII seeks to show that *Killing Time* alludes to, and develops, a symbolic pattern derived from Picasso's *Le Pigeon aux Petits Pois* (Plate 2).[11] The employment of the bull's head in *Meeting Ends* is surely conditioned by Picasso's repeated use of the Bull as a symbol of violent and aggressive male sexuality. The *Vollard Suite* is a major source, but Picasso's work offers many other related examples. *The Minotauromachy* of 1935 is interesting for its juxtaposition of such Warnerian symbols as the candle and the bull, while the *Bull and Horse* (1942) is relevant for its suggestion as to why it is that Agappy should ride the hobby-horse in Act Two Scene Four, and why Ensoff should wonder whether she makes "a hobby of horses" (*ME*, 28; *R*, 224). Her desire to "write an epic about a boy with a horse" (*ME*, 27; *R*, 223) sets up related echoes of such Picasso works as the *Boy Leading a Horse* of 1905. Elsewhere, literary and graphic allusions are combined — as in the use to which materials from Quarles are put — cf. *Emblems* and Plate 1. The ambivalence is there too, in a rather different fashion, in *Maquettes*, insofar as allusions to the writings of Sir Francis Bacon are counterpoised by allusions to the paintings of his modern namesake.

Literature and the visual arts are not, though, the only disciplines put to use in these plays. The sciences are similarly made to bear a part in the allusive structure. Shango's Promethean soliloquy (*ME*, 24–6; *R*, 220–22), for example, takes much of its force from the way in which it exploits the language of mathematics in general and of solvability in particular. Much of *Killing Time* is structured around the details of cerebellar anatomy; so much so that when Squaloid recounts some tales of torture, the name of the alleged victim is chosen very carefully:

> You're damn lucky you're not detailed to combat the Shifta. In North-West Kenya. They cut your balls off and wear them in their buttonholes. I saw them skin a Spaniard called Raymon Cajal alive. Really; I mean it. They took his skin off in strips with razorblades. He looked like meat, screaming.(*KT*, 58; *R*. 182)

It was Raymond Cajal who first established the fundamentals of cerebellar anatomy as a scientific discipline. Astronomy (e.g. *LF*, 5; *R*, 79), genetics (e.g. *KT*, 28; *R*, 152) and physics (e.g. *KT*, 12, 28; *R*, 136, 152) are all called upon, and most of the plays are punctuated by items of arcane zoological knowledge.[12]

Amidst such eclectic materials any reader or viewer is likely to be hopelessly lost if he is not provided with some sort of firm ground, with some kind of reassuring framework. Most drama traditionally has provided such reassurance in terms of character and plot. In Warner's plays, however, these are far from being stable elements. Scarcely any character is explored in terms of psychological consistency, certainly not in such a fashion that his or her sufferings and joys are likely to arouse much emotional reaction in us. Within the *Requiem* plays particularly, the characters are by no means continuous or consistent. Their frequent changes seem to be dictated by some larger consideration than that of psychological 'truth'. Plot is also a relatively minor element here. That is not to say that the plays are without striking incident or action. Far from it; the castrations of Xyster and Ensoff or the murder of Poppaea are all vivid theatrical moments. They stand, though, in relative isolation, rather than functioning as part of any narrative sequence which might hold an audience in suspense or fear. Yet if plot and character do not provide the audience with their firm ground, it need not be assumed that Warner's plays are altogether without their equivalent. Rather, that role is now played by theme and structure; in effecting this change of emphasis Warner merely carries to a further stage an aspect of modern dramatic aesthetics. Its origins can be traced perhaps in Strindberg's Chamber Plays. What Evert Sprinchorn writes about Strindberg's compositional ideas with regard to those plays is truer still of Warner's methods:

> No particular form was to bind the author; theme alone would determine the form; and the playwright could handle the theme in any way he chose as long as he did not violate the "unity and style of the original idea". In short, a chamber play was to be written like a piece of music and to require from an audience attention to theme and its development rather than to plot and character.[13]

Strindberg sought to evolve a dramatic form in which

> feelings could be aroused instantly, as they are in music, without the necessity of spending a great deal of time motivating a situation or etching in all the details in a character portrait to make it as life-like as possible . . . less attention is paid to preparing for the big scenes and building up suspense and more attention is given to drawing parallels between scenes and characters.[14]

It is very much within the tradition of the Strindbergian 'Chamber Play' that Warner works. The musical analogy is an all-important one, if we are to understand the way in which Warner's plays work. *Troat* is declaredly subtitled "A Double Fugue", and Melinda Camber Porter has pointed to the way in which a similar fugal structure governs Act Three of *Lying Figures*.[15] Or consider, for example, the opening scenes of *Light Shadows*. In the first five scenes the characters appear with a rhythmical regularity which owes more to considerations of 'musical' form than it does to 'realism'. In these opening scenes the characters appear as follows:

```
Scene one   : Seneca, Philo.
Scene two   : Seneca, Philo, Lucan.
Scene three : Seneca, Philo, Lucan, Josephus.
Scene four  : Seneca, Philo, Lucan, Josephus, Petronius.
Scene five  : Seneca, Philo, Lucan, Josephus, Petronius, Poppaea.
```

(Tigellinus enters unnoticed during Scene five, but does not speak until Scene six). The formality of these scenes is repeated 'internally' as it were. In Scene two, for example, the speeches of Seneca, Philo and Lucan are disposed in a distinct polyphonic pattern, in which Seneca's twelve speeches are interwoven with the nine each delivered by Philo and Lucan. Scene nine is announced as *"Interwoven Conversations"* (*LS*, 35) and I have discussed the patterning of this scene in Chapter X. In *A Conception of Love*, Act two Scene six presents a particularly clear illustration of this kind of quasi-musical formalism. Throughout the scene:

> The six characters sit in pairs, each pair being one point of a triangle:
> Koinonia and Amatrix, Mara and Fashshar, Gan and Thalassios.
>
> (*CL*, 55)

The formalism of this presentation prepares us for the elaborate permutational polyphony of the ensuing dialogue. A total of 54 speeches is spoken in the scene. If we represent the characters by the initial letters of their names we can see at once that the 54 speeches fall neatly into 9 groups of 6:

1.    AKMFGT
2.    KAFMTG
3.    FAGMTK
4.    AGFTKM
5.    GMKAFT
6.    MKTFGA
7.    KTMGAF
8.    GTMFAK
9.    TGFMKA

Each character has one speech in each set of six. It should also be noted that Group 9 is an inversion of Group 1, Group 8 of Group 2, Group 7 of Group 3, and Group 6 of Group 4, producing a kind of mirror effect. When dialogue rhythms are established in this way, naturalistic patterns of communication are necessarily subordinated to considerations of structure. If further impetus to such a development were needed, Warner may well have found it in the plays of the Surrealists. Gloria Orenstein has drawn attention to Breton's recognition that it was in dialogue that surrealism might best express itself:

Breton saw the possibilities of the supreme use of language as being the surrealist dialogue, one that could eventually compose a surrealist play. Having first claimed that "Language has been given to man so that he may make Surrealist use of it", he went on to add in his *First Manifesto of Surrealism* that "The forms of Surrealist language adapt themselves best to dialogue." ... Breton explains that in a dialogue which is pure surrealist poetry, both interlocutors would address their own internal monologue at, rather than to, each other, each pursuing a portion of his inner soliloquy as a response to the other's questions or statements ... [the result is] the dislocation of language from its usual function of communication to one of simultaneous, discrete, and interwoven monologues.[16]

This is precisely the kind of dialogue we often encounter in Warner's plays, especially the earlier ones (in the two most recent plays characters more frequently talk to, rather than at, one another), where characters frequently appear to deliver their monologues and aphorisms to no-one in particular. An 'exchange' between Actor and Actress in *Lumen* will perhaps make the point clearly:

ACTOR     What distinguishes us one from another is the quality of our vices, our fallings from uniform perfection. And we fall, all of us, in exactly the same way.

ACTRESS   (*Near to tears*) What *could* he have seen in *her*!

ACTOR     This is unfortunate, I must send for the police, they know how to deal with rape. (*Pause. Brightening*) They must teach me! (*Lyrically enthusiastic*) While there is music in the air and oestrogen-pills on prescription.

ACTRESS   I'm going.

ACTOR     The door is on the lock.

ACTRESS   Key!

ACTOR     Why? But consider the possibilities; or at least rule out those things which are less than probable. Are tulips green in a bottle?

ACTRESS   Police! I must fly. A blue bottle?

ACTOR     I normally wear a zip.

ACTRESS   Let me out.

ACTOR     Learn to think of me as your doctor. As one of your gossips round the cradle. Your fishmonger.

ACTRESS   (*In rapture*) My filmstar come true!     (*M*, 44; *R*; 64)

Writing of a play by the surrealist dramatist Radovan Ivsic, Orenstein observes that

each of the four characters represents a voice, a tonal quality, a melody. Addressing their discourse at, rather than to, each other, the characters, as sources of language, harmonize rather than communicate.[17]

The interweaving of monologues is, of course, just one of the characteristically Beckettian patterns of dialogue (e.g. in *Play*) and Beckett's use of musical forms[18] is doubtless another model for Warner's related experiments. Other Beckettian influences are evident — in, for example, the use of mime — and at times Warner's speech rhythms (the dialogue of Laz and Sapphira is a notable example) can sound extraordinarily Beckettian. While Beckett's plays have rarely involved spectacular stage action, they have always evinced a profound sense of theatrical sculpture, an awareness of the power of three-dimensional stage presences. One thinks of Winnie in her mound, a typically Beckettian use of a physical metaphor for the human condition. Others of his plays are 'choreographed' with meticulous precision, e.g. *Footfalls, Theatre II*. Warner's work is more inclined to the spectacular than to the sculptural and static. In terms of stage spectacle his debts are rather to surrealism (perhaps especially to Picasso's two plays, *Desire Caught by the Tail* and *The Four Little Girls*) and to certain aspects of Jacobean tragedy.

Dramatists such as Webster, Chapman and Tourneur, display very marked affinities with that tradition of the Emblem book which has also fascinated Warner, and which gives the title to his very first play. The editors of the New Mermaids text of *The Atheist's Tragedy* offer a pertinent comment upon the death of D'Amville:

> The manner of his death, striking out his own brains with the executioner's axe, is ironic, but it is more than that. There is a symbolic, emblematic quality about the stage-picture of the villain hoist with his own petard, the self-executed executioner, the moral charade. It is the kind of thing one might expect to find in one of the Renaissance Emblem books, accompanied by some motto about purposes mistook falling on the inventor's head.

They comment upon the opening of Act IV where Cataplasma and Soquette (Tourneur's characters have the same kind of punningly symbolic names as are borne by Warner's characters) moralise upon their needlework:

> the dramatic effect is to halt the action for a moment and place before the audience a series of visual examples of the orthodox morality in which the action is set. A similar purpose is served by the skulls, the charnel house, and the ghostly impedimenta in Act IV, scene iii.[19]

This particular scene in *The Atheist's Tragedy* offers a number of suggestive points of contact with Warner's work. Charlemont's ideas as to the most suitable time and place for contemplation are much like Gonad's in *Lying Figures*:

> How fit a place for contemplation
> Is this dead of night, among the dwellings
> Of the dead.   (IV, iii, 3—5)

Languebeau Snuffe and Soquette discuss the pleasures and perils of "generation" in ways which we shall see closely paralleled by Gonad and Epigyne. Their 'courtship', indeed, is conducted in terms of Warner's own favourite patterning of light and dark:

> LANGUEBEAU This is the back side of the house which the
> superstitious call Saint Winifred's church, and is
> verily a convenient unfrequented place,
> Where under the close curtains of the night —
> SOQUETTE You purpose i'th'dark to make me light.
> [SNUFFE] *pulls out a sheet, a hair, and a beard*.
> (IV, iii, 53—57)

After their hasty departure Charlemont encounters two further kinds of 'lying' figures — disguise and death:

> *They run out divers ways and leave the disguise*
> CHARLEMONT What ha' we here? A sheet, a hair, a beard?
> What end was this disguise intended for?
> No matter what. I'll not expostulate
> The purpose of a friendly accident.
> Perhaps it may accomodate my 'scape.
> I fear I am pursued. For more assurance,
> I'll hide me here i'th'charnel house,
> This convocation-house of dead men's skulls.
> *To get into the charnel house he takes hold of*
> *a death's head; it slips and staggers him*
> Death's head, deceiv'st my hold?
> Such is the trust to all mortality.   (IV, iii, 71—80)

The telling emblems continue, as the play's atheist, D'Amville, attempts (in this same setting) the seduction of his daughter-in-law, and the play's virginal heroine, Castabella. He insists that

All the purposes of man
Aim but at one of these two ends, pleasure
Or profit, (IV, iii, 111—113)

an echo of his philosophy as expressed previously at the very beginning
of the play:

Then if death cast up
Our total sum of joy and happiness,
Let me have all my senses feasted in
Th'abundant fulness of delight at once,
And with a sweet insensible increase
Of pleasing surfeit melt into my dust. (I, i, 16—21)

(Guppy offers a very similar argument: "Our bodies are nothing, therefore we may as well abuse them" (*LF*, 32; *R*, 106).) D'Amville seeks,
by specious arguments, to persuade his daughter-in-law to commit
incest with him. (Gonad tells us that he *has* committed incest with his
mother-in-law, but in a play so full of lies, should we believe him? In
any case, since Epigyne tells us that her mother has made lesbian
advances to her, the incestuous circle would appear to be complete,
whether in fact or fantasy). As D'Amville continues his attempted
seduction the use he makes of his surroundings presents as an image
something very close to what *Lying Figures* presents as stage fact in the
skeletal child of its conclusion:

Kiss me. I warrant thee my breath is sweet.
These dead men's bones lie here of purpose to
Invite us to supply the number of
The living. Come, we'll get young bones and do't.
I will enjoy thee. (IV, iii, 155—9)

After Charlemont's rescue of the tormented Castabella the scene
reaches its climax with one of those extraordinary switches (or rather
simultaneities) of mood which offer a very instructive analogy for the
kinds of effects sought in Warner's plays:

CHARLEMONT  My soul is heavy. Come, lie down to rest;
　　　　　　These are the pillows whereon men sleep best.
　　　　　　　*They lie down with either of them a death's*
　　　　　　　*head for a pillow*
　　　　*Enter* [LANGEBEAU]　SNUFFE *seeking* SOQUETTE

LANGUEBEAU   Soquette, Soquette, Soquette! O art thou there?
      *He mistakes the body of* BORACHIO *for*
     SOQUETTE
     Verily thou liest in a fine premeditate readiness for
     the purpose. Come, kiss me, sweet Soquette. — Now
     purity defend me from the sin of Sodom! This is a
     creature of the masculine gender. — Verily the man
     is blasted. — Yea, cold and stiff! — Murder, murder,
     murder.
     *Exit*
     *Enter* D'AMVILLE *distractedly;* [*he*] *starts at*
     *the sight of a death's head.*

Let us leave D'Amville to his own peculiar contemplations upon this
*memento mori*. Tourneur, like Marston, sees the world as a "lodge of
dirt's corruption"[20], a phrase that Warner might have borrowed. One
Jacobean response is a kind of Christian Stoicism (with further admix-
tures of Platonism) of the sort explored by Fulke Greville:

> Oh wearisome Condition of Humanity!
> Borne under one Law, to another bound
> Vainely begot, and yet forbidden vanity;
> Created sicke, commanded to be sound:
> What meaneth Nature by these diverse Lawes?
> Passion and Reason, selfe-division cause.[21]

This is Warner's starting point, too. The same problematical awareness
is eloquently expressed by Sir Philip Sidney:

> our erected wit maketh us know what perfection is, and yet our
> infected will keepeth us from reaching unto it.[22]

If we keep in mind the sexual pun implicit in the first adjective, and if
we give to "will" its full Elizabethan range of meanings,[23] then Sidney's
words will serve as a guide to the antithesis which underlies all of
Francis Warner's plays. The recurrent imagery in which this antithesis
is expressed is the subject of my second chapter. Succeeding chapters
explore the variations upon this antithesis which are offered by the
individual plays.

## Notes

1  *Perennia*'s use of the imagery of the four elements looks forward to *A Conception of Love*.
2  In the Author's Note to *Yeats's Iconography*, F. A. C. Wilson thanks Warner for "much help" in compiling the extensive and learned notes to that book.
3  F. A. C. Wilson, *W. B. Yeats and Tradition*, 1958, pp. 149–50.
4  *The Liturgical Poetry of Adam of St. Victor*, with translations by D. S. Wrangham, 1881, Vol. 3, pp. 190–93. The first ten lines were written by Adam, the last four being the work of a Victorine, John Corrard. Wrangham's occasionally loose translation reads as follows:

> Heir of original sin, a child of wrath too by nature,
> Rightfully banished from God, every man living is born.
>
> Wherefore is man so proud, since in sin his mother conceived him,
> Painful his birth, his life toil, a necessity death?
>
> Vain is the health of a man, vain his beauty, and vanity all things;
> And 'mongst things that are vain, nothing is vainer than man.
>
> While this present life's joys do more and more mock the enjoyer,
> Hence he passes, yea, flies; flies! rather perishes quite!
>
> After man he becomes a worm, after worm, alas! ashes!
> Thus doth our glory return to its original dust.
>
> I, who am laid in this grave, am the poor and pitiful Adam;
> But for one prayer I ask, prayer for the best of all gifts.
>
> Sinful I am, I confess, ask pardon; O spare one confessing!
> Spare him, my father! spare, brethren! and spare him, O God!

5  The phrases translated and used by Warner appear on the painting *L'umana fragilità* by Salvator Rosa, which is in the Fitzwilliam Museum, Cambridge. The painting presents a powerful image of the skeleton of death hovering over a child upon its mother's knee. Having spent a number of years in Cambridge, it is unlikely that Warner does not know the painting.
6  Thomas Kyd, *The Spanish Tragedy*, III, vi, 91–94.
7  Oscar Wilde, *The Picture of Dorian Gray*, Chapter one.
8  W. B. Yeats, *The Cutting of Agate*, 1919, p. 32.
9  F. A. C. Wilson, *W. B. Yeats and Tradition*, op. cit., p. 44.
10  More than merely English traditions are drawn on. Squaloid and Phagocyte share a translation of a poem by Tu Fu, and Kuru puts the poet's name to expressive purposes (*KT*, 29; *R*, 153). *A Conception of Love* draws on Indian traditions (see Chapter IX) and *Killing Time* makes much use of references to matters Egyptian (see Chapter II).

11  My discussion of this pattern of images is indebted to the study of them contained in Chapter 6 of Rosalind Jeffrey's *Chess in the Mirror*, 1980.

12  The variety of such sources is particularly evident in the names borne by characters in the *Requiem* plays. In *Lying Figures* Biblical names (Laz and Sapphira) are opposed to names drawn from a number of scientific desciplines: Gonad, Epigyne, Guppy and Xyster. *Killing Time* is entirely given over to 'scientific' names: *Meeting Ends*, as befits its place in the trilogy's moral argument, pits a single zoological name (Wrasse) against names from Classical (Callisterne) and Biblical (Agappy) Greek, and the Cabbala (Ensoff). Fittingly, the play's evil daemon, Shango, bears a name from a quite different (African) mythological system.

13  August Strindberg, *The Chamber Plays*, translated by Evert Sprinchorn, Seabury Quinn Jr., and Kenneth Petersen, New York, 1962, p. ix.

14  *Ibid.*, pp. x—xi.

15  T. Prentki, ed., *Francis Warner: Poet and Dramatist*, Knotting, 1977, p. 36.

16  Gloria Feman Orenstein, *The Theater of the Marvelous: Surrealism and the Contemporary Stage*, New York, 1975, pp. 19—21.

17  *Ibid.*, p. 59.

18  See Eugene Webb's two volumes: *The Plays of Samuel Beckett*, Seattle, 1972, and *Samuel Beckett: A Study of His Novels*, Seattle and London, 1973.

19  Cyril Tourneur, *The Atheist's Tragedy*, ed. Brian Morris and Roma Gill, 1976, p. xxxii. My quotations are taken from this edition.

20  John Marston, *Antonio's Revenge*, V, ii, 148—9.

21  Fulke Greville, 'Chorus Sacerdotum' from *Mustapha* (1633).

22  Sir Philip Sidney, *An Apology for Poetry*, ed. G. Shepherd, 1965, p. 101.

23  The discussion of the word in Eric Partridge's *Shakespeare's Bawdy* (revised edition, 1968) glosses a number of relevant meanings. Particularly apposite are his remarks with regard to what he calls "the *nexus* between the sexual act and literary creation" in Shakespeare.

# II

# Imagery: Hieroglyphikes of the Life of Man

The emphasis placed in Warner's plays upon quasi-musical virtues has one inevitable consequence: patterns of imagery become primary vehicles of meaning. There is even a sense in which plot and character are made subordinate to such patterns. In one or two instances such a pattern may seem to belong more or less exclusively to a single play: e.g. the cluster, cherry—olive—pea, in *Killing Time*. Where this is so I have reserved discussion for the chapter devoted to the relevant play. Other image patterns, however, are so all-pervasive in Warner's plays, and grow in meaning as their use crosses the boundaries set down by individual plays, that some consideration of them is desirable before moving on to look at the plays individually. The most important of such patterns is structured around the seemingly simple antithesis of light and dark.

Titles such as *Lumen* and *Light Shadows* make clear how important this pattern is in the plays. Quark's ecstatic lyric in *Killing Time* (which, along with Kuru's response, closes Act One) is perhaps the most striking instance of the positive value given to love and light, and will serve as a useful point of departure:

> The universe spins on a shaft of light
> > Whose name is love.
> Flowers of the meadows folded up all night
> > Spread for high strength above
> Them, warming out their secrets till
> Displayed for all to see each world's a daffodil.

23

Full-blown with morning, laughing to the sky
　　With puckered lips
They kiss sun's mastery to catch his eye.
　　No night-jar trips
Among the undergrowth between the stars
For violets and primrose chain the bars.

I took a prism, dazzled as a king,
　　And held it up.
Light shattered into all the flowers of spring.
　　Kingcup
And stalked marsh-marigold, its spendthrift son,
Transfigured all around till night and day were one.

What vision have I seen? Flowers wheel like suns
　　In daisy-chains of dance
Round daffodils, whose green-gold laughter stuns
　　To ignorance
My day-dull thoughts. Then suddently the clue
To all was clear. That source of light is you. (*KT*, 31; *R*, 155)

Quark's very first line should serve to alert us to one of the traditions to which this strand of Warner's thought owes a profound debt, for her line is surely a reminiscence of the Platonic myth of Er in Book Ten of the *Republic*. After their seven days in the meadow the company of souls moved on:

> And on the fourth day afterwards they came to a place whence they could see a straight shaft of light, like a pillar, stretching from above throughout heaven and earth, more like the rainbow than anything else, but brighter and purer. To this they came after a day's journey, and there, at the middle of the light, they saw stretching from heaven the extremities of its chains; for this light binds the heavens, holding together all the revolving firmament, like the undergirths of a ship of war.[1]

Here in Quark's "shaft of light" is the source of Ensoff's sunshaft which opens the succeeding play:

> A sunshaft strikes the steeple by my room,
> Flares the high cock that crowns created day. (*ME*, 1; *R*, 197)

The allusion also gives particular point to his "unchain a ray of light" (*ME*, 44; *R*, 240) near the close of the play.

Quark's second line, however, moves beyond the Platonic myth, for she identifies this shaft of light as love. In doing so she evokes Christian, rather than Platonic, symbolism. The superimposition thus effected is distinctly akin to the kind of reconciliation one finds attempted in, for example, the work of the pseudo-Dionysius, and the many later works produced under its influence. Indeed the affinity between Warner's work and this tradition is so pronounced that only lengthy quotation from Dionysius will make clear the extent and intimacy of the debt:

What shall I say concerning the sun's rays considered in themselves? From the Good comes the light which is an image of Goodness; wherefore the Good is described by the name of "Light" being the archetype thereof which is revealed in that image. For as the Goodness of the all-transcendent Godhead reaches from the highest and most perfect forms of being unto the lowest, and still is beyond them all, remaining superior to those above and retaining those below in its embrace, and so gives light to all things that can receive It, and creates and vitalizes and maintains and perfects them, and is the Measure of the Universe and its Eternity, its Numerical Principle, its Order, its Embracing Power, its Cause and its End: even so this great, all-bright and ever-shining sun, which is the visible image of the Divine Goodness, faintly reechoing the activity of the Good, illumines all things that can receive its light while retaining the utter simplicity of light, and expands above and below throughout the visible world the beams of its own radiance. And if there is aught that does not share them, this is not due to any weakness or deficiency in its distribution of light, but is due to the unreceptiveness of those creatures which do not attain sufficient singleness to participate therein . . . Here I desire to declare what is the spiritual meaning of the name "Light" as belonging to the Good. The Good God is called Spiritual Light because he fills every heavenly mind with spiritual light, and drives all ignorance and error from all souls where they have gained a lodgement, and giveth them all a share of holy light and purges their spiritual eyes from the mist of ignorance that surrounds them, and stirs and opens the eyes which are fast shut and weighed down with darkness . . . This Good is described by the Sacred Writers as Beautiful and as Beauty, as Love or Beloved.[2]

As in the neo-Platonists of the Italian Renaissance, heirs of Dionysius, the light of the sun is repeatedly used in Warner's plays as a symbol either of divine love or of that pseudo-divine love designated by the Biblical *agape*.[3] So at the end of *Killing Time* Chalone addresses Quark:

Let your love lighten upon the waste of our wraths and sorrows.
(KT, 69; R, 193)

Even in the largely loveless climate of *Lying Figures*, when love does make a brief appearance it is in this guise:

> Ah Love, since love has lit through miles and darkness to you,
> Warm me within your naked bed that I may woo you.
(LF, 39; R, 113)

As light is divine love so its denial is necessarily symbolised by darkness. Envy is darkness:

> The walls have shadows that whisper.  (*KT*, 58; *R*, 182)

Those who live in darkness naturally fear the light. So Shango's torture is at its worst when his darkness is thrown into relief by the light he refuses:

> *Please* no more shadows; no, no more. Light's seeping in. No one should be asked to bear this pain . . . LIGHT! I can't bear it.
(ME, 24–6; R, 220–2)

Loveless sexual activity is a deed of darkness in these plays. Gan's disturbing story recognises it as such:

> Back in the twenties this old lady had been to a house-party exactly like the one she's giving next week. A man in a velvet jacket had chatted her up, and later in the evening, during a game of 'Murder', she had gone into a dark place with him. They were silent, except for the fact that at one point in a melancholy tone he had recited a poem to her, an obvious invitation to make love, after which, still in silence, they did . . . When she reached for the light afterwards and switched it on, she found it was not her flatterer in the velvet coat at all but her brother.  (*CL*, 29–30)

In *Lying Figures* the movement towards sexual intercourse in the dialogue between Epigyne and Gonad is complemented by a simultaneous movement towards darkness:

| EPI | Marriage makes strange bedfellows. (*Sighs*) |
| GONAD | Both sides of the blanket. I don't want to make you succumb. But you might acquiesce. |
| EPI | (*Giggles*) There's many a true word broken in jest. *Lights begin to go down.* |

GONAD    I've watched your expression change with interest. It ranged from golf ball to rugger ball. (*Tenderly*) You are the gossip-columnist's dream. If it's good about me you discount it, and yet if bad, however preposterous, you swallow it whole.

EPI    Come here, my sweet.

GONAD    (*To audience*) The milkmaid, pulling away at her cow, dreams of her boyfriend.

EPI    It was nearly tragic.

GONAD    Nonsense. Tragedy comes when passion exceeds competence. (EPIGYNE *giggles*) When a man's tested at his weakest point. (*She giggles more. They begin embrace.*)

*TOTAL BLACK. After a pause, flare of struck match. Lights back up again to bright sunny day as before.*

EPIGYNE *is now in the tree, smoking a cigarette,* GONAD *in hanging basket chair.*

EPI    Why do you always watch to see if I light up afterwards?
                                             (*LF*, 30; *R*, 104)

(A similar movement, and moment, is observable in *Lumen* between Actor and Actress (*M*, 48; *R*, 68), where the striking of a match is given the same symbolic value). Earlier in *Lying Figures* the ephemeral light of the match and the cigarette has already been used as a measure of the transience of sexual pleasure. Epigyne approaches Gonad with the words:

Light my cigarette. Go on. You are irresistible to women. Know that? Irresistible.   (*LF*, 19; *R*, 93)

At the beginning of the same play Gonad lights a cigarette as he handles the two corpses; he even drops his cigarette ash in the mouth of one of them. At the end of the play it is a candle that he lights and his behaviour has much more of the ritual about it. The contrast is telling.

The match measures the triviality of human desire — its flickering light reveals the surrounding darkness, but fails to illuminate it:

I made a man's love the centre of my life. My own selfish passion of universal importance! When it failed, chaos came . . . I was walking in black down a rainy street like a burnt match thinking how nettles grow and breed.   (*ME*, 32–3; *R*, 228–9)

If love is a shaft of light it is scarcely surprising that loveless sexuality should be envisaged in precisely opposite terms:

| SAPPH | Holy innocents! what a bloodbath childbirth is. |
| LAZ | Through no fault of its own, forced into being by its lusting parents. |
| SAPPH | (*With rapture*) A night of love! |
| LAZ | The shafting darkness.  (*LF*, 45–6; *R*, 119–20) |

Laz's phrase takes its force in part from its inversion of the Platonic myth. So, in a slightly more oblique fashion, does Fashshar's crudity:

I'll leave to shaft Mara.  (*CL*, 50)

In the instances we have so far considered light and dark have been handled in a simple antithetic relationship which has distinctly Manichaean overtones. For Mani the spirit is light, and matter (or flesh) is darkness. The teachings of Mani are fundamentally dualistic. They are not without their seductive attractiveness and when Stanley Hopper writes of them that their

ultimate perspective consists in the dramatic opposition of darkness and light[4]

we may feel that his chosen adjective has a relevance beyond his own purposes. James Knowlson has demonstrated the central presence of such a contrast in the work of Samuel Beckett. He writes of

the key images of light and dark . . . that have recurred throughout Beckett's work[5]

and when he reproduces a page from Beckett's manuscript notebook written for the 1969 Berlin production of *Krapp's Last Tape*, it is clear that Beckett's mind has been operating in exactly this area of Manichaean dualism:

Note that Krapp decrees physical (ethical) incompatibility of light (spiritual) and dark (sensual) only when he intuits possibility of their reconciliation intellectually as rational-irrational. He turns from fact of anti-mind alien to mind to thought of anti-mind constituent of mind. He is thus ethically correct (Signaculum sinus) through intellectual transgression, the duty of reason being not to join but to separate (deliverance of imprisoned light). For this sin he is punished as shown by the aeons.
Note that if the giving of the black ball to the white dog represents the sacrifice of sense to spirit the form here too is that of a mingling.[6]

Beckett here alludes very specifically to the Manichaean (and Hermetic) notion of particles of spiritual light imprisoned within material darkness. Mani's mythology accounts in a poetical manner for this imprisonment, and views it as the purpose of morality to achieve liberation of these particles:

> The way to accomplish this was by severe asceticism, including abstention from meat-eating, and abstention from sexual intercourse, which in generating new bodies, promoted the continued imprisonment of light particles or souls in the demonic material world.[7]

Here in Beckett we have, if we want one, an obvious channel for the Manichaean element in Warner's work. Paul Hewison was surely near the truth when he described *Lying Figures* as

> almost Manichaean in its belief in the fundamentally dark and irredeemable nature of Man;[8]

but viewed as a whole Warner's work is most decidedly *not* Manichaean, whatever use it might make of the "dramatic opposition" which lies at the centre of that body of ideas. No Manichaean could take as an epigraph the text chosen by Warner as epigraph for *Meeting Ends*: "Yet in my flesh shall I see God".

Indeed, the more closely one looks at Warner's use of the imagery of light and dark the clearer it becomes that he is not content to employ such images merely as part of that simple antithetical structure which we have so far observed him using. In Manichaean tradition the darkness is irredeemably wicked. The kingdoms of light and dark are coeternal and irreconcilably hostile. It makes even starker the Zoroastrian dualism of Ormazd and Ahriman. In Warner's work, however, the darkness is more important not as evidence of evil but, in a seeming paradox, as evidence of the existence of the good.

In Warner's plays the darkness largely takes the form of shadows, and we may echo Donne's observation that if a shadow is to exist then "a light and body must be here".[9] As the title of the play about St. Paul tells us: light shadows. Amatrix knows that

> a shadow lives because I block the light     (*CL*, 11)

and though the light may be blocked, its existence is conclusively demonstrated by the presence of the shadow. When Kuru tells us

> I'll lose my laughter when I lose my shadow    (*KT*, 47; *R*, 171)

she surely implies that to lose sight of one's shadow is to lose one's certainty that the divine light exists. Ensoff's light may shadow forth the dramatic world which 'crucifies' him, but Phagocyte characterises Chalone as

> a ruler who can't bear the sight of his own shadow.    (*KT*, 22; *R*, 146)

Of course, our earlier interpretation of the significance of the sun in these plays makes it only logical that the shadow should take on this related meaning.

Many of the most beautiful passages in the plays are evocations of precisely these effects of light and dark. Taking just one or two instances, all from the same play, one might put side by side Griot's words at the beginning of Act Two:

> A fallen tree — its roots can form my backrest — slants morning shadows in this spring wood . . . Endlessly changing light through the branches on the water, in the hollows and humps and trunks and undergrowth    (*CL*, 40)

and Koinonia's remarkable line:

> See! The light fails on the dark water there.    (*CL*, 72)

It is in such a context that we must consider Griot's final dismissal of Fashshar:

> The shadow in the brook. Let him go.    (*CL*, 75)

At the centre of the web of images drawn from sun and shadows there stands, naturally enough, the emblem of the sundial. The very first of Warner's plays bore the title *Emblems*. We have no excuse if we fail to observe the author's debt to the tradition of the Emblem book. I should like to draw attention to one particular volume in that tradition which offers, if not necessarily a source, then a revealing analogy, for this whole nexus of images. The book I have in mind is the second and smaller of Francis Quarles' volumes — the *Hieroglyphikes* of 1638. It takes as its central theme a comparison between the life of a man and the burning of a candle. How that particular analogy is used by Warner I shall discuss in a moment. More immediately I wish to draw attention to just one plate from Quarles' volume, reproduced here as Plate 1.

Gathered together in it are a number of the central props and images in Warner's dramatic language: the sun, the sundial, the hour-glass, the candle and the skeleton. The sundial is a prominent symbol in these plays because by its play of shadows it measures the movement of the sun. It registers, that is, the light of love in a pattern of darkness. It first appears in *Lying Figures*. In Act Three Epigyne instructs Gonad that he must do some gardening to prove his love, and she produces an hour-glass by which to measure his efforts:

GONAD *brings out from behind tree a square of obviously plastic, artificial lawn.* EPIGYNE *is sitting back in her hanging basket chair, relaxed, swinging her legs gently.*
Rake!
GONAD *mimes the various tools.*
Now the wire rake. Yes, the leaves. Good. In a heap. Stupid! Now the edges. Use the grass-clippers, not the shears. Put all that in the wheelbarrow.
*As he does so* EPIGYNE *turns the hour-glass and rests it on her knee.*
Watch the sands.
GONAD, *astonished at how the time has passed, hurriedly wheels off imaginary wheelbarrow into wings and returns.*
Now the roller.
GONAD *sweats with the weight of the imaginary roller as he drags it to and fro, pushing it and pulling it.*
Mind the sundial!    (*LF*, 26; *R*, 100)

As Epigyne sits swinging in her swing-chair she offers an unmistakeable reminder of the skeleton on the swing at the close of *Emblems*. For all her attractive flesh she is a powerful emblem of mortality. The hour-glass she holds, since it needs no light, suitably measures the time-scale of that darkened human world which conducts its activities without benefit of the light of love. The hour-glass rests solidly on Epigyne's shapely knee, the sundial is invisible. In the second play of the trilogy even Quark can

only see the future in distortion, like a sundial in water.
(*KT*, 15; *R*, 139)

Fittingly, it is only in the final play, and in the final moments of that play, that the sundial is made actual. The acting area throughout *Meeting Ends* is circular. It is not, however, until Act Two Scene Four that the full significance of that circle is revealed:

ENSOFF . . . *walks downstage centre to nearest point of stage
circle to audience, bends down, grips the stagecloth with both
hands, and in one steady movement walks backwards upstage
and off left taking the stagecloth with him. Underneath, the stage
is revealed to be a sundial (no centre upright).*   (*ME*, 45; *R*, 241)

The revelation is made immediately before Ensoff's meeting with
Wrasse and Callisterne, and before his mutilation by Shango. After
his castration he sits in the centre of the sundial, becoming the missing
upright (though not sexually) whose shadow gives eloquent evidence
of the light. Before that moment has been reached he has, in words
adapted from the Book of Kings, announced to the two women that:

It is a light thing for the shadow on the sundial to go down ten
degrees, but you ask me to let the shadow return back as much.
                                          (*ME*, 45–6; *R*, 241–2)

His punning on the word 'light' is a pointer to an essential ambiguity
in the word, as used in this series of plays. It may remind us of the
inversion of a verse from St. John's Gospel with which *Lying Figures*
closes:

Darkness encroaches on the light, and in lightness we dare not
comprehend   (*LF*, 47; *R*, 121)

or even of the Actor's prayer in *Lumen*:

Darken our lightness.   (*M*, 49; *R*, 69)

Human lightness (this dramatic world is peopled by light men as well as
by light women) is but a grotesque parody of the light of love. It is the
product of a failure to recognise shadows for what they are – the
insubstantial evidence of a substantial reality. Mistaking the shadow for
the substance man lives in lightness rather than in light. The 'darkness'
of this particular Platonic cave of shadows paradoxically takes the form
of 'lightness'.

It will naturally be expected that darkness too should be employed
in ways which go far beyond any simple Gnostic duality. Darkness
may indeed embody evil (it is with savage irony that Squaloid is made to
bastardise the Nicene Creed when he remarks "Those Very lights are
hell" (*KT*, 6; *R*, 130)), but it is, simultaneously, capable of an almost
precisely opposite meaning. Earlier in this chapter we saw Dionysius
the Areopagite writing of God as light. In doing so he makes use of the

vocabulary of what he calls the "affirmative expressions of God". In a different spiritual vocabulary, God is He who "has made Darkness His secret place"[11]:

> Unto this Darkness which is beyond Light we pray that we may come and may attain unto vision through the loss of sight and knowledge.[12]

In this 'negative' spiritual language, darkness bears a radically different significance. Rather than hymning Light, Dionysius now asserts that:

> the simple, absolute, and unchangeable mysteries of heavenly Truth lie hidden in the dazzling obscurity of the secret Silence, outshining all brilliance with the intensity of their darkness.[13]

When the newly blinded Quark affirms that

> God is best seen when all the sky is dark    (*KT*, 58; *R*, 182)

or when Agappy instructs

> To be initiated, close your eyes    (*ME*, 7; *R*, 203)

it is from this 'negative' spiritual vocabulary that their words take their meaning. In *Light Shadows* Luke says of Paul that

> his sight has little light in it since that last flogging    (*LS*, 41)

but Paul has 'light' enough to make his contribution to Nero's 'Symposium'. The paradoxical relationship is stated comically:

> my Supervisor droned on about Sir Walter Raleigh and the School of Night in the sunshine    (*CL*, 36)

and with a wit which is not merely comic:

> PHILO    If we die, we are martyrs, we go to the Eternal Light, our Father in Heaven — like the sun in the sky, the source of all life.
> SENECA    The shades. Yes.    (*LS*, 4)

"The dazzling eyes of God" (*KT*, 45; *R*, 169) may dazzle by excessive light or by excelling darkness. The simple dualities of Mani's system are not, then, simply imported wholesale. They are refined and explored within a larger scheme of dramatic and poetic development.

After the sundial (which stands in opposition not only to the hour-glass but to all that is implied by Wrasse's "menstrual clock" (*ME*, 42; *R*, 238)) the most telling and sustained of this cluster of images is the candle. Again it is used with vitalising ambivalence. It plays an important part in the closing moments of *Lumen* — just as it is to be an important image (and symbol) at the close of both *Meeting Ends* and *Light Shadows*.

The candle had a long and distinguished career in those emblem books from which Warner so often draws his symbolic language. Quarles' *Hieroglyphikes* has already been mentioned, and in the very same year that this volume made its appearance (1638) there also appeared Robert Fairlie's *Lychnocausia or Lights Morall Embleme*.[14] For both authors the candle is an emblem of human life, as, of course, it had earlier been for Macbeth, whose

> Out, out brief candle!
> Life's but a walking shadow, a poor player
> That struts and frets his hour upon the stage
> And then is heard no more.[15]

provides Warner with one of the models for his extended punning on 'shadow'. Self-consuming, and easily snuffed, readily extinguished by the gusts of sorrow, Quarles finds in the candle a fit emblem of mortality:

> No sooner is this lighted Tapour set
> Upon the transitory Stage
> Of eye-bedarkening night,
> But it is straight subjected to the threat
> Of envious windes, whose wastfull rage
> Disturbs her peacefull light,
> And makes her substance wast, and makes her flame less bright.[16]

Less pious spirits in the same century found in the candle an emblem of a more specific kind of mortality. In an anonymous Restoration dialogue, for example, we find the old whore, Mother Creswel, instructing the relatively innocent Dorothea:

*M.C.*   Hast thou never observed, when a Candle burns down

into the Socket, and when the flame begins to want nutri-
ment, how it is sometimes up, and sometimes down, one
while it seems quite extinct, and then of a sudden it makes
a faint resurrection?

*Dor.*     That I have often remarked, for it always happens, if the
Candle is suffered to burn down, and a Save-all wanting.

*M.C.*     Then, Child, thou hast seen the natural Emblem of an
Old Man's vigour.

*Dor.*     Ha, ha, ha. I fancy you have given me a lively representation on't.[17]

The wit of this passage largely resides in the way that the author does
not allow us, by his use of words such as "resurrection" and "natural
emblem" (perhaps even "Save-all"), to forget the larger moral significance of the candle. Other, coarser, spirits are content to direct our
minds only to the candle's obvious phallic meaning, as is Suckling in
a peculiarly unpleasant poem:

There is a thing which in the light
Is seldom us'd; but in the night
It serves the maiden female crew,
The ladies, and the good-wives too:
They use to take it in their hand,
And then it will uprightly stand;
And to a hole they it apply,
Where by its goodwill it would die;
It spends, goes out, and still within
It leaves its moisture thick and thin.[18]

Phallic symbol, and emblem of mortality, the candle's other major
symbolic value is, of course, as a figure of the illumination of the
human soul — too universal a value to need specific exemplification
here.

When Laz and Sapphira, in their mortuary fridges, talk of the
candle they have in mind a resurrection which belongs in the world
of Mother Creswel, rather than the Life Eternal:

SAPPH     (*Excited*) Have you a candle for me, for when my fridge
is off?

LAZ     In your vanity bag.

SAPPH     That's where you always push it. (*Sighs*) But it's not the
same.   (*LF*, 42; *R*, 116)

When the Actor and Actress of *Lumen* move towards their moment of sexual darkness, the candle has an obvious phallic significance (*M*, 47; *R*, 67), but when it has been lit it begins to take on a more ambiguous meaning:

> ACTOR   Flame.
> ACTRESS   (*Sitting up*) Old.
> ACTOR   That which distinguishes us from the brute creation.
> $\qquad\qquad\qquad\qquad\qquad\qquad\qquad\qquad\qquad\qquad$ (*M*, 48; *R*, 68)

*An* old flame is, of course, a former lover; *the* old flame which "distinguished us from the brute creation" sounds more like the inner light of the human soul. It is in a related manner that the phallic candle of Laz and Sapphira is succeeded, shortly afterwards, by the candle used by Gonad in his almost silent ceremony performed over the skeleton of his child. (Though not so explicit verbally, this episode performs the same dramatic function as is fulfilled by Aunt Christine's candle-ceremony performed over the body of Maurice at the close of Scene V of Solzhenitsyn's neglected play *Candle in the Wind*. Solzhenitsyn's play was originally to be titled 'The light which is in thee', a meaning implicit in Alex's declared desire

> to help pass on to the next century one particular baton — the flickering candle of our soul.[19]

When Gonad leaves the stage he takes with him the candle: "*the only source of light*" (*LF*, 47; *R*, 121); but the candle he takes with him is still lit. Some light may be brought to bear on the darkness offstage, by means of this flickering candle.)

Certainly the movement of *Meeting Ends*, as it completes the *Requiem* cycle, is towards the affirmation of light, embodied in the circle of six candles above, and then behind, Ensoff's head. Unable any longer to rise sexually, Ensoff does rise to his feet, helped by Callisterne. Having helped him up, Callisterne lights the candles. This is the Candlemas to which Quark had alluded, and with which she had identified herself long before in *Killing Time* (*KT*, 56; *R*, 180). Ensoff's desire to "search out Edinburgh (*Or wherever play is being performed*) with candles" (*ME*, 44; *R*, 240) is in part fulfilled. (His words adapt those of *Zephaniah*, 1:12). The light of these candles may "search out" others as Shango is searched out by the light which torments him in his Promethean tortures. In the final scene of *Light Shadows* Paul is led off to execution by Tigellinus. The last stage direction reads as follows:

*Enter Tigellinus with lit candle to lead Paul to execution. Exeunt,
leaving candle on stage. Lights down until only the outline of a
dark figure with an axe can be seen. This figure slowly raises his
axe; and, as he brings it down, the candle's flame, the only source
of light, is extinguished.* (*LS*, 61)

The twin symbolic meanings of the candle are relevant here. That
candle which is the individual life of Paul within history has been
extinguished with his execution; that flame of illumination which
transcends both the individual and the limitations of history has not been
extinguished — that we are watching the play is evidence enough of that.

Leaving aside for the moment the candle as phallic symbol, we can
see that Warner uses the candle in a manner that belongs firmly within
the Hermetic tradition: it is seen as that light within an individual which
corresponds to, gives answer to, the originating light of the divine sun.
It is to Warner's emblem of the sun that we must now return. Recognition of the sun as an emblem of divine light (and love) is central to
our understanding of a number of the other recurrent images in Warner's
plays. This is particularly the case with the many images of flowers and
birds. Time and again the celebratory lyrics in these plays, lyrics more
often than not in celebration of light, simultaneously celebrate the
flower. Quark's lyric quoted at the beginning of this chapter is one
important instance. Callisterne, throughout *Meeting Ends*, "wears two
large daisy-rings on her left hand" (*ME*, 2; *R*, 198) and thus gives
special point to Ensoff's lyric:

> Summer walked in last week
> With daisies on her fingers, and a shawl
> Of fresh-lost music scattered down her form.
>     I rubbed my eyes
> But still the sunbeams danced.  (*ME*, 31; *R*, 227)

Without treating them in too rigidly allegorical a fashion it is probably
safe to say that flowers in these plays are, traditionally enough, symbols
of innocence and of renewal and hope. Certainly this is so when Quark
tells us that

> Snowdrops are emblems of the Feast of Lights!  (*KT*, 56; *R*, 180)

and that

> The infant daisies in January down by the river are so small in the
> grass they look like the remains of frost.  (*KT*. 56; *R*, 180)

This last observation counterpoises frost and flower at the very moment of transition, the instant of balance between frozen immobility and the new life of spring. The two-fold image is taken up by Ensoff in the final lines of the *Requiem* cycle:

> Yet at my feet a snowdrop breaks moon's winter
> Its secret yellow trussed up in green gauze
> Traced round and rimmed with white, and all enfolded
> By three white lips that shield it out of doors,
> Weighing down like a bell from a sheathed splinter
> This surge of life the icy dust has moulded.   (*ME*, 48; *R*, 244)

Of course this cluster of images — frost, flower, spring — is a profoundly traditional language for the expression of the hope of resurrection. A single passage from St. Bernard of Clairvaux will make the point:

> You must see the splendours of the Resurrection rather as flowers of the age of grace but now begun, blossoms of the new springtide of creation which, in the general resurrection at the end of time, will bear their boundless and eternal fruit. 'For lo, the winter is past,' says the Bride, 'the rain is over and gone, the flowers have appeared in our land.' By these words she would have us understand, summer has come with Him Who, loosed from out death's winter into the springtide of the risen life, declares, 'Behold, I make all things new.' For, sown in death, His Body has in His resurrection flowered anew; to greet its budding fragrance our life's parched plain grows green, the glaciers melt, the dead return to life.[20]

At the beginning of Act Three of *Lying Figures*, Epigyne swings gently in her hanging basket chair, snipping the heads off tulips. Her sensual scorning of that hope of resurrection which the flowers symbolise is perfectly encapsulated in this one moment of silent action. Quark's ecstatic lyric in *Killing Time* is answered by Kuru in counterbalancing floral terms:

> Close, close tight buds, now parting ends the day
>     Laughter must cease
> Colours fade, and withering winter come.   (*KT*, 32; *R*, 156)

In their attitude to flowers can be judged the moral perceptiveness of Warner's characters. Quark's innocence is measured by flowers, so is Bride Two's shallowness by her abuse of them:

We call it a daisy-chain sandwich, in the best wife-swapping circles.

(*M*, 12; *R*, 32)

In the lyrics, images of flowers and the sun are repeatedly associated with images of birds. Quark will again serve as a point of departure. Kuru tells Squaloid, quite simply: "She's like a bird" (*KT*, 42; *R*, 166) and when Chalone is reminded of her presence at the very end of the play, reminded of her continued existence by her innocent words of love, his startled recognition of her is beautifully expressed in the same terms:

A feather dropped from the plumage of heaven!   (*KT*, 69; *R*, 193)

When Kuru, surrounded by the presence of death and its attendant ceremonies, feels the need to reassert the values of life she does so in words which once more establish a relationship between the bird and the sun:

> KURU *seizes* PHAGOCYTE's *hand, to his astonishment, and drags him downstage.*
>
> KURU           Give me life! Give me life! Hold my hand, hug me!
> PHAGOCYTE This is an appalling shock to morale.
> KURU           I'm your new horizon! Anything's better than that dust down the throat. Let me feel alive again! When a chick breaks the eggshell, it comes out chirping as loud as it can. I can't stand all this death!
>
> (*KT*, 45; *R*, 169)

"Dust down the throat" takes us back to the very beginning of *Lying Figures*, but her image of the chick emerging from its shell is taken from the Egyptian *Book of the Dead*, more specifically from the Hymn to the Sun known as "The Adoration of the Disk by King Akhnaten and Princess Nefer Neferiu Aten":

> The chick within the egg, whose breath is thine,
> Who runneth from its shell, chirping its joy,
> And dancing on its small unsteady legs
> To greet the splendour of the rising sun.[21]

As positive symbols in Warner's plays "birds are divine remembrancers" (*KT*, 70; *R*, 194). It is this awareness which lies behind Koinonia's beautiful words spoken at the very moment when all must assimilate the news of Broomy's death:

| | |
|---|---|
| GAN | The dark angel has touched once more. |
| GRIOT | If we lament a death, life for us must have meaning. We must pick up the fragments of order left behind. |
| KOINONIA | Listen! It's gone very quiet. Like birdsong early on Christmas morning. (*CL*, 74) |

Birdsong is evidence of something beyond the merely human. When Shango's tortured soliloquy moves towards some kind of tentative recognition of God his language brings together sun and bird once more:

> There is a God after all! At least pain asserts the power of human pity, if only for oneself. First light of day — God, I'm trembling — birds sleepily begin their duty. Streak of sun through the wineglass of water by my bed. (*ME*, 26; *R*, 222)

The birdsong is used with grim irony when it introduces — on a brightly lit stage — the 'dark' confessions of Wrasse (*ME*, 34–6; *R*, 230–2). At the opening of Act Two of *A Conception of Love*, however, it sets the tone of the succeeding scene quite without irony:

> Birdsong all around. Lark . . . blackbird . . . thrush . . . bullfinch and willow-piper. Stillness caresses their song. (*CL*, 40)

In the Groom's lyric which closes *Emblems* the thrush's song, however painfully it may be wrung from the bird's throat, is an assertion of light in the dark:

> Home, home immortal breakers urge.
> Grey mountains open to the piper's note.
> Dusk brings the darkness, embers mark the end,
> Yet what contortion leaps the . . . thrush's . . . throat?
> (*M*, 21–2; *R*, 41–2)

Of course the imagery of birds is not allowed to play a uniformly affirmative role. If, for example, the cock and the cuckoo are "remembrancers" it is only indirectly that they remind us of the divine. For Yeats the cock is

> the symbol of *Hermes psychopompus*, and it is a reincarnation symbol, . . . representing the rebirth of divinity into the world. Yeats found it used in this special sense in G. R. S. Mead's book on Hermes Trismegistus, where 'the crowing of the cock' 'which plays so

important a part in the crucifixion story in the Gospels' is traced back to Egyptian theurgy as a symbol for the beginning of a new Platonic year and for the hour at which 'the Virgin gives birth to the Aeon' (Godhead).[22]

The cock is used at the very beginning of *Meeting Ends* as an emblem of a kind of spiritual vigilance closely related to this Hermetic interpretation. At the close of *Killing Time* it had been used in a fashion which holds in balance its twin significances of betrayal and hope.[23] Elsewhere it is used less ambivalently as a symbol of faith betrayed. It functions thus in *Troat* (*M*, 33; *R*, 53); as such it is paralleled by the use of the cuckoo as the traditional emblem of another kind of betrayal. The Actor's lyric in *Lumen* is greeted by the call of the cuckoo (*M*, 46; *R*, 66) and when, in the complex sexual politics of *Lying Figures*, Gonad suspects that he has been outmanoeuvred, the image recurs:

> Very clever, dearest; the perfect excuse. So the cuckoo is deftly fielded to my nest. (*LF*, 31; *R*, 105)

While never attaining the complexity and richness which it has in, for example, the work of Yeats, the symbolic language of birds has a considerable expressive range in Warner's plays. One extreme might be marked by the "exultation of larks" in *Meeting Ends* (*ME*, 15; *R*, 211: see also *LF*, 39; *R*, 113), simultaneously collective noun, description, and symbolic meaning. At the other extreme stands the ominous owl, foreboder of death in *Lying Figures* (*LF*, 7, 14–15; *R*, 81, 88–9) as surely as in any Jacobean tragedy.[24]

The related images of animals are mainly employed, not surprisingly, to evoke man's subordination to the physical, rather than his capacity for the spiritual. In the godless world of *Lying Figures* it is the animal kingdom which provides the most insistently reiterated imagery. Married life is lived in "the bridal sty" (*LF*, 25; *R*, 99) since

> once embarked on the gadarene slope of matrimony you might as well eat like a pig. (*LF*, 32; *R*, 106)

This is the world of the crablouse (*LF*, 16, 28; *R*, 90, 102), a world where

> the female praying mantis during copulation bites off the head of her love; who, all the same, still continues to thrust away with undiminished fervour. (*LF*, 18; *R*, 92)

It is the world of the bitch (*LF*, 21, 23; *R*, 95, 97), the limpet (*LF*, 20; *R*, 94) and the cow (*LF*, 30; *R*, 104), of the stallion with "farcy in the glanders" (*LF*, 18; *R*, 92). Indeed the animals are not merely emblems of human sexual appetites, they serve as measures of those appetites, measures which reveal the full extent of human lust and corruption:

> Animals are not bestial. The silver fox is on heat only eight days a year. And those are in February.   (*LF*, 18; *R*, 92)

If the fox's relative celibacy passes damning comment upon human lustfulness, its propensity for violence can later serve as an emblem of human viciousness, as Chalone's opening speech demonstrates:

> Perhaps there is a greatness in man only brought out in war. What a frail hope. We are more like severed worms, caravans of weasels. When two dogs fight and one of them can grip no longer, he rolls over and offers his throat, and the other turns away. It's a natural instinct that prevents all dogs fighting to the death. Even wolves have a code for killing their kind. But man and the fox are deformed. (*Takes off his hood to reveal his face*) The fox kills far beyond his need for food, for pleasure, until exhausted. And the human baby is anonymous until his teeth grow. Then the shape of the jaw gives the parents' likeness. He can bite. There is no innocence save lack of experience; and man, being a questing creature, cannot accept life on those terms, so war is a fever in our brain.   (*KT*, 1–2; *R*, 125–6)

There are those for whom the expression of power involved in killing a fellow man is a moment of sexual fulfilment; the two become related acts of predation:

> Your first man, it's like catching your first pike. Death makes a man of you.   (*KT*, 3; *R*, 127)

Imagery of this kind is central to *Troat*. Here in *Killing Time* Chalone's opening speech makes it disturbingly clear why trenches should be called "Foxholes" (*KT*, 4, 33, 36, 38; *R*, 128, 157, 160, 162). The associations give a special power to a conversation between Broomy and Gan, where the flowers of innocence and hope are juxtaposed with the destructive power of the fox:

> BROOMY Now look at these fritillaries. Beautiful! White, or
> snake-speckled purple flower-bell hanging down. Look

> at this white one! Six green streaks along the vein of
> the bell, and six green stamens inside.
>
> GAN       Have you ever seen a fox in this garden?   (*CL*, 27)

Man at war exceeds the destructive power of the fox, if for no other
reason than that he has a greater variety of means at his disposal. The
animals cannot compete:

> Even the animals have fled. There are no birds in the sky
>
> (*KT*, 1; *R*, 125)

or as Squaloid puts it:

> It's everyone for himself now. The embassies have closed, the rats
> have left — even the brothels are shut . . . There's no such thing as
> politics. Only politicians. And I hate them as vermin.
>
> (*KT*, 35; *R*, 159)

In a world of "moles and . . . bats" (*KT*, 34; *R*, 158), of "rat-shit"
(*KT*, 7; *R*, 131), of teachers who give birth to puppies (*KT*, 11; *R*,
135), of women who indulge in "whores' play" (*KT*, 25; *R*, 149) and
who want their men "wild as a camel on heat" (*KT*, 28; *R*, 152) the
capacity for suicide might indeed appear to be a redeeming quality.
In *Meeting Ends* there are at least some characters able to reject the
bull's head of sexuality which Shango flaunts so arrogantly. Wrasse
and Shango may still live in a world of pigtroughs (*ME*, 19, 23; *R*, 215,
219) and mousetraps, but Callisterne triumphantly escapes from her
kennel before the play is over. In *Light Shadows* Nero is both lion
(*LS*, 1, 24) and "the beast of the Apocalypse" (*LS*, 21). It is a Rome
where dogs go for the throat (*LS*, 22), since they are 'human' dogs.
It is a Rome where

> in the morning our fellow humans are torn to meat by bears and
> lions; at noon they are thrown to the spectators.   (*LS*, 6)

It is a Rome where

> bears eat men, and we eat the bears from the arena     (*LS*, 42)

and where the chief of the Praetorian Guard is a "jumping rat" (*LS*,
41). At least, though, it is a Rome where Philo, remembering his Plato,
is wise enough to observe that

the charioteer has lost control of the white horse    (*LS*, 53)

immediately after Tigellinus and Nero have announced their intention
of racing "the horses by torchlight" (*LS*, 52) and Nero has brutally
slaughtered Poppaea. Above all, the redeeming hope of which Paul is
the embodiment and the spokesman is confidently expressed in language which adds a further dimension to this kind of imagery:

> Nothing can come between us and the love of God. Shall tribulation,
> or distress, or persecution, or famine, or nakedness, or the sword?
> As the loveliest of all our poets, the Psalmist, sang, 'For thy sake are
> we killed all the day long. We are accounted as sheep for the slaughter'.
> (*LS*, 32)

This is only the most explicit, the most triumphant, expression given
to the motif of the sacrificial lamb, alluded to more glancingly at a
number of other points in the plays. The motif has an evident relation
to the sheep and goats of the Last Judgement (*cf M*, 32; *KT*, 20; *ME*,
25; *R*, 52, 145, 221). Such allusions, though, cannot outweigh our
sense that Epigyne's vision of

> human beings as lascivious insects, lovingly stinging each other to
> death during their little stay    (*LF*, 18; *R*, 92)

is an all too accurate description of what we see in the first two plays
of the 'Requiem' trilogy, and the first two plays of *Maquettes*. Her
vision is made literally true in the death-bringing venereal disease
which pervades this world of fallen sexuality. The fate of Shango is
evoked, along with that of all the 'lying figures' when the Old Man and
the Young Man in *Troat* talk (ironically enough) of flowers:

> OLD MAN      You have a flower called Venus' Claptrap?
> YOUNG MAN    Oh, I know what you mean, Venus' *Mouse*trap!
> (*M*, 30; *R*, 50)

In *Lying Figures* the permutations, both sexual and mathematic (though
these figures don't lie) ensure that Xyster's syphilis will "kill four
stones with one bird" (*LF*, 3; *R*, 77), that Epigyne will come, however
belatedly, to recognise that

> each man has two women, each woman two men.
> All eight of us poisoned by delight.    (*LF*, 37; *R*, 111)

Not surprisingly, the imagery of venereal disease permeates *Killing Time* (eg. *KT*, 27, 41—2; *R*, 151, 165—6) and is by no means absent from *Meeting Ends*. Callisterne finds work as a stripper "like living in a ward of terminal syphilitics" (*ME*, 10; *R*, 206). Even in the comic world of *A Conception of Love* its presence is felt, and must be exorcised. Mara sees it as evidence of 'real' life, placing one 'community' against another:

FASHSHAR    I did go on a fourteen-day trip to Casablanca once. We went into Las Palmas, which must be the most popular place for men in the hemisphere. The Green Doors in Catalina Square. Tourists only know the square as a market, but it's where nine out of ten laundry-boys have their first sexual experience. I overheard them borrowing the £7 from the chief laundry-man.

MARA    Only to have to pay it back on sub-day, I suppose. Yes, everyone knows when they have it. They don't appear to be sick, yet they're not allowed to work in the catering section. A list used to go up in the mess of those who'd caught it; only to be crossed off when cured. As a result, most of the boys didn't report it, and it spread like wildfire. (*Pause*) What do these students know of real life?     (*CL*, 46)

This chapter has traced, in outline, a few of the most sustained themes of imagery to be found in these plays. Of course there are many more such themes, some of them intricately interwoven with those already discussed. We have seen, for example, that the hymning of the sun in *Killing Time* derives from one of the Egyptian Hymns to the Sun. It is, then, a witty piece of counterpoint that Egypt should be used several times in the plays as an emblem of the excessively worldly. Phagocyte's murder of the girl Solange (ironically performed with the words "Let's throw some light on this by opening a window" (*KT*, 5; *R*, 129)) takes place in Egypt. Josephus recounts brutalities in Egypt (*LS*, 12) and Griot tells Broomy that "Egypt means 'black'" (*CL*, 2). Once again Warner makes use of a traditional symbolic value. Ultimately Biblical, Egypt was frequently used as a symbol of that which held man back from the spiritual light:

First we must leave Egypt behind, first we must cross the Red Sea . . . He who desires that food of heavenly solitude let him abandon Egypt both in body and heart, and altogether set aside the love of the world. Let him cross the Red Sea, let him try to drive all sadness and bitterness out of his heart, if he desires to be filled with inward sweetness . . . First the foods of Egypt must fail, and carnal pleasures he held in abomination before we may experience the nature of those inner and eternal pleasures.[25]

Warner's plays counterpoint elements from two distinct symbolic traditions whenever their characters speak of Egypt and things Egyptian.

The inhabitants of these dramatic worlds are very much given to the acting of roles and to the playing of games of the sort written about by Eric Berne. Images of acting and the theatre, and of games of many different kinds, therefore abound. It would be tedious to enumerate all such instances, but a few of the more striking may be pointed out. The language of chess is used very frequently. Phagocyte observes that "we are the pawns of night manoeuvres", having moments before enquired of Quark "do you play chess in the mirror?" and talked of "our bishop" Gregor Mendel (*KT*, 15; *R*, 139). Chalone has earlier told him that he has "mated unchecked" (*KT*, 14; *R*, 138). Epigyne plans her adultery as a "game":

> Well! I too can play games    (*LF*, 9; *R*, 83)

and talks of it as such to her lover Guppy:

| EPI | Will you marry me? |
|---|---|
| GUPPY | We have reached the stage where most couples are thinking of divorce. |
| EPI | Stale, mate? |
| GUPPY | Dead heat!    (*LF*, 10; *R*, 84) |

Though Nero and Tigellinus are players of chess (*LS*, 50), like the torturers of *Killing Time* (*KT*, 60; *R*, 184), their tastes are more for the games of the amphitheatre. The chess image does, though, appear with beautiful appropriateness in Mara's final words in *A Conception of Love*:

> We are in a game of chess, and I must mate with an unseen king.
>
> (*CL*, 75)

Images from acting and the theatre are perhaps even more frequent. The allusion brings to life (if that is not an inappropriate phrase in this context) two rather hackneyed phrases in the opening speech of *Killing Time*:

In the theatre of war a soldier must take life as it comes.

$$(KT, 1; R, 125)$$

Chalone declares

I'm not a character in a play, I'm a human being     $(KT, 62; R, 186)$

but after his deception of Phagocyte, when Squaloid congratulates him, "You acted well" $(KT, 67; R, 191)$ one feels that one's approbation ought to be extended to his histrionic, rather than his moral, performance. He is an actor in a theatre, not only of war, but of cruelty. Well might he say at the close of the play:

The parts of actors are like the flames of matches, blown out in the wind and vanished.   $(KT, 70; R, 194)$

This relates to Agappy's description of immortality earlier, and is perhaps an indirect reminder, too, that when Warner talks of 'shadows' he frequently uses the word to refer to actors (*cf*. OED, 6b). It forms, thereby, a link with that network of light/dark images with the consideration of which this chapter began. In these plays individual hieroglyphics are never merely isolated. Patterns of contrast and parallelism operate eloquently both within individual plays and across Warner's work as a whole. It is this quasi-musical sense of structure and pattern in the use of imagery which gives an imaginative coherence to the eclectic material from which these plays are made.

## Notes

1   Quoted in the translation by F. M. Cornford, *The Republic of Plato*, 1941. The myth of Er exerted a potent fascination on Yeats, and Warner's use of the myth may be influenced by that example; *cf*.

    Who talks of Plato's spindle;
    What set it whirling round?
    Eternity may dwindle,
    Time is unwound,
    Dan and Jerry Lout
    Change their loves about. ('His Bargain').

2   Dionysius the Areopagite, 'The Divine Names', in *The Divine Names and The Mystical Theology*, trans. C. E. Rolt (1920), 1972, pp. 91–5.

3   See Chapter VIII.

4   S. R. Hopper, 'The Anti-Manichean Writings', in *A Companion to the Study of St. Augustine*, ed. R. W. Battenhouse, New York, 1955, pp. 148—174. The quotation occurs on page 150.

5   James Knowlson, *Light and Darkness in the Theatre of Samuel Beckett*, 1972, p. 40.

6   Knowlson, *ibid.*, p. 47.

7   Ninian Smart, *The Religious Experience of Mankind*, 1971, p. 450.

8   P. Hewison, 'Theology in the Plays' in *Francis Warner: Poet and Dramatist*, ed. T. Prentki, Knotting, 1977, pp. 53—66. The quotation occurs on page 66.

9   *A Nocturnall upon S. Lucies Day, being the shortest day*, line 36.

10  2 Kings 20:10 *ff.*

11  Dionysius the Areopagite, *op. cit.*, p. 192.

12  *Ibid.*, p. 194.

13  *Ibid.*, p. 191.

14  Interesting short accounts of both books can be found in Chapter V of Rosemary Freeman's *English Emblem Books*, 1948.

15  *Macbeth*, V. iii. 23—26.

16  Francis Quarles, *Hieroglyphikes of the Life of Man*, 1638, p. 11.

17  Anon., *The Whore's Rhetorick, Calculated to the Meridian of London and Conformed to the Rules of Art in Two Dialogues*, (1683), reprinted 1960, p. 107.

18  *Minor Poets of the Seventeenth Century*, (Everyman), 1931, p. 231.

19  Solzhenitsyn, *Candle in the Wind*, trans. K. Armes in association with A. Hudgins, (Penguin), 1976, p. 148.

20  St. Bernard, *On the Love of God*, (*De Diligendo Deo*), trans. by A Religious of C.S.M.V., 1961, pp. 21—22.

21  Trans. Robert Hillyer in *An Anthology of World Poetry*, ed. M. Van Doren, 1929, p. 218. There is an obvious analogy here with the moment when Quark is released from the guillotine.

22  F. A. C. Wilson, *W. B. Yeats and Tradition*, 1958, p. 185.

23  See Chapter VII.

24  I reserve discussion of the pigeon/dove images for Chapter VII.

25  Richard of St. Victor, *The Four Degrees of Passionate Clarity*, quoted from the version in F. C. Happold, *Mysticism*, 1970, pp. 243—4.

# III

## *Emblems:* Here Come the Brides

Like the other plays in *Maquettes*, *Emblems* opens with a long silent
scene. Against a paradoxical background of rain *and* sun,[1] a camera of
old-fashioned tripod design flashes away at an empty stage. Offstage an
organ plays the opening of 'Here Comes the Bride'. Tape-recorded
applause and cheers sound from offstage. A perfectly archetypal bride
appears — "fully dressed in white, blushing, etc." (*M*, 9; *R*, 29), the
'etc.' presumably intended to suggest that she should be all that a
producer can think of as conventionally bridal. She makes her curtsies
to the audience, and the rain continues to sound while she stands
beneath the "warm sunny lighting". Conventional and unconventional
are already disturbingly juxtaposed. She is joined on stage by her
bridegroom. Naturally there are more bowings and curtseyings. Naturally
they pose for the photographer and the camera flashes again. That it
had previously taken a photograph of an empty stage makes us wonder
how empty its present subject is. Look beyond the conventional trappings and will there be anything more substantial, anything not capable
of being registered upon a photographic plate? A second bride enters
and takes the groom's other hand. Applause and photographs follow
precisely the same pattern as before. While their spirit is grotesquely
distorted, the conventions are politely upheld so far as externals go.
Now all three can bow and curtsy to the audience — now cast in the
roles of family and congregation at this unusual wedding. The groom
kisses each bride chastely on her forehead[2] — not so much the kiss of
a happy groom on his wedding day as the kiss of a bored businessman
off to work. Indeed, having bestowed these no more than emblematic
kisses, the groom "disengages" (*M*, 10; *R*, 30), and sits down to read his
*Daily Mirror*.

49

The title of the play ought to have prepared us for this elaborate episode — or at least for something like it. For what is it but a dumb-show, and it is surely true that

> the dumb show of the stage is in both form and function only a much more elaborate version of the pictures in an emblem book.[3]

Warner's dumb-show here (as with the dumb-shows which open *Troat*, *Lumen*, and *Lying Figures*) is characterised perfectly by a sentence from another writer on emblems:

> In a sense the dumb-show is the *inscriptio* to the *pictura* of the whole play.[4]

This *inscriptio* introduces us to marriage, adultery, paradox and mirrors — all of them to play important parts in the ensuing *picturae*. The hidden cameraman and the convenient black box upon which the Groom sits to read his newspaper will both of them turn out to be important features of the most potent emblematic *pictura* of this particular play.

As soon as the dialogue begins our sense of the two Brides as mirror inversions of one another is reinforced:

> BRIDE ONE    Good morning.
> BRIDE TWO    Good afternoon.
>              *They shake hands. Clock strikes twelve.*
> BRIDE ONE    I'm sorry, I should have said "Good afternoon".
>              It's not my day.
> BRIDE TWO    It was morning.
> BRIDE ONE    (*Startled*) Mourning? At our wedding?
>
>                                        (*M*, 10; *R*, 30)

The two Brides appear as a morning and an afternoon separated by the sound of the clock — a sound which chimes and ticks insistently at a number of points in this play. Their patterned disposition here repeats the visual pattern of the dumb-show where the two brides (in white) had stood either side of the groom (in black). Yet it is also the striking of the clock which frees them from the frozen formalities of greeting. It is Bride One who is immediately on the defensive — the rest of the play will show us Bride Two as the dominant woman. Her apology is, of course, uncalled for. She was quite right. Her pathetic "It's not my day" has ambiguous overtones. It is conventional to refer to the wedding

day as the Bride's 'special' day. But in this instance the day has turned
out to belong to more than just her. Another meaning is evident. If
the two Brides (morning and afternoon) can be seen as forming a whole
day, it is not one which belongs to Bride One. Bride Two's conciliatory
"It was morning" can only be misunderstood by the now harassed Bride
One: "Mourning? At our wedding?". The pun (*cf.* Kuru's "Morning,
son" (*KT*, 25; *R*, 149)) begins that juxtaposition of the ceremonies
of marriage with the rituals of death which is a recurrent feature of
the succeeding plays. It looks forward, for example, to Sapphira's
"Mine was a white funeral" (*LF*, 2; *R*, 76) or to Epigyne's black wedding
dress with black bouquet" (*LF*, 8; *R*, 82). Startled by the thought of
death, Bride One falls back on a handy phrase — "At our wedding".
But to whom does the 'our' refer? Used conventionally it ought to refer
to Bride (One) and Groom; and so it does. In the context of this
particular wedding, however, it must refer to all three 'partners'. In the
light of later developments it can be seen to have still another meaning.
The Groom has already 'disengaged' himself from his two brides. Later
events will exclude him from the marriage in a version of that "law of
the excluded middle" (*KT*, 63; *R*, 187) of which Squaloid talks. The
"our" refers to the two Brides, since the wedding ceremony binds them
together more effectively than it binds either of them to the Groom.
Bride Two is soon pointing out that marriage has given them the same
name:

> BRIDE ONE     What did you say your name is?
>
> BRIDE TWO     Don't be silly. The same as yours, of course. When
> you marry a (*With disgust*) 'man', you take his
> good name even as he has taken yours.
>
> BRIDE ONE     You have taken *my* name?
>
> BRIDE TWO     A name has reference only in the context of a
> proposition.    (*M*, 11; *R*, 31)

Allusions to Wittgenstein do not long remain a hallmark of Bride Two's
conversation. Soon her language is becoming ingratiatingly persuasive:

> Now don't be silly, dear; two girls who've been
> through what we've been through today have a
> great deal in common. Let's make the best of a
> good job and . . .    (*M*, 12; *R*, 32)

she is interrupted at this point by the Groom, but events later in the
play make it easy to imagine how her sentence might have ended. The
mirror invertibility of the Brides is confirmed when the Groom rejoins

the conversation at this point. His "Have you two met before?" produces a precisely mirrored response:

| | |
|---|---|
| BRIDE ONE | No. |
| BRIDE TWO | Yes. |
| GROOM | I beg your pardon? |
| BRIDE ONE | Yes. |
| BRIDE TWO | No.   (*M*, 13; *R*, 33) |

That the two women are a complementary pair has already been made clear:

| | |
|---|---|
| BRIDE TWO | He asked me to envelop whoredom with ceremony. |
| BRIDE ONE | (*Shyly*) I wanted to be his mistress as well as his wife. |
| BRIDE TWO | And I his bride as well as his whore.   (*M*, 11; *R*, 31) |

After Bride Two's long monologue it is she who ushers Bride One back on to stage:

BRIDE TWO *brings* BRIDE ONE *on again with a gesture of hand held out.*   (*M*, 18; *R*, 38)

The gesture repeats a moment from the dumb-show, when the invitational role was played once by the Groom:

GROOM, *still holding* BRIDE'S *hand, turns half round and extends his left hand to welcome* BRIDE TWO *from curtains upstage centre.*
(*M*, 10; *R*, 30)

Previously we have seen Bride One playing the same game of invitation:

BRIDE *turns towards upstage centre where curtains meet and extends her left hand.* BRIDEGROOM *enters upstage centre and takes her hand.*   (*M*, 9; *R*, 29)

These two earlier instances involved a Bride and the Groom. Now when Bride Two brings on Bride One with the same gesture their union, and the exclusion of the Groom, are simultaneously confirmed, in terms of stage spectacle. This time the gesture is not greeted with offstage applause and cheers. It is only natural, under the circumstances, that their conversation should turn to matters incestuous (their burgeoning relationship is surely a startling addition to the repertoire of incest) and to Solomon, whose own experiences are not without their relevance here:[5]

| | |
|---|---|
| BRIDE TWO | Our first marriage was only a civil one, so this is our church ceremony. And naturally, under these circumstances, he is free to marry you. |
| BRIDE ONE | Holy Mother of God! |
| BRIDE TWO | The Mother of God must also have been His daughter. We must stick to Solomon, who knew rather better how to cope.   (*M*, 19; *R*, 39) |

Bride Two may be intrigued by the paradoxes of the incarnation, paradoxes that have fascinated better minds than hers,[6] but they remain merely fragments of wit for her, she can see no significance in them, obtain no understanding from them. Having encouraged Bride One to tears in persuading her to give a narrative of her courtship by the Groom, she prefers to concentrate on sensual matters and to ensure that she gets the sexual initiative firmly into her hands:

| | |
|---|---|
| BRIDE TWO | Let me take off this absurd long dress. And you don't mind short hair, do you. I loathe a wig. (*Takes off wig to reveal masculine haircut*) *She wears masculine woman's clothes under bridal gown. Deposits bridal gown about two feet left of downstage centre.* There now, that's better. And you, out of that get-up. *Takes* BRIDE ONE'S *bouquet while she undresses, to reveal pretty, miniskirted, and attractive young lady.* BRIDE ONE *deposits bridal gown about two feet right of downstage centre. She takes back her bouquet, and then, both together, facing audience, drop their bouquets on their own discarded bridal gowns, giving a stage effect of nipples placed on a pair of white breasts.*   (*M*, 19–20; *R*, 39–40) |

Bride Two's desire to assume the masculine role is here made literal. The patterning of sexual roles is, of course, a repeated concern in Warner's plays and here the discarding of one set of clothes (the virginal white of the wedding dress — absurdly inappropriate for Bride Two in any case) reveals another emblematic suit — the caricatured 'butch' clothes of the dominant lesbian. Another powerful emblematic picture is produced when the two women throw down their bouquets to form the image of a pair of breasts. The breasts, formed from the discarded trappings of a bizarre marriage, and acting as the prelude to a lesbian relationship, serve as an emblem of that feminine role of motherhood which the two brides have scorned in preferring one another to the Groom. Fittingly this 'marriage' (at least it involves only two partners) is recorded for posterity just like the earlier one(s):

> BRIDE TWO	Pose for the photographer.
> *Each puts arm round the other's waist. Flash.*
> (*M*, 20; *R*, 40)

The Groom may have settled for a chastely formal kiss, but Bride Two demands "a real one" (*M*, 20; *R*, 40). Bride Two enjoys her pseudo-masculine dominance as much as it is enjoyed, at least temporarily, by Epigyne and Wrasse in the later plays. She comments: "God, men are lucky!" (*M*, 20; *R*, 40) and lights a cigar in dubiously convincing celebration and confirmation of her newly found sexual role. The final exchange between the two women, before they exit in a lovers' embrace asserts their different understandings of the relationship:

> BRIDE ONE	In you I have found him.
> BRIDE TWO	Through him you have found me.	(*M*, 20; *R*, 40)

The only relationship we actually see on stage is thus a lesbian one. It has been symbolically enacted in another of the play's small dumbshows:

> GROOM	Organist! Do the bride backwards.
> BRIDE ONE *turns to face offstage right*, BRIDE TWO *to offstage left, both in one movement. At the same time the lights dim. Organ music for the first two bars of Here Comes the Bride, played backwards.* (*M*, 12-13; *R*, 32-33)

The Groom's command is, on one level, fulfilled by the organist who plays in reverse those two bars of Here Comes the Bride which we had earlier heard him play during the dumb-show (*M*, 9; *R*, 29). The phrasing of the command does, though, have disturbing sexual overtones, suggestive of sodomy. In the immediate context (assuming the organist to be male) it suggests male-female sodomy. It serves, though, as a reminder. in the language of masculine homosexuality, of the lesbian relationship of the two Brides. When they turn their backs upon one another they provide an emblem of that denial of sexual function which we have already discussed. During the black-out they turn to face one another; their meeting is possible, and the Groom can ask them "Have you two met before?"    (*M*, 13; *R*, 33)

Against the sterility of lesbianism the play invites us to consider the heterosexual conventions of marriage. What the ceremonies of marriage might mean or what they might conceal is made clear enough by the opening dumb-show, and by the Groom's rapid loss of interest in the two women now that they have become his wives. Retrospective accounts by his two Brides suggest that his interest in them was perhaps never very insistent. Consider Bride One's account first:

> I loved him from the day we walked beneath the trees. He said my cheeks were as soft and fragile as the eggs of a blackbird. But he would go away. Oh, I grew so *lonely*. Night after night I'd be alone. Then I went to an evening class, and a doctor sat by me. He was so understanding. He took me to a party where I laughed and danced, and he said my eyes were like fishpools and my breasts like clusters of grapes. So I showed him them, as he was a doctor; though he wasn't practising, but he said he was the son of a Prime Minister, and he said more beautiful things about me as I showed him more until he had all he wanted; twice. Then, next morning when I returned, *he* was looking for me. He saw through my lies and turned me away. (*Near to tears*) He said it was the third time in a year and it was the end. So I begged him to marry me, so I wouldn't be lonely and tempted, and for our wedding he's given me you.   (*M*, 19; *R*, 39)

The speech does more than confirm our sense of Bride One's naivety. Her hilarious account of the doctor's courtship makes beautifully ironic use of the good doctor's apparent habit of creative pastiche. His version of the *Song of Solomon* (it follows immediately upon the other Bride's allusion to Solomon, and incorporates phrases from Chapter Seven, verses four and seven, of its Biblical original) is here made to function in much the same way as January's use of the same source in the *Merchant's Tale*. January's lyric, in another context, would be beautiful; so would the doctor's paraphrase. As it is, the narrating Merchant can only comment:

Swich olde lewed wordes used he.[7]

The same has to be said of the amorous doctor. Such allusive evocation of the Biblical ideal of heterosexual love serves only to damn the triviality of the inhabitants of *Emblems'* dramatic world. It is no surprise to find that the motives for Bride One's marriage have little to do with such ideals — rather the marriage is a confession of weakness and a plea for protection against that weakness. Bride One has turned to marriage in the hope that it might provide an effective sanction against her promiscuity. The terms in which she makes the confession are delightfully ironic. She hoped that by marrying the Groom she would no longer be lonely and no longer be tempted. The Groom has certainly solved the first problem for her — by providing her with a wifely companion. It is that companion, however, who will provide the very temptation she had sought to avoid. "For our wedding he's given me you" — again the phrase "our wedding" is heavily ironic.

Bride One's retrospective narration of her dealings with the Groom constitutes a mirror inversion of the much longer monologue delivered before it by Bride Two (*M*, 14–18; *R*, 34–8), a monologue interrupted only by a voice offstage. Her account of her second marriage to the Groom (David):

Now the birth of our wedding was conceived on the ruins of our divorce    (*M*, 14; *R*, 34)

has the same kind of startling compression about it that one finds else-where in Warner's juxtapositions of birth and death. The simultaneity of apparent contraries is an important part of the surreal world of *Emblems* where the passage of time is telescoped into an intensely contradictory present:

GROOM         (*Looking up from newspaper*) Darlings, when you
              two have quite finished would one of you fetch
              the breakfast and the other bring my dinner? Get
              me up and come to bed?
BRIDE ONE     (*Bird-twittering. She listens a few moments*) The
              dawn chorus!
BRIDE TWO     (*Bell. She listens a few moments*) Waiter! There's
              the bell for compline. Bring us the bill and call a
              taxi!    (*M*, 12; *R*, 32)

When Bride Two has the stage to herself she reenacts the sordid rituals of her adultery. She sits (in mime) at her (imaginary) dressing table like a seedy Belinda. As she sits there her long monologue moves through a kaleidoscope of moods and associations of thought. She thinks of her lover Brendan with his "rolled stick" and she toys with her lipstick, and naturally remembers his "gorgeous lips" (*M*, 15; *R*, 35). As the soliloquy opens she is certain that she is pregnant by her lover:

> It's not coming, that's clear. Twelve days overdue, and sick as a child.   (*M*, 15; *R*, 35)

As the soliloquy progresses, however, we begin to realise that her period is not the only thing which is overdue in this play so thoroughly marked by the pressure of time. Brendan himself is overdue:

> Oh Brendan come on, you must have left the city long ago and you said you'd be here, *ages* ago! ... Oh DEAR! Brendan, where are you? ... Brendan! Where are you now? Why in hell's name did I come early? ... Hell and blast him! Half the night's going; and if he's much later we'll never go out at all. What could be keeping him? ... You know I'm going to hate you, Brendan, if you're not here soon. This is the last straw. I've been finding you more and more unsatisfactory. You're thick, that's what you are. What do you think you are doing, keeping me waiting like this? I'm not dancing to your tune ... Brendan, darling Brendan, please come ... If Brendan comes now ... Perhaps he never meant to come at all! ... You have left me high and dry when I most needed you, you, you despicable coward! I'm through with you and thank God at last ...
> (*M*, 16–18; *R*, 36–38)

The knock at the door which follows may (or may not) signal the arrival of Brendan — Bride Two's next words are "So he divorced me ... " (*M*, 19; *R*, 39). Brendan's belated arrival — if that is what it is — is paralleled by the belated arrival of her period. A sequence of interlocking motifs heralds its arrival. She tells us "I've had a shower" (*M*, 15; *R*, 35) in preparation for Brendan's arrival. When he fails to appear she panics momentarily:

> He's had an accident! Yes, that's it. Oh that lovely hair matted with blood! Nonsense. He's so damned careful he makes love with a book in his hand. *Hell*! It's come. Ah, what a mess. The bath that's done it.
> (*M*, 17; *R*, 37)

The shower intended to prepare for one arrival (Brendan) has actually prompted a different arrival — her period. The blood she imagines streaming from Brendan in a car-crash now streams from herself. Her 'curse' for her period "*Hell*!" and her glib use elsewhere of religious diction — "My God he can love" (*M*, 16; *R*, 36), "Why in hell's name

did I come early" (*M*, 16; *R*, 36), "I'm through with you and thank
God at last . . . " (*M*, 18; *R*, 38) — confirms our sense of her essential
triviality and lack of moral or spiritual vision. Her "mysterious dark
glasses" (*M*, 14; *R*, 34) only serve to ensure that for her "the light is
dark" (*KT*, 15; *R*, 139). Her dismissive

> What's the book? Oh, one he used to read me. Gideons. Never does
> now. We used to have such fun: he whispering in the boats, always
> early in his best shoes to meet my train     (*M*, 17; *R*, 37)

not only confirms her own shallowness, but stands in important contrast to the moment near the end of the play when the Groom produces
a book and holds it up to the audience during his closing lyric.

Bride Two is alternately confident in her sexuality and aware that
her period is indeed a curse which excludes her from her Eden of sexual
pleasure. Beneath her veneer of self-assurance there is little of substance.
Her emotions and her attitudes towards the two men in her life (at
present) flicker and change repeatedly, and are apparently quite without
any stable foundation in any kind of self-knowledge. Her uncertainty
is characterised by her contradictoriness as to quite where she left the
note for her husband. First she tells us "He'll be finding it on the
kitchen table now" (*M*, 15; *R*, 35) and then she wonders:

> But would David have seen the note? I left it on the fridge.
>                                                    (*M*, 17; *R*, 37)

The note itself mentions their son Jonathan, as she does again later in
the monologue:

> I'm cold and lonely, and Jonathan will be wanting his tea and David
> is hopeless putting him to bed . . . (*M*, 16; *R*, 36)

The collocation of these two names — David and Jonathan — offers us
a reminder of their Biblical prototypes. As an allusion to homosexuality
it stands in opposition to Bride One's allusion to the heterosexuality of
the Song of Solomon. Before Bride Two can take on her own lesbian
role as substitute Groom she can find no comfort for her loneliness.
Her pathetic lies to the hotel servant reveal the misery of her position:

BRIDE TWO         *Knock at the door.*
                  (*In startled anticipation*) Who is it?
MAN'S VOICE       (*Offstage, slow, measured, courteous but sardonic
                  voice*) May we turn down the beds?

| | |
|---|---|
| BRIDE TWO | (*Disappointed*) No, no, come back later, we're going out for a bit. |
| VOICE | Will you be wanting a call in the morning, madam? |
| BRIDE TWO | No, thank you. |
| VOICE | (*Pause*) Tea, madam? |
| BRIDE TWO | Er, no thanks. |
| VOICE | Any papers? |
| BRIDE TWO | No, no, nothing at all, thank you. |
| VOICE | Sorry to have bothered you, madam. |
| BRIDE TWO | Oh, oh, oh (*Stamps foot*) Oh! David, why ever did I leave you?   (*M*, 17–18; *R*, 37–8) |

Bride One, in her naivety, and Bride Two, for all her seeming sophistication, are both lonely, both quite unable to find the contentment they seek either inside or outside the bounds of marriage. Their lesbian relationship may be sterile, but it is entered into with more conviction than they can muster for their heterosexual relationships.

The dramatic pattern, though, makes it clear that without the Groom the Brides will necessarily be incomplete. The pattern can be seen in microcosm in an early dialogue:

| | |
|---|---|
| BRIDE ONE | (*Primly*) We must master our needs. |
| BRIDE TWO | Our needs are masters. Morality is very largely glandular. |
| GROOM | (*Centrestage, taking each by the hand*) We need our glands to master morality.   (*M*, 12; *R*, 32) |

Bride One's thesis and Bride Two's antithesis are united in the Groom's synthesis, the stage business mimicking the logical progression. The pattern is repeated on a larger scale: the narratives of the two Brides are succeeded, once they have left the stage, by the Groom's lyrical statement.

The Groom has played little active role during most of the play. In his detachment he plays a role not unlike some of the later figures in the plays — notably Ensoff. The parallel, however, is only approximate. The Groom is not so much above passion as merely outside it. His detachment only succeeds in ensuring that his two brides are married one to another and both of them to sterility. As he sits and reads his *Daily Mirror* he reminds one of Shango reading his *Times* within the mousetrap. Still, if there is any wisdom to be found in *Emblems* it is to be found with the Groom. As we have seen it is he who makes the positive statement in the logical chain quoted above. His speech continues:

The way of convention leads to patriotism, but the way (*Looks in turn at* BRIDE ONE *and* BRIDE TWO *with a smile*) of understanding leads to the creation of children, not the destruction of life.  (*M*, 12; *R*, 32)

Insofar as he possesses any kind of vision of a "way of understanding" he is markedly different from his two brides. However tentatively, he does perhaps have some vision of, as it were, a marriage of true minds, transcending the picture of marriage as it is otherwise presented in the play. If he does have any glimmer of superior understanding it is because of the sense of human mortality which his final lyric reveals. The sobriety consequent upon this awareness puts him in a different world from the women's triviality. The final moments of the play are left to the Groom alone. To facilitate discussion we can consider his words and his actions to some degree separately; for a theatre audience the verbal and the visual are, of course, indivisibly linked. His lyric, stripped of its accompanying stage business, reads as follows:

> Beneath this scalp within this skin a skull
> Out of which peer two globes that clutch the light.
> A dropped jaw parts two lips, and nostril holes
> Rake in the pollen of a July night.
> Red bones that clasp a book pull white in sinews.
> Nails protrude to gather up the dust.
> The valve-fed engine thrums its tambourine.
> To galvanize a vagrant's wanderlust.
> Home, home, immortal breakers urge.
> Grey mountains open to the piper's note.
> Dusk brings the darkness, embers mark the end,
> Yet what contortion leaps the . . . thrush's . . . throat?
>
> (*M*, 20—22; *R*, 40—42)

The first line constitutes a kind of two-fold allusion, adapting, as it does, Eliot's lines on Webster in "Whispers of Immortality":

> Webster was much possessed by death
> And saw the skull beneath the skin;[8]

Both prongs of the allusion are relevant. Webster's two major tragedies are apt analogies for Warner's plays insofar as they expose human viciousness in a manner which can readily lead to their being misunderstood as the work of sensationalist playwrights who handle these horrors with little or no moral purpose, save that of exciting and amusing the audience.[9]

The charge would be as unjust where Warner is concerned as it is where Webster is under discussion. The world of Eliot's early poems is also, in slightly different ways, related to the world of Warner's plays. The poem to which Warner's lyric alludes juxtaposes the attitudes of Webster and Donne with those of modern man. George Williamson writes of Eliot's poem:

> Possessed by death, Webster and Donne saw beyond the flesh; possessed by flesh we take refuge in abstractions to conceive any life beyond the physical.[10]

The problems, and much of the poem's argument prompted by them, are precisely those of the *Requiem* plays and their *Maquettes*.

The Groom's awareness of mortality leads him to strip the image of humanity to those organs by which it preys upon the natural world — clutching the light, raking in the pollen. When he pulls a book from his pocket his argument moves on a stage.[11] The presence of the flesh is still assertively stated — "red bones" — but the book itself is a kind of emblem, since it represents one crucial form of human immortality, one means by which man might transcend the limitations of his flesh. The Groom's gesture, brandishing the book at the audience (as a torch will be brandished in the third of the *Maquettes*), becomes, in its context, a wordless affirmation of Milton's resounding assertion:

> A good book is the precious life-blood of a master spirit, embalmed and treasured up on purpose to a life beyond life.[12]

It is after this gesture, and after reflections on the heart, frail source of the precious life-blood, that the Groom reveals the cameraman for what he is — and has been throughout the fleshly proceedings — a skeleton. More silently than his counterparts in *Lying Figures* he has watched and recorded the absurd activities of the busily sensual. In the final emblematic *pictura* the skeleton is made to serve as an emblem of undifferentiated humanity. When first revealed it wears a sanitary towel; to this there is later added the Groom's top hat. The skeleton is thus invested with the symbolic properties of public masculinity and private femininity, or, to put it another way, the trappings of public ceremony and the necessities of sexual reality. The Groom's moving of the skeleton is described thus:

*Gently, as though helping a very old person, he leads it across stage to place it in the swing.*   (*M*, 21; *R*, 41)

This "very old person" is placed in a child's swing. Once there the Groom's words

Grey mountains open to the piper's note

make an unmistakeable allusion to what Browning subtitled "A Child's Story" — *The Pied Piper of Hamelin*. Man, woman, old person, child — all of them meet in the skeleton.

The skeleton swings to and fro, the chains of the swing producing a ticking sound, just as their movements visually imitate the pendulum of a clock. The allusion to Browning's poem offers a glance at the kind of timeless paradisal world which that poem's piper promises the children:

For he led us, he said, to a joyous land,
Joining the town and just at hand,
Where waters gushed and fruit-trees grew,
And flowers put forth a fairer hue,
And everything was strange and new;
The sparrows were brighter than peacocks here,
And their dogs outran our fallow deer,
And honey-bees had lost their stings,
And horses were born with eagles' wings.

It can only be a glance, however. *Emblems* can offer no such land of transformation. The bleaker truth is that

Dusk brings the darkness, embers mark the end.

Yet this is not quite the end: the Groom's lyric has one more line, and it is a line which suggests (however tentatively) that the darkness is not total, that, however precariously, the light survives. The closing line is surely as much exclamation as it is question, despite the text's furnishing it with a question mark. It is an exclamation at the survival of beauty, a wondering recognition of the intimate links between beauty and pain. It may remind us of the legend of the Nightingale and the Rose,[13] or even of Hardy's 'Darkling Thrush'. Their themes both of necessary sacrifice and of the survival of a seed of optimism and light in encircling darkness are both relevant here. However hesitantly, the closing line is an affirmation at parting — an affirmation whose further meaning is clarified if one bears in mind Chalone's words near the end of *Killing Time* — "Birds are divine remembrancers" (*KT*, 70; *R*, 194). It is on this precarious note of balance that the play ends; the stage has been set, and our expectations have been upset.

## Notes

1 cf. Kuru's description of her "last husband": "The reigning son" (*KT*, 51; *R*, 175).
2 The kiss which Shango bestows upon Callisterne in Scene One of *Meeting Ends* is here foreshadowed.
3 R. Freeman, *English Emblem Books*, 1948, p. 15. The analogy has been more fully explored by Dieter Mehl, *The Elizabethan Dumb Show*, 1965, and A. Schöne, *Emblematik und Drama im Zeitalter des Barock*, 2nd. revised edition, Munich, 1968.
4 P. M. Daly, *Literature in the Light of the Emblem*, 1979, p. 151.
5 cf. "Solomon had seven hundred wives and three hundred concubines. The wisest of men was also the most highly sexed. You can't judge a man by his private life. The creative are also the fecund" (*ME*, 39; *R*, 235).
6 e.g. Donne, *La Corona*, Sonnet 2:

> yea thou art now
> Thy maker's maker, and thy father's mother,
> Thou hast light in dark; and shutt'st in little room,
> Immensity cloistered in thy dear womb.

7 Chaucer, *The Merchant's Tale*, IV, (E), 2149.
8 T. S. Eliot, 'Whispers of Immortality', *Poems*, 1919.
9 Charles Kingsley, 'Plays and Puritans', *North British Review*, 1856; quoted thus in G. K. & S. K. Hunter, *John Webster*, 1969, p. 52.
10 George Williamson, *A Reader's Guide to T. S. Eliot*, revised edition, 1967, p. 96.
11 In the original production the book used was a copy of Francis Quarles' *Emblems* — source, presumably, of the play's title.
12 Milton, *Areopagitica*.
13 I have in mind the versions in Hafez, and in Wilde's 'The Nightingale and the Rose'.

# IV

## *Troat:* The Sweetest Canticle

*Emblems* closes with a twelve line poem spoken in concert with the sight of a skeleton upon a child's swing. Its two closing lines assert and question:

> Dusk brings the darkness, embers mark the end,
> Yet what contortion leaps the . . . thrush's . . . throat?
>
> $\qquad\qquad\qquad\qquad\qquad\qquad\qquad$ (*M*, 22; *R*, 42)

The opening of *Troat* immediately takes up several of the notes struck here. This second Maquette begins in darkness on a stage lit only by embers: "a brazier of coals, glowing" (*M*, 25; *R*, 45). In silence the solitary figure of the Nightwatchman drops fresh coals upon the fire, patting each one into place. He "blows on embers" (*M*, 25; *R*, 45). The very title of this second play appears to echo the closing word of *Emblems*. OED lists 'throat' as a seventeenth-century variant of 'troat'; 'troat' is one of the many terms from venery used by Warner in these plays. It is a verb meaning to cry or bellow and has particular reference to the cry of a buck at rutting time. It thus carries associations both of hunting and of sexuality. Both themes are prominent in the play.

The opening words of *Troat* take the form of a Shakesperean sonnet spoken by the Old Man. Attention is drawn to the form of the sonnet by the way in which the Old Man pauses after each of the three quatrains. The longest silence and the most violent action (the capture and strangling of the mouse) are placed between octave and sestet, so as to further reinforce an audience's awareness of the form. The perfect regularity of the sonnet serves both as a prelude and as a model of constructive

64

impulses to put against the impulse to destruction which it both surrounds and is surrounded by. The effect and purpose, in this respect,
are not unlike those of the sonnets in *Romeo and Juliet*. Discussion of
*Troat*'s opening sonnet will perhaps be easier if it is temporarily isolated
from its context of action and gesture:

> Imagination's huge, informing strength
> Raised with a thought; and with a word endowed
> Into the quality, and feel, and length
> Of anything I choose out from the crowd.
> I am this elm; from frailest stalk to root;
> Pervade, and thicken through warm sap to bark;
> Creak the wind's strain, press out in rings that shoot
> Bud-surging thrusts, while trembling limbs are stark.
> I am an old man staring at the coals,
> Seeking sensations while the brain runs rife.
> Staring through eyes that swoop on beasts in holes.
> Inhabit each last strangled cry for life.
> Companion thoughts; protean, unconfined.
> The spawning cancers of a dying mind.   (*M*, 25–26; *R*, 45–46)

The first line offers eloquent statement of that theme of imagination
which is so important throughout the six plays of *Maquettes* and
*Requiem*. The whole of the first quatrain raises a number of questions
about creative imagination — about kinds of creation and kinds of
imagination. The first line's eloquence, in phrasing which echoes both
Shakespeare and Yeats, requires us to see imagination as a noble, perhaps vital, faculty. Imagination as esemplastic power is not far away.
With the second line, however, one begins to feel less certain of the
essential nobility of the imaginative faculty. The imagery becomes
expressly sensual, perhaps specifically sexual. The "feel" and "length"
are revealingly concrete words in this context. The allusion to the
phrase "never mind the quality, feel the width" conjures up the image
of a kind of Old Testament Ancient of Days measuring out his creation
in a dim light. Certainly in this dramatic world the act of creation is
bound to carry sexual implications: "Raised with a thought" carries
inescapable overtones of sexual erection. Imagination, in this Old Man
at any rate, seems to be turning into something dangerously close to
sexual fantasy, and it is no surprise when the ensuing play illustrates
at length the ferocity of his sexual imaginings. At the same time, however, the second line prompts thoughts of other kinds of creativity. The
phrase "with a word endowed" simultaneously points us to the poetic
use of language (giving "to airy nothing/A local habitation and a

name") and to the Johannine doctrine of the Logos. We are encouraged
to see the Old Man as in some sense a type of both Poet and God. The
second quatrain of his sonnet shows us the kind of limited identificatory
use to which the Old Man does, in fact, put his power of imagination.
Even here the sexual overtones are present. The language is reminiscent
of Donne's *Loves Growth*:

> Gentle love deeds, as blossomes on a bough,
> From loves awaken'd root do bud out now

but the Old Man's tone is more violent than Donne's. "Surging thrusts"
and the "stark" "trembling limbs" reinforce one's sense that there are
continuing elements both of the phallic and the violent in the Old
Man's imagination. Certainly the nobility of the sonnet's opening line,
already somewhat tarnished, is thoroughly shattered by the actions
which punctuate the break between octave and sestet:

> *Pause. Then sees mouse cross stage . . . Catches it. Holds it up.*
> *Strokes it gently, smiling. Strangles it viciously between legs. Holds*
> *up by tail so audience can see . . . Then slowly swings it round in*
> *clockwise direction with right hand by tip of tail three times, the*
> *third letting it go so that it rises into air and lands among audience.*
> *Shuffles back. Sits, oblivious.*   (M, 26; R, 46)

The apparent tenderness turns to violence. The mouse is strangled
between his legs. The sexuality of his imagination is shown to have a
violent edge.

Not surprisingly the tone of the sonnet is much changed in the
remaining sestet. Dominant now are his isolation and his fascination
with death. His thoughts are his only companions and they are "spawning cancers". His sonnet completed he "goes into reverie" (M, 26;
R, 46) and the Young Man enters. There is much here to encourage one
in the belief that the Young Man (and therefore the Woman and the
Boy too) is a creation of the Old Man's imagination. We have already
seen that the Old Man is presented as a type of the creator. It is when
he falls into a reverie, having talked of his "spawning" thoughts, that
the Young Man enters. We may choose to interpret all that follows as
the imaginative articulation of the Old Man's subconscious, as well as
being a presentation of the artist's relation to his creations, and of the
relationship of God and man. *Troat* is in some ways an earlier sketch
for the later treatment of some similar themes in Chalone and Ensoff.
The text of *Troat* stops short of any explicit assertions with regard to
these possibilities. We are left to decide for ourselves how 'real' the
remainder of the play is.

The Young Man, whose tenor voice we may take as being counter-pointed with the bass voice of the Old Man, enters with the phrase "Excuse me" (*M*, 26; *R*, 46). The later inhabitants of *Troat*'s imaginative world both enter with the same phrase on their lips (*M*, 28, 31; *R*, 48, 51): one aspect of that quasi-musical formality in the play's structure which is hinted at when the play is described as "a double fugue" (*M*, 23; *R*, 43). (Since the Young Man is explicitly said to have a "tenor voice" (*M*, 26; *R*, 46) and the Boy sings in a "treble voice" (*M*, 35; *R*, 55), it seems reasonable to assume that the Old Man provides the bass and the Woman the alto, so that we have the vocal resources for a four-voice fugue.)

At the Young Man's entry the Old Man immediately takes on a military role. He becomes, not a guardian of holes in the road, but a sentry. His "Who . . . goes . . . there?" is spoken "with great deliberation" (*M*. 26; *R*. 46), perhaps after the fashion of a man remembering a role with which he is now less familiar than he used to be. Imagination, creative power, becomes merely a matter of memory. Soon the Old Man is reminiscing:

They put up a white rag on the end of a rifle. Waved it over the pill-box. Yes. Mud. I went up and they said 'Mein Herr, wir surrender!' 'Gut,' I said, took out the pin and lobbed in a grenade. (*Chuckles*) What a bang! Couldn't be fussed with prisoners. (*Pause. Chuckles*) What a bang!     (*M*, 27; *R*, 47)

By now we ought not to be surprised either by the content of the Old Man's reminiscences, or by the relish with which he recounts acts of violence. Before this point has been reached the Old and the Young Man (since both are so insistently designated in this way, would it be altogether inappropriate for us to think of the Young Man as a kind of fantastic memory of the Old Man's younger self?) have acted out a small but intricate cameo of strained communication:

| | |
|---|---|
| OLD MAN | Who . . . goes . . . there? I said. |
| YOUNG MAN | I know . . . |
| OLD MAN | Of course *you* know, unless you are someone else. It is I who wish to know. |
| YOUNG MAN | What a strange gentleman you are. |
| OLD MAN | I am not a gentleman. |
| YOUNG MAN | You may watch the road, but you are not a sentry. There isn't a war on, you know. |
| OLD MAN | Several.  (*M*, 26–7; *R*, 46–7) |

The misunderstanding which pivots on the word 'know' is particularily telling so early in the play. Any knowledge, slippery enough in itself, proves still more slippery if it must be expressed verbally. The Young Man uses words more for reasons of social politeness than for reasons of accuracy. The Old Man, more concerned for the accuracy of the tongue, and inclined to take people's words literally, rejects the epithet 'gentleman'. His isolation from society perhaps leads him to take at face value those important words which a trivial society has debased. We are given a clear instance of this later when the Woman responds "Good God!" to his description of the carnivorous flower. "You have great faith" comments the Old Man (*M*, 30; *R*, 50). In this earlier exchange with the Young Man, the Old Man fluctuates between reminiscence and fantasy, both involving the same dual fascination with slaughter and fornication. His fantasies initially focus on the ludicrous desire for a filing cabinet — this Old Man's equivalent of that trip to Sidcup, to collect his papers, which sustains Davies, the old man of Pinter's play *The Caretaker*. This initial fantasy serves only to set his mind free to indulge in its dreams — dreams which naturally involve the celebration (with allusions to inappropriate songs) of predators and predacity:

> I could evict my tenants, sell their houses, and fish in the Gulf of Mexico. Yes! See it? Bonito! That great predator. Hot, calm for miles, then, watch! Suddenly a great hand plunges up out of the ocean scattering handfuls of small fry like silver coins in the sun. He's hungry! After him, in among the minnows! Speed bonny boat! . . . The great predatory chain of nature.   (*M*, 28; *R*, 48)

The manner in which he anthropomorphises the process of predation — "suddenly a great hand" — creates the sense of a huge god–like figure (with whom, of course, the Old Man identifies himself) actively destroying his creation, and doing so with enormous gusto. The Old Man's "the great predatory chain of nature" ironically invokes the whole philosophical tradition of the *scala naturae*, 'the Great Chain of Being'. We have, however, moved a long way from a merely classificatory system. Doubtless the Old Man would agree with Plotinus in the observation that

> the animals devour each other: men attack each other: all is war without rest, without truce[1]

and in drawing the conclusion that

this devouring of Kind by Kind is necessary.[2]

The Old Man's observations, however, are imbued with a greater degree
of sheer enthusiasm than is compatible with philosophical analysis. At
the same time, though, we ought to bear it in mind that the concept of
the 'chain of being' has traditionally contained within it the implication
of a possible upward return by man:

> The scale of nature set
> From center to circumference, whereon
> In contemplation of created things
> By steps we may ascend to God.[3]

The argument, as presented, for example, in Bellarmino's *De ascensione
mentis in Deum per scalas creaturarum* is that through the observation
of the imperfections of all around us we shall conclude that

> all things other than God are vanity and vexation of spirit, which
> have no existence, but only appear to have, and do not afford solace,
> but only affliction.[4]

The resultant meditation leads us to an 'ascent' of the material and
spiritual ladder which leads to God. *Troat* is concerned with both the
Young Man's and the Old Man's perceptions of human inperfection (*cf.*
*M*, 32, 35; *R*, 52, 55); but in neither case does this perception function
as envisaged by such philosophers as Bellarmino. One clue as to why,
we may find in one of the most powerful of eighteenth-century medi-
tations upon the *topos* in Edward Young's *Night Thoughts*. His vision is
of a Nature which is "neat gradation all"; an important question must
be posed, however:

> But how preserv'd
> The chain unbroken upward, to the realms
> Of incorporeal life? Those realms of bliss,
> Where death hath no dominion? Grant a make
> Half-mortal, half-immortal; earthy, part,
> And part ethereal; grant the soul of man
> Eternal; or in man the series ends.
> Wide yawns the gap; connexion is no more;
> Check'd reason halts; her next step wants support;
> Striving to climb, she tumbles from her scheme.[5]

"Check'd reason halts" — throughout the *Maquettes* and the *Requiem* plays there is much for which this phrase might stand as epigraph; the limitations of human reason, and with them the horrors of a society trapped within those limitations, are illustrated and analysed at length in these plays.

When the Young Man concedes "And you as part of it find your place" (*M*, 28; *R*, 48) he sees the Old Man primarily as predator. The remaining lines which they share before the entrance of the Woman confirm the sexual dimensions of that imagination which is presented here. At the Woman's entry the Young Man's attempt to return to the language of polite discourse ensures that once more the Old Man will refuse the offered title:

> I am not a gentleman.   (*M*, 29; *R*, 49)

His sombre statement

> I have been part of a regiment, and am now alone   (*M*, 29; *R*, 49)

sets up important resonances. On the most limited of levels it gives a degree of pathos to the Old Man's isolation. We have already found some reason, however, for viewing him as in some sense a God-like figure. By now it ought to be becoming clear more precisely what kind of God he is, or rather what kind of conception of God he represents. He is a God who remains at an emotional distance from his creatures; in his solitude he keeps watch; we are encouraged to think of his moral standards as being those of military discipline rather than those of compassionate concern. He has, in short, a more than passing resemblance to the Old Testament God of Wrath. In the Old Testament's presentation of Yahweh, figures of speech taken from military language are amongst those used most frequently. In *Exodus* (15:3) we are told that "The Lord is a man of war"; in *Psalms* (24:8) he is "the Lord strong and mighty, the Lord mighty in battle". We might do well to remember that evolution from polytheism towards monotheism which seems to have taken place amongst the ancient Israelites. In emerging from the cult of familiar gods and becoming "Sole Lord" it might well be said of Yahweh that he was once "part of a regiment" and is "now alone". The Old Man assuredly possesses those qualities of wrath and jealousy which the Old Testament attributes to Yahweh. At the same time the Woman's immediate "you remind me of my father" (*M*, 29; *R*, 49) offers a reminder of a rather different aspect of God. However, the Old Man's response — "Incest" — hardly encourages us to see in him an exemplum of spiritual fatherhood. He treats the Woman's sentimentality with scorn. For her 'nature' is not a "great predatory chain" but a matter of hearing the rustle of the leaves, feeding the rabbits, watching the dawn.   (*M*, 29; *R*, 49)

For the Old Man nature necessarily involves a chain of sexual predation too. He tells his companions

Come on you two. Hurry up and get it over.   (*M*, 29; *R*, 49)

He prompts the Woman and the Young Man to that for which he will later punish them. The Old Man is recognisable as a distorted picture of Yahweh. In part the distortion lies in the apparent prurience of the Old Man's imagination:

Here, alone in the night, sitting beside the road works, you think of women?   (*M*, 27; *R*, 47)

As a God figure the Old Man obviously asks to be compared with Chalone and Ensoff — and his seemingly arbitrary cruelty links him with Nero. The contrast between Ensoff and the Old Man is the most revealing. Ensoff is a creator who can share the sufferings of his creation; he can, above all, view his creations with both wonder and tenderness. When Callisterne says to Ensoff

I think of you as a father

*he* replies

I will not importune, not yet desert you. I am your close friend and will never hurt you.   (*ME*, 46; *R*, 242)

Shango's castration of Ensoff follows immediately and afterwards the stage direction reads:

ENSOFF *sitting position, where he fell, in centre of sundial.*
CALLISTERNE *is sitting beside him. He has an arm around her, but they must not at any point kiss.* (*ME*, 46–7; *R*, 242–3)

We must put against this the analogous episode in *Troat*:

OLD MAN        It's an urban civilization. A woman of the world is
               very largely a woman of the streets.
WOMAN          No, I like you and won't be put off. Tell me what
               you think about here at night

WOMAN *crouches beside him, downstage, daughterly snuggle up to him.*

WOMAN          With time passing. How many pendulums has a grandfather clock?

OLD MAN          Two weights and a pendulum. (*To* YOUNG MAN) Just like a man.   (*M*, 29—30; *R*, 49—50)

The two incidents have very different preludes and reveal very different things about their protagonists. In *Meeting Ends* the fatherly embrace (devoid of all sexual connotations) takes place upon that sundial which is a potent symbol in the play, measuring the movements of divine light and standing in opposition to the kind of purely temporal world symbolised by the 'grandfather clock'. The asexual dimension of compassion evident in *Meeting Ends* is opposed to the prurience of the Old Man in *Troat*; the Woman's question jars somewhat clumsily against the relative naturalism of dialogue in which the play has so far been couched. Thematically it is important in that it is also part of an increasing use of family terms and names which is to build up to a climax in the later "child's game" (*M*, 34; *R*, 54) version of the Prayer Book. Before long the Woman is calling the Old Man "Grandpa" (*M*, 31; *R*, 51); the boy is calling her "Mum" (*M*, 33, *R*, 53), but insisting "don't mother me" (*M*, 33; *R*, 53). Because their God is not a father, or perhaps because he *is* a father only of a rigorously restrictive kind (here the comparison with Chalone is most pertinent), these people see no meaning in such familial terms. Marriage must necessarily be a meaningless concept for them, as their parody of the Book of Common Prayer's "Table of Kindred and Affinity" vividly demonstrates.

More immediately upon her "snuggling" beside the Old Man, the Woman serves to introduce what is perhaps the most telling pattern of literary allusion to be found anywhere in the *Maquettes*:

WOMAN          . . . Don't leave just because I've taken notice of our watchman of the night. I have to find . . .

OLD MAN          The nightly parliament of stars, resplendent rulers, bringing heat, and colds, by turns.  (*M*, 30 *R*, 50)

The Woman's "our watchman of the night" points inescapably to the Book of Isaiah:

The burden of Dumah. He calleth to me out of Seir, Watchman, what of the night? Watchman, what of the night?  (*Isaiah*, 21:11)

The Old Man's words take us in a different, but closely related, direction. The words I have quoted are a direct translation of famous lines near the beginning of the Watchman's speech which constitutes the Prologue to Aeschylus's *Agamemnon* and thus to the Oresteian trilogy as a whole. The suggestion is clear — we are invited to see *this* nightwatchman as being related to, or even identified with, these two other nightwatchmen. Let us consider the Isaiah reference first.

Isaiah Chapter Twenty-One is a prophecy which describes the siege and capture of Babylon by the troops of Elam and Media. The prophet suffers as he undergoes his visionary experience:

> A grievous vision is declared unto me; the treacherous dealer dealeth treacherously, and the spoiler spoileth. Go up, O Elam: besiege, O Media; all the sighing thereof have I made to cease.
>
> Therefore are my loins filled with pain: pangs have taken hold upon me, as the pangs of a woman that travaileth: I was bowed down at the hearing of it; I was dismayed at the seeing of it.
>
> My heart panted, fearfulness affrighted me: the night of my pleasure hath he turned into fear unto me.  (21:2—4)

The watchman referred to in Isaiah is the prophet himself when in that condition of trance which is the precondition of his 'seeing'. The whole background of war has an obvious and straightforward relevance to *Troat*, but in the question the watchman is asked, and the answer he gives, there is something of even more direct relevance:

> Watchman, what of the night? Watchman, what of the night?
>
> The Watchman said, The morning cometh, and also the night: if ye will inquire, inquire ye: return, come.  (21:11—12)

The watchman's reply is ambiguous. The night of Edom's troubles will find the day — "the morning cometh" — but night will return. Is the watchman unsure which force will achieve supremacy? Will the offer of light be scorned? Will there be light for some and darkness for others? In *Troat* we are watching another world of night which also waits the light; the Young Man insists that "light is not now far away" (*M*, 31; *R*, 51); the Boy is on his way to begin his dawn delivery of newspapers; we hear the cock crow (*M*, 33; *R*, 53); the Woman announces to the Young Man:

> I'll share your coat, and we can sit by the fire while he [the Boy] sings in the new day.  (*M*, 35; *R*, 55)

The 'song' is the *Nunc Dimittis*, but the light comes only in the form of the fire of wrath. The blackout upon which the play ends is more than a matter of theatrical convenience. Even the 'embers' which illuminated the play's opening are extinguished at its close.

The allusion to (or rather, quotation of) the Aeschylean watchman invokes a related thematic pattern.[6] The setting of the original speech has been well described by E. T. Owen:

> his actual position, the scene that is called up in his words, expresses visually the keynote of the whole trilogy — waiting in darkness for the light of deliverance.[7]

The whole of the watchman's speech constitutes a prayer for release, a prayer for light — the first of many others throughout Aeschylus's trilogy. His particular plea is for the flash of the beacon which will indicate the capture of Troy — the motif of the besieged city we have already seen in the passage from Isaiah. The light comes (as fire) but like so many other 'lights' in the Oresteian trilogy it brings not deliverance, but further disaster. Eventually a true light will shine out. All the deceptive lights are subsumed in the light which bathes the end of the *Eumenides* — the procession of torches which escorts the Eumenides to their new Athenian home. The movement towards light is imitated in Warner's plays — the ring of candles which surround Ensoff at the close of *Meeting Ends* taking the place of the music and lighted torches of Aeschylus.

These two allusions, one to Isaiah and one to Aeschylus, have produced a pattern of theme and image which both contains and expands the significance of this particular nightwatchman we can see on stage, and our sense of his importance in Warner's *Requiem* cycle. We must, though, bear in mind one important respect in which this watchman differs from his fellow in *Agamemnon*. He is the custodian of the beacon (or in his case, brazier) rather than the seeker for it. He has the fire at his disposal, and we shall see that he has no hesitation in putting it to use.

With the entry of the Boy we find the play modulating into a different key. A new register enters the play. We hear talk of "the sacrificial lamb" and the statement that "Christ was a fisher" (*M*, 32; *R*, 52). Allusions to the crucifixion are much in evidence. Confronted with the Boy's desire for bait, the Old Man responds:

Why hast thou forsaken the lot of us?     (*M*, 32; *R*, 52)

and only a little later the Boy himself, asked about "the boss", states

"Oh, he's finished" (*M*, 32; *R*, 52). Invocation of the Passion reminds us of a standard against which we might measure the Old Man's insufficiency as a type of God, and against which we might also judge the behaviour of the other inhabitants of this darkened world. It is only a few moments later that we are to hear the crowing of the cock:

| OLD MAN | The boss is a bloody fool. |
| WOMAN | (*To* BOY) Yes, how is he? Isn't he in a very bad way these days? |
| BOY | Oh; he's finished. (*Pause*) He's dead. |
| WOMAN | (*Goes over to* YOUNG MAN *and takes him by the hand*). I feel we all need each other, all four of us gathered round the fire. *A cock crows* |
| OLD MAN | What illusions!    (*M*, 32–33; *R*, 52–53) |

The crowing of the cock follows on the bluntness of the Boy's denial and the triteness of the Woman's sentimentality. Unlike their Biblical prototype, however, no one is moved to go and "weep bitterly". Undaunted, their superficiality continues unabated. The betrayal of God is only reinforced by the juxtaposition of their mockery of the Prayer Book alongside the Boy's reading the lesson (*M*, 35; *R*, 55) and his singing of the *Nunc Dimittis*. The 'lesson', couched in effectively Biblical tones, runs as follows:

And the Lord saw man as beautiful and imperfect, and stripping away the imperfections found only a shadow of the man he had thought so beautiful.   (*M*, 35; *R*, 55)

We must put this 'lesson' alongside some earlier lines from the play — the Young Man's 'witty' reflections:

I suppose none of us is perfect. If we were we'd be indistinguishable. Our fallings from perfection, our vices, are what make us individuals; so in the name of common humanity we should cultivate our faults.
(*M*, 32; *R*, 52)

The theme is continued and restated with an important variation in *Lumen*:

What distinguishes us one from another is the quality of our vices, our fallings from uniform perfection. And we fall, all of us, in exactly the same way.   (*M*, 44; *R*, 64)

*Troat* itself is primarily concerned with two aspects of that 'fall': the human propensities for indulgence in sex and violence. The boy's talk of bait links the two motifs, as does the behaviour of the Old Man. As well as that bait which the Boy requires for his fishing, the play is permeated by the presence of another sort of bait. The link might be forged in our minds by a poem such as Donne's 'The Bait'. When Wyatt renounces love he renounces its "bayted hookes" and, most forcefully, Shakespeare, in Sonnet 129, sees lust as being

> Past reason hunted; and no sooner had,
> Past reason hated, as a swallow'd bait
> On purpose laid to make the taker mad.

Where this kind of bait is concerned the Old Man is the fisherman. We have traced already the obsessively sexual cast of his imagination; more than this, he seeks to put flesh on the sexual words of his imagination. In his own impotence that flesh must be the flesh of others: all three of the other characters. His opening sonnet, let us remind ourselves, talked of his

> Seeking sensations while the brain runs rife     (*M*, 26; *R*, 46)

and of things "with a word endowed" (*M*, 25; *R*, 45). The particular kind of incarnation he has in mind is patently more carnal than it is Johannine. He uses the very same terms when he half taunts, half encourages, the Young Man:

> Make love to her, man. Come on, Narcissus. Endow her with your fantasies and hug your reflection to yourself. It's dark enough.
> (*M*, 33; *R*, 53)

Long before this he has sought to influence the Young Man's imagination, his power of 'interpretation', immediately before the Woman's entrance:

> OLD MAN        . . . See that over there? Two lovers kissing? See? See? (*Pause*) It's a pollarded willow.
> YOUNG MAN    By Heaven, so it is! Well, it looked just like . . .
> (*M*, 28; *R*, 48)

Both of the Old Man's incitements are centered upon the power of fantasy. *Lumen* will take up explicitly the suggested strategy of the first quotation, and the pollarded willow (cropped so as to be more 'creative') would appear to foreshadow some of the 'mutilations' of later plays — notably that of Ensoff. Only a few lines after the Woman's entrance the Old Man is insisting bluntly:

Come on you two. Hurry up and get it over.　(*M*, 29; *R*, 49)

He views them, inevitably, as a young couple eager to copulate (*M*, 30; *R*, 50). Before long his persuasions:

Let him satisfy your wasps' nest of regret　　(*M*, 31; *R*, 51)

are having an effect, but the effect is not to bring the couple together, but rather to make the Woman masturbate. *Emblems* has already shown us a lesbian marriage; *Troat* has shown us the Young Man's insistence that he is "self sufficient" (*M*, 27; *R*, 47) and his effeminacy has been emphasised. With the entry of the Boy following immediately upon the Woman's masturbation, we are told that the Young Man is "a ruddy queer" (*M*, 31; *R*, 51). The Old Man continues to encourage the sensuality of those around him, continues to seek the fleshing forth of his imaginings. He expects

the boy and the lady to play 'chest nuts'　　(*M*, 33; *R*, 53)

a remark accompanied by gestures directed towards her breasts and the Boy's genitals. In the midst of all these perversions, and after the incestuous permutations of the child's game played with the Prayer Book, there is something almost innocent, attractively fresh, about one of the first moments of contact to occur in the play:

WOMAN　　　　　...(*To* YOUNG MAN) I'll share your coat, and we can sit by the fire while he sings in the new day.　(*M*, 35; *R*, 55)

Of course such fleeting innocence as the moment may possess is quite outweighed by the darkness and corruption that surrounds it.

The world we have seen in the play is a world which has denied God, which has consciously chosen darkness. It persists, however, in expecting "the new day". Light is invoked in the clear voice of the Boy as he sings the *Nunc Dimittis*. Here is *Troat*'s equivalent to those prayers for light which we have seen alluded to in the reference made to the *Oresteia*; at the same time it foreshadows those prayers which, in a variety of forms, constitute the closing words of *Lumen* and *Killing Time* and it announces the chord of imagery upon which, in very different modes, *Lying*

*Figures*, *Meeting Ends* and *Light Shadows* all close. Since Sir Francis Bacon is to make an important and early appearance in the final play of this trilogy of *Maquettes*, there is much aptness here in some words of his with regard to the Nunc Dimittis:

> Above all, believe it, the sweetest canticle is "Nunc dimittis", when a man hath obtained worthy ends and expectations.[8]

These preconditions have not here been met; the "sweetest canticle" will be made to reveal its bitter side.

The Boy gets no further than "To be a light to lighten":

> Lord, now lettest thou thy servant depart in peace according to thy word.
> For mine eyes have seen thy salvation,
> Which thou hast prepared before the face of all people,
> To be a light to lighten the Gentiles.

The mockery is complete: they are *not* God's servants; their eyes have not seen or understood the salvation. They have yet to learn (instruction is close at hand) that there is, to borrow a Shakespearean phrase, such a thing as the "abusing of God's patience":

> Be not deceived; God is not mocked: for whatsoever a man soweth, that shall he also reap.
> For he that soweth to his flesh shall of the flesh reap corruption.
> *(Galatians* 6: 7–8)

The Old Man, ambiguous and jealous Yahweh of this little dramatic universe, gives his people the light they request. It is a light, however, which is here manifested as the flame of both vengeance and purification:

> *As he reaches 'To be a light to lighten' the* OLD MAN, *who has slowly been coming nearer and nearer, his gloves on, suddenly seizes the brazier full of red-hot coals and with one swift movement lifts it up and thrusts it down inverted on the heads of* YOUNG MAN *and* WOMAN *who were about to kiss. Violent scream.*
> *(M*, 35; *R*, 55)

The Old Man may have been a creator when the play began; by now he is unquestionably a dealer out of death and destruction. Later, more

Pauline, plays of Warner's will explore the making metaphorical of what is here literal:

> Dearly beloved, avenge not yourselves, but rather give place unto wrath: for it is written, Vengeance is mine; I will repay, saith the Lord.
> Therefore if thine enemy hunger, feed him; if he thirst, give him drink: for in so doing thou shalt heap coals of fire on his head.
> Be not overcome of evil, but overcome evil with good.
>
> (*Romans*, 12: 19–21)

Here the burning coals are all too literal. Even their 'light' cannot prevent the play's ending in darkness. The next play is called *Lumen*.

### Notes

1 Plotinus, *The Ethical Treatises*, translated by Stephen MacKenna, 1921, Vol. II, p. 28. To the Young Man's "There isn't a war on, you know" the Old Man has earlier replied "Several" (*M*, 27; *R*, 47).
2 Plotinus, *ibid*. Interestingly the whole of this section of the *Enneads* is built around the metaphor of life as a stage-play.
3 Quoted thus in A. O. Lovejoy, *The Great Chain of Being*, New York, 1965, p. 89. Warner's use of this symbol may perhaps be influenced by its use in Agrippa, and in Lull's *Liber de Ascensu et Descensu Intellectus*. See Warner's essay 'Das Gedankengebäude des Agrippa von Nettesheim', *Antaios*, V, (1963), 122–142.
4 Lovejoy, *op. cit.*, p. 92.
5 Edward Young, *Night Thoughts*, Book VI.
6 The words will be taken up again by Ensoff in Act Two Scene Seven of *Meeting Ends* (*ME*, 47; *R*, 243).
7 E. T. Owen, *The Harmony of Aeschylus*, Toronto, 1952, p. 64.
8 Bacon, *Essays*, 'Of Death'.

# V

## *Lumen:* Lux, etsi per immunda transeat, non inquinatur

The title of the third maquette naturally and necessarily alerts us to a number of possible themes and motifs. The world we have seen in the first two plays has certainly been sadly in need of enlightenment. Will this play show us what that enlightenment might be? Some of the imagery used towards the end of *Troat* has prepared us to look for light in a particular form. "The sacrificial lamb" and "Christ was a fisher" (*M*, 32; *R*, 52) are phrases which predispose us to look in this final maquette for light in the form of Christ incarnate. *Troat*, as we have seen, made a number of allusions to the opening verses of the Gospel according to St. John. Only a few words into *Lumen* we find very clear reference to the same text:

| ACTRESS | That word! |
| ACTOR | Made flesh; stable produce.   (*M*, 40; *R*, 60) |

Taking up the hint (a pretty plain one) we may look to the Gospel text both for confirmation of the identity of this play's 'lumen' and some suggestions as to the way the play may present men's reaction to that light:

> In the beginning was the Word, and the Word was with God, and the Word was God.
> The same was in the beginning with God.
> All things were made by him; and without him was not anything made that was made.
> In him was life; and the life was the light of men.

And the light shineth in darkness; and the darkness comprehended it not.

There was a man sent from God, whose name was John.

The same came for a witness, to bear witness of the Light, that all men through him might believe.

He was not that Light, but was sent to bear witness of that Light.

That was the true Light, which lighteth every man that cometh into the world.

He was in the world, and the world was made by him, and the world knew him not.

He came unto his own, and his own received him not.

But as many as received him, to them gave he power to become the sons of God, even to them that believe on his name:

Which were born, not of blood, nor of the will of the flesh, nor of the will of man, but of God.

And the Word was made flesh, and dwelt among us (and we beheld his glory, the glory as of the only begotten of the Father), full of grace and truth.[1]

The play opens in darkness. Light does, literally, arrive. A single spotlight illumines the centre of an empty stage. The movement will be repeated in an exactly inverted form at the play's close. The overall movement of the play is through light from darkness to darkness. It is a bare theatrical analogy for human life.

The play opens with a sequence of tableaux, interleaved with fades and darkness. The empty, spotlit, stage is first replaced by a darkness flooded by

*Loud, unidentifiable discothèque music.*     (*M*, 39; *R*, 59)

That darkness ceases, enabling us to see two sides of meat hanging on stage; with the 'interruption' of several moments of darkness we see, first:

*upstage right flank of meat with a pair of men's Y-front underpants pinned on, and upstage left flank with bra and panties.*

(*M*, 39; *R*, 59)

and then a naked actor and actress seated in front of these 'clothed' joints of meat. The final tableau presents the two pieces of meat stripped of their garments, which have now been transferred to the actor and actress. In outline (though not in precise detail) this sequence too will be reversed at the end of the play. As an analogy with human life we may see it as a movement from nothingness and darkness to meat, and to the acting of roles, and back through meat to darkness and nothingness. The vision is a bleak one; any light would certainly be welcome.

Individually, these tableaux are striking visual compositions. In sequence they offer, as it were, a very 'physical' background against which we must necessarily place, and judge, the dialogue of the unnamed man and woman which is framed by the opening and closing dumb-shows. Indeed, they can scarcely even be called dumb-shows: there is no activity to be seen, merely a sequence of 'snapshots', alternating with a darkened stage. We are reminded of that camera (and cameraman) encountered in the very first of these *Maquettes*.

The spoken proceedings open with a rapid game of word associations, or at least that is one's first impression. The speed and insistence of this early quibbling suggests a trivialisation of language. These appear to be wordgames played without due seriousness by their practitioners. At the end of the play the actress will observe, regretfully, "we shouldn't have joked" (*M*, 49; *R*, 69). The word-association game they play is a poor substitute for real human communication. Their later failure to touch hands (*M*, 49; *R*, 69) is here foreshadowed verbally. Their opening conversational 'movement' turns out on closer examination, however, to be perfectly designed both in terms of its own structure and in terms of its relevance to the major themes of the tetralogy. It will bear closer scrutiny:

| | |
|---|---|
| ACTOR | (*After a pause*) Cold. |
| ACTRESS | (*With contempt*) You are! |
| ACTOR | Cold, that proves I exist. Hot? Therefore you do not. |
| ACTRESS | Hottentot. |
| ACTOR | The sparrow has found her a nest where she may lay her young; and the tot of the Hottentot his pot where it |
| ACTRESS | He |
| ACTOR | May deposit its, or his — |
| ACTRESS | Excrement. |
| ACTOR | Ah! The language remains stable. We have not yet sunk to stable language. |
| ACTRESS | The staple produce of a stable is sh . . . |
| ACTOR | Dung. |
| ACTRESS | That word! |
| ACTOR | Made flesh; stable produce. |
| ACTRESS | Bacon. |
| ACTOR | All path to power *is* by a winding stair. |

| ACTRESS | Spiral. |
| ACTOR | Stone, doubtless, stone steps in the form of a |
| ACTRESS | (*With relish*) Screw. |
| ACTOR | Child! |
| ACTRESS | Chilled. |
| ACTOR | Cold. |
| ACTRESS | You are! |
| | (*Pause*).   (*M*, 40–41; *R*, 60–61) |

The Actor's opening word is presumably an initial observation upon the circumstances in which he finds himself. Reflection on the ability to feel cold at least serves to persuade him of the reality of his own existence. But the Cartesian formula has gone down in the world somewhat: 'I am cold, therefore I exist'. Even before this evidence of the actor's flawed powers of reasoning, his meditation has been interrupted by the Actress' contemptuous "You are!", a dismissal of him for his failure to provide sufficient sexual fire to satisfy her appetites. The Actor continues to develop his dubiously logical propositions. If his 'coldness' proves his existence, then her (sexual) heat must prove her non-existence. The Actress not unfittingly responds with a word whose association is purely one of sound. The Actor's masquerade of logic has had little more than this to offer. One of the play's main themes has already received embryonic statement: the extent to which our human relationships depend upon words (this is the most 'verbal' of all Warner's plays, the one which pays least attention to characters and action) and the extent to which this vital medium has been debased.

In the next stages of the exchange a theme of even greater centrality is stated. The Actor's response takes the form of a Biblical allusion:

The sparrow has found her a nest where she may lay her young.

As so often with Warner's Biblical references it is wisest to return the text to its original context if we wish to understand its purpose in its new one. In this case that original context is to be found in Psalms:

My soul longeth, yea, even fainteth for the courts of the Lord: my heart and my flesh crieth out for the living God.

Yea, the sparrow hath found an house, and the swallow a nest for herself, where she may lay her young, even thine altars, O Lord of hosts, my King and my God.

Blessed are they that dwell in thy house: they will still be praising thee. Selah.[2]

The first of these verses eloquently expresses that state of mind which has been so noticeably absent from the characters we have met in the first two maquettes, but which will, at any rate, be hinted at by the conclusion of this third play. In Warner's adaptation of the second verse quoted above the sparrow seems not to have its usual symbolic value as a bird of lechery; rather its finding a nest for its young, understood in terms of its Biblical context, contrasts with the reiterative cuckoo we are to hear later (*M*, 46; *R*, 66). In the Actor's speech the sparrow's 'laying' of young is immediately juxtaposed with the "tot of the Hottentot" and his 'laying' of his excrement. The juxtaposition looks forward to a passage in *Lying Figures*:

SAPPH          We drop children into the world like . . . like . . .
LAZ            Turds.  (*LF*, 5; *R*, 79)

Here in *Lumen* the beauty of the Biblical paraphrase is immediately debased; firstly by the crude jingle of "the tot of the Hottentot his pot" and secondly by the pedantic refinement of the characters' elusion of the word 'shit'. The juxtaposition of spiritual with crudely earthy is reinforced formally. The Biblical paraphrase is allowed uninterrupted and attractively cadenced statement; the words about the Hottentot are allowed only fragmented and clumsy statement.

The Actor's self satisfied assertion

Ah! the language remains stable. We have not yet sunk to stable language

betrays an over-confidence which will later be punished. Their own manner of talking has already made us doubt the stability of their language; if it has such 'stability' it is surely only because they have not yet tried to make it bear the weight of real conversation:

ACTRESS          The staple produce of a stable is sh . . .
ACTOR            Dung.
ACTRESS          That word!
ACTOR            Made flesh; stable produce.

Their bland refinement leads to the Actor's hurried "Dung" and the actress' "That word!". But their blindness takes on a more serious form too. Their debasement of the Johannine text at least serves to remind us that in one important sense Christ is, indeed, "stable produce" — a clear allusion to the circumstances of the nativity. Here, surely, they are close to some kind of perception of that event which might make sense of their juxtaposition of the earthly and the spiritual. A perception of the incarnation would effect not only a reconciliation of these two elements but make visible that 'light' for which we are waiting. It is not to be, however. The vertiginous game of word associations to which they have reduced human conversation will allow no pause for meditation on the weight of the words they have so casually used.

The associations of "flesh" and "stable produce" (as well, of course, as the flanks of meat hanging on the stage throughout) lead on inevitably to the next phase of the game:

ACTRESS      Bacon.
ACTOR        All path to power *is* by a winding stair.

For them the Johannine doctrine of the Word made flesh can mean no more than becoming a side of meat. In the quick-moving but shallow minds of these two 'shadows' the word bacon, once enunciated, naturally takes on a double meaning. It becomes a proper name and the actor replies with a borrowing from the works of the Viscount St. Albans. The Actor seems to be remembering a sentence from Bacon's Essay 'Of Great Place':

All rising to great place is by a winding stair.

Of course the kind of power the Actor has in mind is sexual power. The linguistic game continues, via spiral and its definition, enabling the Actress to reassert her sexual desires, transforming "screw" from noun to verb. The Actor readopts his air of superiority in dismissing her as childish, and through an easy series of transitions we are back to an exact repetition of the opening of the whole trope. The "spiral" and "screw" of the verbal exchange are now revealed to be not only parts of the trope, but descriptions of the whole of it. All their verbal agility has led them no further than their own point of departure. At the mid-point of the exchange of words they came within distance of an all-important realisation, but failed to make the realisation. All their words seem so readily interchangeable as to be devoid of any specific gravity of meaning.

This "set of wit" has, though, served to establish for them, to their own satisfaction at least, that they are an Actor and Actress. That being established they can now begin to take on an equally vertiginous succession of roles. Nowhere in the cast-lists of these *Maquettes* are the characters given names; but in the first two plays they have at least borne generic titles — Bride, Groom, Old Man, Young Man and so on. Here in this third play we meet only Actor and Actress, Man and Woman. As such we see and hear them. Chained as he is to his flesh, brother to the flank of meat behind him on the stage, it is as an actor that he can establish his humanity. Just as all their words seem to have an equal weight, so all the roles that they can imagine for themselves seem to have an equal reality. They can thus explore something like the full range of the *dramatis personae* we shall meet in the *Requiem* plays. The Actor can be husband and lover, bishop and prime-minister, God and fishmonger, doctor and landlord (amongst others). The Actress' roles include tart and mother, housewife and business woman. We have entered the world of Eric Berne's *Games People Play*, the world of transactional analysis.

At first this particular man and woman remain acutely conscious that they are Actor and Actress. They can thus address some of their remarks directly to the audience:

| | |
|---|---|
| ACTOR | (*It should be clear that in this speech he is not telling the truth*) Tired. A busy day, the . . . telephone never stopped ringing. Not a minute! |
| ACTRESS | (*To audience*) Why does he sit there in his under-clothes acting a part? |
| ACTOR | You are alluding to an illusion. |
| ACTRESS | Not *another* restful night! (*Sighs*). (*M*, 41; *R*, 61) |

"Acting a part" says the Actress. The previous speech we know to have been a lie; does she refer only to that? Does she seek a reason — acting apart — why he sits there in his underclothes? Does she merely observe that here is a man sitting on stage playing an actor who is acting a role? Is she merely concerned that he is "acting *apart*", that the two of them are unable to do anything more than exchange words at a distance? The ambiguities abound, as they necessarily will when we are brought face to face with the uncertainties which ensue when an actor plays an actor, when an actress plays an actress playing . . . The device mimics an experience of the 'real' world, a world where to be human is to be simultaneously a flank of meat and a set of masks. Where is the 'real' person, where does the human remain? The Actor's "You are alluding to an illusion" plays upon these uncertainties, but the Actress' "Not *another* restful night" returns us to what appears to be an unchanging reality for her, her sexual appetite.

Before long the two figures are exchanging and manipulating identities as abruptly and energetically as they had previously manipulated words. The games played include both the taking of a role upon oneself:

I am the Prime Minister and God and am entitled to read your gas-meter   (*M*, 42; *R*, 62) and the projecting of roles upon others:

> Married with children not his own.
> Probably a split-level architect.   (*M*, 42; *R*, 62)

We have to perfection an illustration of that technique which the Old Man in *Troat* advised the Young Man to adopt:

> Make love to her, man. Come on, Narcissus.
> Endow her with your fantasies and hug your reflection to yourself.
> It's dark enough.   (*M*, 33; *R*, 53)

The solipsism inherent in erotic fantasy is a recurrent motif in Warner's plays. Most of Warner's lovers are brothers to Marston's Pigmalion:

> Hee was amazed at the wondrous rarenesse
> Of his owne workmanships perfection.
> He thought that Nature nere produc'd such fairenes
> In which all beauties have their mantion.
>    And thus admiring, was enamored
>    On that fayre Image himselfe portraied.[3]

When the Actress tells us that "the marriage licence is a charter for violation" (*M*, 42; *R*, 62) we are alerted to another possible interpretation. Does all this take place within a marriage, are these all fantasies to which husband and wife are driven by the 'bonds' of marriage? Are we dealing with something akin to the relationships of Richard and Sarah (and 'Max') in Pinter's *The Lover*? The ensuing dialogue encompasses both marriage and its prelude.

The actress has earlier displayed her sexual appetite and her contempt for his sexual inadequacy, but the rules of the game determine that she should, even so, reject the Actor's blunt approaches:

> ACTOR     Let me have it then.
> ACTRESS   No.   (*M*, 43; *R*, 63)

The next stage requires a new departure, the "reason game":

> ACTOR     Let us then play the reason game, shall we?
>           Great nature's bounty? Stored gifts waste? Rot?
>           Frustration? (*Pause*) Compliments, date, cinema,
>           chocolates, snog, finger, front-room, row, parents,
>           wedding, brat, a whore, semi-forgiveness, repeat
>           endlessly, death?

| ACTRESS | (*Faraway*) Security, legal aid, grandchildren. |
| ACTOR | Flesh, words, promise kept under pressure, result — new flesh, words, flesh, word, flesh grows up and then all the fumbling and bumbling all over a-fondling-gain.  (*M*, 43; *R*, 63) |

The rules require persuasion and the Actor perfunctorily provides it. The perfunctoriness is, of course, quite unimportant since the Actress requires only the pretence and not the reality of persuasion. The Actor's resultant performance is, of course, a travesty of reason's function. In a kind of pseudo-philosophical shorthand he crudely summarises the traditional arguments which underlie, for example, Comus's speech of persuasion to the Lady. Or we might prefer to think of Shakespeare and of Adonis' response to a Venus who has used just such arguments as those to which the Actor here alludes. Adonis objects:

> You do it for increase: O strange excuse,
> When reason is the bawd to lust's abuse!
> Call it not love, for love to heaven is fled,
> Since sweating lust on earth usurp'd his name.[4]

The kind of distinctions made by Shakespeare's poem are clearly absent from the minds of Warner's characters, though they are certainly not absent from the dramatist's.

The Actor states his 'philosophical' premises, his 'rational' justification. His pause effects the transition to the particular means which the Actress' (and society's) expectations will require him to employ. The laconic brevity of his expression in these two speeches evokes the constriction of that sequence he lists. We have here all the sense of energy and creativity confined and imprisoned both by "lust's abuse" and by a society which uses marriage as no more than a sanction for sexual appetites — "a charter for violation". Here in words we have what we later meet in visual terms; we look ahead to Gonad (similarly clad in his underpants) sitting "*in the vulva of a hollow tree-trunk*" (*LF*, 16; *R*, 90) and to Shango in his mousetrap in *Meeting Ends*. Underlying this reiterated pattern is the question posed by the Old Man in *Troat*:

> Because a man lies with a woman once, must he the rest of his life?
> (*M*, 33; *R*, 53)[5]

We might note that this question is not answered directly there, but is followed by the suggestive exchange:

| WOMAN | (*To Boy*) I'll make sure you have your bait. |
|---|---|
| BOY | Oh, thanks a lot, Mum. Can I have it now? |
| YOUNG MAN | (*Mimics*) 'Can I have it now?' |
| OLD MAN | (*To Young Man*) Go on, take it man! |

(M, 33; R, 53)

The pre-echo here of the actor's "Let me have it then" confirms the identity perceived by the Old Man; the Woman uses the bait to entrap the Boy in the same way that the Actress uses her sexual bait to imprison the Actor. In each case the woman acquires sexual power; she uses the winding stair (the "screw") more successfully than the man. This is why the stage direction insists that throughout the "reason game" the Actor should grow *"more sombre, she happier"* (*M*, 43). Accepting his fate the Actor adopts a new, more domestic role:

> And I'll do a nice little bit of shopping and tidying up before she gets back from work, she will be pleased. (*M*, 43; *R*, 63)

As the fantasies continue the Actor attempts to retrieve the position. That the sexual power game is never simple and, indeed, is necessarily ambivalent is clear from the complex relationship between the Actress' words and her attitudes:

> Do what you like with me. Rape me, hang me up and I'll say no all the time. (*M*, 43; *R*, 63)

It is part of the Actor's desire to regain his lost power that he should think himself the philosopher of the partnership. It is he who offers us the 'wise' words:

> What distinguishes us one from another is the quality of our vices, our fallings from uniform perfection. And we fall, all of us, in exactly the same way. (*M*, 44; *R*, 64)

The statement would gain no great praise as an exercise in logic. His statements are of dubious philosophical value elsewhere:

| ACTOR | The infinite variety of the eyeball, when the lid is down, successfully excludes the light. The knee is capped. |
|---|---|
| ACTRESS | We know so much! |
| ACTOR | (*Correcting her*) Enough to know how little. (*Sadly*) Adequate to realize our outrageous inadequacy. |

ACTRESS      No dear. That for which we grieve should make us
             rejoice.

ACTOR        (*With determined naivety*) We must seek ever to
             know more!

ACTRESS      This I speak with tears, our knowledge is curtailed
             lest we should despair.   (*M*, 45; *R*, 65)

The wisdom here is with the Actress, though the Actor may have the
knowledge. His knowledge, symptomatically, concerns a means of
excluding the light. His lids are, it seems, very firmly down. Spiritual
light has been effectively excluded. The idioms of the Actress, however,
while not embracing any full comprehension of that light do at least
hint at an apprehension of it. The theme of a limit placed upon human
knowledge will shortly be taken up again, and after the actor's earlier
speculation about the 'fall' its mention can hardly help but imply the
presence of a God able to "curtail" human knowledge "lest we despair".
Even more explicitly the actress invokes a traditional theological
analysis of Eden (the story of the first naked actor and actress) when
she insists:

No dear. That for which we grieve should make us rejoice.

Behind her words lies a whole tradition of Christian theodicy. For most
modern readers the paradox will be most familiar in the form in which
it is expressed in Book XII of *Paradise Lost*. The words are spoken by
Adam:

> O Goodness infinite, Goodness immense,
> That all this good of evil shall produce,
> And evil turn to good — more wonderful
> Than that which by creation first brought forth
> Light out of darkness! Full of doubt I stand,
> Whether I should repent me now of sin
> By me done or occasioned, or rejoice
> Much more that much more good thereof shall spring —
> To God more glory, more good will to men
> From God — and over wrath grace shall abound.[6]

As a tradition of thought it lies right at the paradoxical centre of
Christian faith. Professor Lovejoy has traced the idea to a passage in
the Roman Liturgy:

In the service for Easter Even (Holy Saturday) there is a hymn, sung
by the deacon in the rite of blessing the paschal candle, which bears

the title of *Praeconium* but is better known, from the word with
which it opens, as the *Exultet* (*exultet iam angelica turba caelorum*).

For the author of this hymn

> Adam's sin was not only a 'happy fault' but 'certainly necessary' —
> necessary to the very possibility of the redemptive act, which, it may
> be supposed, was by the author of the hymn conceived as itself a
> necessary, and the central, event in the divine plan of terrestrial
> history.[7]

A candle is shortly to be lit here in *Lumen*; but it is scarcely lit with
benedictions, and it would be giving way to fanciful optimism if we
were to regard it as a Paschal candle — a candle, that is to say, blessed
and lit during the service for Holy Saturday and remaining on the altar
till Ascension day. The incarnation has been hinted at at several points
in this play; the Actor's cynical account of married life has invoked it
only a few moments earlier:

> Flesh, words, promise kept under pressure, result — new flesh,
> words, flesh, word, flesh grows up and then all the fumbling and
> bumbling all over a-fondling-gain.  (*M*, 43; *R*, 63)

None of these hints seem to produce any real or lasting illumination in
the characters who issue or receive them; more markedly, the play is
devoid of even a hint of the Passion. If the Actor and Actress can
conceive of the Incarnation at all it is only as a vision of a Christ who
does no more than become corrupt. St. Augustine's commentary on
St. John's Gospel insists that

> Lux, etsi per immunda transeat, non inquinatur[8]

but the nearest the Actor and Actress can come to this understanding
is in the Actress' momentary allusion to the *felix culpa*. There is a
glimmering here, and the glimmer is made literal when the actor lights
a candle. However, between the words and the action comes that which
must radically qualify any suggestion that the two of them are close to
any full apprehension of spiritual light. Shortly after the Actress'
moving realisation:

> This I speak with tears, our knowledge is curtailed lest we should
> despair   (*M*, 45; *R*, 65)

the two of them relapse into the trivial playing of roles, and into their
playing of perverse sexual games. The Actress is now a lonely and
frustrated housewife: "It's lonely in the kitchen" (*M*, 45; *R*, 65) and
the Actor is a sexual predator acting out both fantasy and memory in
actions and words which combine, but fail to unite, tenderness and
violence. The Actress and a side of meat are exchanged, so that the
Actor's tender love lyric is addressed to a flank of meat. His words are
words of love, but their debasement is made complete when they are
commented upon by the adulterous cry of the cuckoo:

> Then, as dusk curls
> His shimmering smoke-light round the apple-trees
> And plucks each stem with darkness from its bough
>     Then come with me
>   Warm in acticipation's tensity
> Where only windowed moonlight's eye can pry
>     Upon such secrecies
> Disclosed in flower-filled summer's stroking breeze
>     As make night fall
> And our soft bird his breathing song of bridal call.
> *Lights down as cuckoo calls, twice*.   (*M*, 46; *R*, 66)

The cuckoo's comment here embodies the betrayal of human love as
assuredly as the sound of the cock-crow in *Troat* (*M*, 33; *R*, 53) signi-
fied another, related kind of betrayal. It leads immediately into the
powerful visual presentation of a peculiarly violent act of sex, where
the stage equivocation over meat/Actress is made to yield more effectively dramatic results than in some of the earlier scenes. It is after
this that the Actor first holds the candle in his hands. The violent
sexual play has offered the Actress a new kind of titillation:

ACTRESS          (*Reluctant smile, chin down, eyes looking slowly
                  up at him*) It's new.   (*M*, 47; *R*, 67)

In this context the candle would seem to have more phallic than
paschal significance. Well might the Actor tell us "The tallow is soft"
(*M*, 47; *R*, 67) and the Actress clasp the candle in her lap, while staring
at it fondly (*M*, 48; *R*, 68). The act, though, has brought them still
nearer to silence, made their language an even more inadequate, an even
more fragmentary, means of communication. Despite this, and despite
the initial act of violence, the two find in themselves an increasing
capacity for tenderness. The tenderness increases in proportion to the
breakdown of their words. The whole movement is very delicately

handled, in some of the most attractively cadenced writing to be found
in the play:

| | |
|---|---|
| ACTOR | The tallow is soft. |
| ACTRESS | I don't really think it's allowed. |
| ACTOR | (*Still holding candle in right hand*) Silent then. |
| | *Pause*. |
| ACTRESS | It is fortunate that we . . . |
| ACTOR | The day broke early that morning. |
| ACTRESS | In our comings and goings . . . |
| ACTOR | No earlier than the previous day, I suppose, but it seemed early as I was not accustomed to walking to the station in the dark. |
| ACTRESS | Know that the fingers of bone leaf the faded pages. |
| ACTOR | (*To her*) I don't really think it's allowed. |
| ACTRESS | (*To him*) Unfortunately the day broke. |
| ACTOR | In our comings and goings. |
| | *With increasing tenderness*. |
| ACTRESS | No earlier than the previous day, I suppose, but it seemed early. |
| ACTOR | Know that the fingers |
| ACTRESS | It is fortunate that we |
| ACTOR | Silent then. |
| | *Blackout. Once the audience's eyes are accustomed to the dark., ACTOR, strikes a bright match and lights candle. ACTRESS is leaning back on her stool, legs apart, head back. Warm lighting to aid candle, but no more than is necessary. Maintain low warm pool of light to include the centrestage area but little more*. |
| ACTOR | Flame. |
| ACTRESS | (*Sitting up*) Old. |
| ACTOR | That which distinguishes us from the brute creation. |
| ACTRESS | Old as the crags. |
| ACTOR | The vultures, the pain. |
| ACTRESS | The eyes!   (*M*, 47–8; *R*, 67–8) |

The movement of time is very effectively evoked, as the actor approaches
the final realisation that "we have left it too late" (*M*, 49; *R*, 69). As
their tenderness increases it is embodied in the cadences of their phrasing,
as they use words with lexical referents which are not necessarily tender.
The blackness which follows represents that wordless state in which
their love (and now, surely, it appears to deserve that name) is expressed

and consummated; the match which lights the candle is unable to throw light upon the huge darkness which surrounds them, but at least it is a candle which is lit, rather than the post-coital cigarette lit by Epigyne (*LF*, 30; *R*, 104). There is, in *Lying Figures*, a more comprehensive, more irredeemable betrayal of love than anything we have met in *Lumen*. The sensual triviality of the cigarette is poised against the ritual significance (at any rate potentially) of the candle. It is, after all, the candle which will be used to evoke images of eternity at the close of *Meeting Ends*, in the final moments of the whole sequence. The giggling of Epigyne and "all the grotesquerie of sexual politics" (*LF*, 22; *R*, 96) are largely absent from this moment in *Lumen*. Laz's reflection on sex is that

> with joy, tenderness and delight we transform ourselves into beasts.
> (*LF*, 45; *R*, 119)

The Actor and Actress find something a little different. When the candle has been lit, their immediate words are terse:

| | |
|---|---|
| ACTOR | Flame. |
| ACTRESS | (*Sitting up*) Old. |
| ACTOR | That which distinguishes us from the brute creation. |
| ACTRESS | Old as the crags. |
| ACTOR | The vultures, the pain.   (*M*, 48; *R*, 68) |

Their sexual activity reminds them that each is, as far as the other is concerned, 'an old flame'. Each embodies a flame of lust which has now burned itself out. But if that flame dies, does not its associated 'shadow' die too? The play is over when the lights go out:

> The parts of actors are like the flames of matches, blown out in the wind, and vanished.   (*KT*, 70; *R*, 194)

The flame of lust may throw out light, but as *Troat* has suggested, it is a light which offers little illumination. While love has a purely earthly focus it produces not light but darkness. Yet the ability to perceive this may itself constitute a means of dispersing the darkness. The allusions to Prometheus are echoed elsewhere in the related plays (most notably in the figure of Shango in *Meeting Ends*); here they continue the play's earlier concern with the necessary limits placed upon human knowledge. For all that the candle has been lit, the darkness increases. The Actor finds both light and heat decreasing: his 'part' is almost over:

> It grows dark. I need my coat.   (*M*, 48; *R*, 68)

Their act of love has produced darkness out of light. Dante gives to Virgil some words on love which are of great relevance here:

> Però che tu rificchi
> la mente pur alle cose terrene,
> di vera luce tenebre dis picchi.[9]

Though their thoughts have been with "things of earth" the Actor and Actress have not been without glimmerings of light. The Actor's desperate attempt to find another part to play, with his switch to a *"Blimpish voice"* (*M*, 48; *R*, 68), cannot hide an unmistakable reference forward to the Reveille which closes *Meeting Ends*:

> The army can be summoned. If necessary, by bugle.   (*M*, 48; *R*, 68)

But darkness and blindness outweigh such moments of light. The single candle retains a poignant force, handed on as it is from Actor to Actress. It is during the Actor's absence from the stage that the Actress gives expression to her poignant realisation that her 'part' too is almost over, and that her prospects of 'rebirth' are poor. She observes that

> Only the actions of the just smell sweet, and blossom in their dust.
> (*M*, 49; *R*, 69)

The Actress here quotes the beautiful conclusion to one of Shirley's most exquisite lyrics:

> The glories of our blood and state
>      Are shadows, not substantial things;
> There is no armour against fate;
>      Death lays his icy hand on kings:
>           Sceptre and crown
>           Must tumble down,
> And in the dust be equal made
> With the poor crooked scythe and spade.
>
> Some men with swords may reap the field,
>      And plant fresh laurels where they kill;
> But their strong nerves at last must yield;
>      They tame but one another still;
>           Early or late
>           They stoop to fate,
> And must give up their murmuring breath,
> When they, pale captives, creep to death.

The garlands wither on your brow;
   Then boast no more your mighty deeds;
Upon Death's purple altar now,
   See, where the victor-victim bleeds:
     Your head must come
     To the cold tomb:
Only the actions of the just
Smell sweet, and blossom in their dust.[10]

The Actor and Actress are coming to the "cold tomb" as the military
men of *Killing Time* will come to it. When the actor returns to the stage
to invite the Actress to join him in the darkness offstage — "Come, to
bed" (*M*, 49; *R*, 69) — he surely invites her to share his bed of earth.
When she recognizes the lateness of the hour and her weakness, the
candle is extinguished. Their 'parts' are almost complete, their roles are
nearly exhausted. Some fundamental humanity, beyond their manifold
roles, presses them to seek comfort in one another. Their actions, however, have not been just. They will not blossom in their dust as the
snowdrop *will* blossom from the cold dust at the close of *Meeting Ends*.

The Actor and Actress, though, are able to recognise the inadequacy
of their condition, and, above all, they are able to acknowledge both
the need for prayer and the existence of that to which they might offer
their prayers:

ACTOR       We have left it too late.
ACTRESS    We shouldn't have joked.
ACTOR       Darken our lightness.
ACTRESS    Bear with our weakness.  (*M*, 49; *R*, 69)

In their 'bareness' they plead "bear with our weakness", for they have
discovered by bitter experience that which is offered (and scorned) as
instruction to Ford's Giovanni at the beginning of his play.

   nice philosophy
May tolerate unlikely arguments,
But Heaven admits no jest.[11]

The self-knowledge acquired by Actor and Actress comes much too
late. Recognising their "lightness", their triviality, the actor inverts a
collect:

Lighten our darkness, we beseech Thee, O Lord; and by thy great
mercy defend us from all perils and dangers of this night.[12]

In these closing words of the first trilogy there comes the realisation that "lightness" of mind is an inadequate defence against the very real perils and dangers of the surrounding night. The Actor's plea is for a 'darkness' or seriousness of mind which might make enlightenment possible. The trilogy closes on a note of simple and honest acknowledgement of human fallibility. The acknowledgement is not, in itself, enough. The Gospel according to St. Luke tells of the divine mission

> To give light to them that sit in darkness and in the shadow of death.[13]

The light has been glimpsed, but the shadows predominate. On stage, as the lights dim, the area of shadow increases, till all is dark:

> The glories of our blood and state
>    Are shadows, not substantial things.

Shirley's lines seem forcefully appropriate here. The insubstantiality of the Actor and Actress has been stressed throughout by the counterpointed presence of the two flanks of meat. All the roles these two figures project for themselves are, indeed, no more than shadows. "The best in this kind are but shadows" and shadows can have but insubstantial pleasures:

> Are they shadows that we see?
> And can shadows pleasure give?
> Pleasures only shadows be,
> Cast by bodies we conceive,
> . . .
> But these pleasures vanish fast
> Which by shadows are expressed,
> Pleasures are not, if they last;
> In their passing is their best:
> Glory is most bright and gay
> In a flash and so away
> . . .
> When your eyes have done their part,
> Thought must length it in the heart.[14]

Daniel's wonderful lines alert us to some of the ambivalent significances of this shadow play which closes *Maquettes*. At the end of the trilogy these shadows which are actors are overtaken by the shadow of death. Shadow encroaches until the stage is entirely dark and empty. It is *Lying Figures* which closes with an inversion of Chapter One, Verse Five of the Gospel according to St. John:

Darkness encroaches on the light, and in lightness we dare not comprehend.  (*LF*, 47; *R*, 121)

Gonad's words, in the play which succeeds *Lumen*, indicate the path that must be travelled if we are to move from the vanished and solitary glimmer of *Lumen* to the ring of burning candles and the reveille which will bring the whole *Requiem* cycle to a close.

## Notes

1   *St. John's Gospel*, I, 1—14.
2   *Psalms*, 84, 2—4.
3   John Marston, *The Metamorphosis of Pigmalions Image*, (1598), St. 3.
4   *Venus and Adonis*, ll. 791—4.
5   The aphorism is borrowed from Shadwell. Cf. *The Squire of Alsatia* (1688), II, i:

> What a Devil should I do? if a man lies once with a Woman is he bound to do it for ever?

*Works*, ed. M. Summers, 1927, IV, p. 288. I am indebted to Mr. Martin Woodhead for this information.
6   *Paradise Lost*, XII, 469—78.
7   A. O. Lovejoy, 'Milton and the Paradox of the Fortunate Fall', *Essays in the History of Ideas*, 1948, pp. 277—95.
8   St. Augustine, *In Johannis Evangelium Tractatus CXXIV*, 5, 15.
9   *Purgatorio*, XV, 64—66. Dorothy Sayers translates the lines as follows:

> Because once more thy mental reach
> Stops short at earthly things, thy dullard mood
> From truth's own light draws darkness black as pitch.

10   *The Contention of Ajax and Ulysses*, 1659.
11   John Ford, *'Tis Pity She's a Whore* (1633), I, i, 2—4.
12   *The Book of Common Prayer*, 'The Third Collect, for Aid against all Perils'.
13   *St. Luke's Gospel*, I: 79.
14   Samuel Daniel, *Tethys' Festival*, 1610.

# VI

## *Lying Figures:* Many Inventions

The historian Langlois tells a nice story of a certain philosopher called Maupertius. During a visit to the ossuary of the Cordeliers of Touloise he was asked why skeletons appear to laugh. "The dead are apparently laughing at us, the Living" replied Maupertius.[1] This first full length play of Warner's *Requiem* presents us with the dead's view of the living.

Sapphira and Laz are not, however, mere skeletons. Nor, indeed, is laughter their only response to the 'living' they see around them. It is Laz who assures us that

> from the perspective of death, life looks a little grave
>
> $\qquad\qquad\qquad\qquad\qquad$ (*LF*, 46; *R*, 120)

and Sapphira has earlier made the suggestion "Let us sing a requiem for the living" (*LF*, 4; *R*, 78). Still the view from their perspective does occasionally stimulate them to a response akin to that of the skeletons described by Maupertius:

> LAZ $\quad$ . . . (*Laughing suddenly*) And that rude grafoetus thinks life a permanent fixture! Weeping mankind fooled by its follies into bedlock. (*LF*, 5; *R*, 79)

In *Lying Figures* the observation is mutual: the living watch the dead as much as the dead watch the living. Gonad extols the virtues of the occupation:

99

So I thought I'd take a job where I could read at nights . . . But I always liked the night-time. Hear the owls on the hospital lawn. Yes. Imagine things . . . I like a full moon. Warm by the electric fire. Blanket. Doze off. Read a bit. Slip out for an hour or two. See a nurse. Sunday's best for that, they're bored, feel their week-end's nearly gone. Snow. Sun on the ditches. I like crisp grass in the early morning. Then walk home. Yes, there's a lot to be said for watching the dead.　*(LF*, 6–7; *R*, 80–81)

The mirror-effect is clear. Act One offers a number of such mirror-like juxtapositions, and it is worth noticing that the play's larger structure has more than a little of the mirror about it, with the two outer scenes in the mortuary and the two inner in the 'living' world, while the opening and closing moments of the play reflect one another even more closely. Within the play the living and the dead constitute one mirror image:

The world after death is all back to front.　*(LF*, 12; *R*, 86)

In the theatre, we have it on the highest authority, the purpose of playing is to hold "as 'twere, the mirror up to nature". The play's epigraph should alert us to the kind of reflections this mirror will offer:

And I will wipe off the face of the earth every living thing that I have made.

The verse is taken from Chapter VI of *Genesis* and its full significance and relevance can best be appreciated if we return it to its original context:

And God saw that the wickedness of man was great in the earth, and that every imagination of the thoughts of his heart was only evil continually.
And it repented the Lord that he had made man on the earth, and it grieved him at his heart.
And the Lord said, I will destroy man whom I have created from the face of the earth; both man, and beast, and the creeping thing, and the fowls of the air; for it repenteth me that I have made them.
But Noah found grace in the eyes of the Lord.
These are the generations of Noah: Noah was a just man and perfect in his generations, and Noah walked with God.
And Noah begat three sons, Shem, Ham, and Japheth.

The earth also was corrupt before God, and the earth was filled
with violence. And God looked upon the earth, and behold, it was
corrupt; for all flesh had corrupted his way upon the earth.

And God said unto Noah, The end of all flesh is come before me;
for the earth is filled with violence through them; and, behold, I
will destroy them with the earth.  (*Genesis*, 6: 5—13)

It is thus that the play's epigraph is introduced in *Genesis*, and Warner's
play develops a number of motifs evident here. Its world is a world in
which "the wickedness of man" is "great in the earth"; in which "every
imagination of the thoughts of his heart was only evil"; it is too a world
which allows the possibility of divine grace even in the midst of a time
when "all flesh had corrupted his way upon the earth". We might
notice that in the Biblical account divine grace was extended to the
man who was "perfect in his generations": *Lying Figures* explores the
fate of those who are wholly imperfect in their 'generations'. The play's
very title will bear a number of relevant interpretations. 'Lying' may be
adjective or noun; 'figures' may be noun or verb. The punning has
begun. Here is a play in which figures lie to one another. Presumably
they do so because they believe that telling lies 'figures' — makes sense.
Here is a play in which figures lie with one another in sexual pleasure, and
in which figures lie down in death; the death bed figures as prominently
here as does the bed of pleasure. If we add up what we see and are told
we may suspect that the figures tell lies — that the accounts do not
balance. The central puns of the play, and it is a play to some extent
hinged upon wordplay, are those of Shakespeare's Sonnet 138:

> When my love swears that she is made of truth
> I do believe her, though I know she lies,
> That she might think me some untutor'd youth
> Unlearned in the world's false subtleties.
> Thus vainly thinking that she thinks me young,
> Although she knows my days are past the best,
> Simply I credit her false-speaking tongue:
> On both sides thus is simple truth suppress'd.
> But wherefore says she not she is unjust?
> And wherefore say not I that I am old?
> Oh, love's best habit is in seeming trust,
> And age in love loves not to have years told.
>> Therefore I lie with her, and she with me,
>> And in our faults by lies we flatter'd be.

In Chapter One of this study I pointed out some of the ways in which

*Lying Figures* has affinities with the work of Tourneur, and we might here consider a more modern artistic analogy which throws an interesting light upon the play. Tim Prentki has pointed out the way in which the play's title and development evoke the work of, among others, Francis Bacon.[2] Warner has never made any secret of his admiration for the paintings of Bacon, and in connection with this first play of Warner's trilogy, so deeply immersed in the shadow of death, we might do well to consider some remarks of Francis Bacon's in an interview with David Sylvester:

> FB    I think you once said to me that people always have a feeling of mortality about my paintings.
>
> DS    Yes.
>
> FB    But then, perhaps I have a feeling of mortality all the time. Because, if life excites you, its opposite, like a shadow, death, must excite you. Perhaps not excite you, but you are aware of it in the same way as you are aware of life, you're aware of it like the turn of a coin between life and death. And I'm very aware of that about people, and about myself too, after all. I'm always surprised when I wake up in the morning.
>
> DS    Doesn't that belie your view that you're essentially an optimistic person?
>
> FB    Ah well, you can be optimistic and totally without hope. One's basic nature is totally without hope, and yet one's nervous system is made out of optimistic stuff. It doesn't make any difference to my awareness of the shortness of the moment of existence between birth and death. And that's one thing I'm conscious of all the time.[3]

The tension between pessimism and optimism is that tension which the *Requiem* dramatically embodies; more particularly, *Lying Figures* is concerned with

> the shortness of the moment of existence between birth and death.

Laz observes (happily)

> We are born in excrement and even so we decompose
>
>            (*LF*, 4; *R*, 78)

and Sapphira shares with him this observation from their 'grave' perspective:

SAPPH          We drop children into the world like . . . like . . .
LAZ            Turds.  (*LF*, 5; *R*, 79)

The languages of sex and death, procreation and excrement, are fused
in this play as part of a vision of a world of vanity — giving to that word
the full weight that it bears in *Ecclesiastes*. In Act Three Gonad sardoni-
cally requests of his wife:

Let me kiss your open grave

and, logically enough, receives the reply

Your end is near.  (*LF*, 18; *R*, 92)

A life dedicated to the pursuit of sexual pleasure can lead only to
death-in-life, symbolised by the skeletal child of the play's conclusion.
The route by which we arrive at that concluding horror must first be
traced.

Act One takes place in the mortuary and juxtaposes the ceremonies
of death with the ceremonies of marriage — a juxtaposition familiar to
us from the opening of the parent play, *Emblems*. Both Laz and Sapphira
are well pleased with the rituals of their deaths:

SAPPH          (*Far away, with quiet pride*) Mine was a white funeral.
LAZ            (*Modest self-satisfaction*) You should have seen my
               death-certificate. A collector's item. Unique. I
               shouldn't be at all surprised if it went for thousands
               of pounds in the next Book Auction Records.
                                              (*LF*, 2; *R*, 76)

Sapphira's "white funeral" is the mirror partner of Epigyne's "*black
wedding-dress with black bouquet*" (*LF*, 8; *R*, 82), and in its immediate
context constitutes a kind of counterpoint with Gonad's account of
his stag night and marriage. His words debase that sacrament as his
earlier actions (for he opens and closes the act) have already debased
the rituals of death. When Gonad opens a corpse's mouth to tap in the
ash from his cigarette, the Prayer Book's "ashes to ashes" is subjected
to a grotesque parody. Still, these particular corpses *do* take on a new
life, even if it is scarcely that promised in the Prayer Book's 'Order for
the Burial of the Dead'. Since the living have apparently dedicated
themselves to death-in-life, it is only fitting, in a play of mirror-
paradoxes, that the dead should be granted a kind of life-in-death. It
is a life devoid of 'ability' ("Let's pretend we are able . . ." suggests

Sapphira) but possessed, by virtue of its detachment, of a certain choric superiority. Their minds cannot, however, escape the narrow pathways which confine human imagination as seen in this play. It is clear what Sapphira has in mind when she calls upon Laz to do his "death duty":

| | |
|---|---|
| SAPPH | I've the most shocking stomach-ache. (*Radiant*) I feel marvellous! |
| LAZ | Now woman, you've put a period to all that. |
| SAPPH | (*In a low voice, warm and encouraging*) Come on Laz, do your death duty.   (*LF*, 3; *R*, 77) |

Laz's "The organ's softer now" (*LF*, 3; *R*, 77) relates triply to Sapphira's observation "Our music is unwound" (*LF*, 4; *R*, 78), to Laz's own physiological state, and to his memories of his own funeral service: "You should have heard *my* funeral" (*LF*, 3; *R*, 77). Sexual fantasy and personal pride are still hopelessly interwoven: Laz's "deep feeling of sadness as the old roots stir" (*LF*, 3; *R*, 77) takes us back to the Old Man in *Troat*, a figure we shall see evoked rather differently at the end of this Act. The whole of Act One operates as a kind of overture for the complete trilogy. Sapphira, indeed, announces its title: "Let us sing a requiem for the living" (*LF*, 4; *R*, 78) and the titles of the second and third plays in the sequence are also alluded to during the course of *Lying Figures*: Guppy recommends sexual activity as a good way to "kill time" (*LF*, 33; *R*, 107) and Epigyne, disappointed that her husband and lover don't fight over her, comments:

And now I bring you together, the two live ends don't fuse!
(*LF*, 35; *R*, 109)

In Act One of this first play a number of the sequence's recurrent motifs are introduced: the lighting of the cigarette, the skeleton, menstruation, venereal disease, the stars, and many others. One of the most characteristically Warnerian chords, a harmony of Biblical and sexual languages, is powerfully struck:

| | |
|---|---|
| SAPPH | I'd lived with him for three years, and there was still little prospect of his proposing marriage, so I decided to go to Rome and take a lover. |
| LAZ | Kill four stones with one bird? |
| SAPPH | To kiss the Pope. |
| LAZ | Did they go together? |
| SAPPH | It was a pious assumption, but (*Coyly*) the conception was not immaculate. |

LAZ                    (*Feeling his genitals*) Jesus! body-snatchers.
                       There's a stone missing.   (*LF*, 3; *R*, 77)

The puns on 'stone' and 'conception' give power to the ambiguous
references to the raising of Lazarus and, indeed, to the raising of Christ.
Invocation of the Virgin constitutes its own ironic comment on the
world in which the invocation has been made, and the two contrasting
terms of such a dramatic moment will serve as points of reference for
the succeeding plays. If the women here are far from virginal, it is
through female agency that a kind of salvation will be perceived in
*Meeting Ends*. When Gonad re-enters his reaction tells us much of the
world he represents: "Holy God, these stiffs sprung up again?" (*LF*, 5;
*R*, 79) is a question which owes more to a professional knowledge of
rigor mortis and a capacity for sexual pun than it does to any spiritual
apprehension of the possibilities of resurrection. With the stage to
himself Gonad reminisces in a fashion very like that of the Old Man in
*Troat*. Like him Gonad prefers the darkness:

I always liked the night-time. Hear the owls on the hospital lawn.
Yes. Imagine things.   (*LF*, 6–7; *R*, 80–81)

The owl will appear on stage before long, and the direction of his
"imaginings" is clear from his account of his nocturnal activities:

Slip out for an hour or two. See a nurse. Sunday's best for that,
they're bored, feel their week-end's nearly gone.   (*LF*, 7; *R*, 81)

Act Two moves us from the world of life-in-death to that of death-
in-life, to the adulterous world of Epigyne and Guppy. The music
which introduces Epigyne, and the props with which she shares the
stage, make her moral significance clear enough, as does the black
wedding-dress that she wears. What could be more appropriate for a
woman wedded to death? Her rationalisations of her infidelity are too
trivial to bear consideration. "Plaisir d'Amour" says much more. The
prose style is well calculated to demonstrate the shallowness of her
mind, but finds room too for moments of absurd fantasy:

Why, but for him I might by now have been anything. A Mother
Superior.   (*LF*, 9; *R*, 83)

There is room also for the striking of a few deeper notes which contrast
her shallowness of concern with the deeper concerns of the play as a
whole. When, for example, she says of her lover:

> *Frozen*, in his car for me, poor darling, waiting beyond the trees,
> watching until it's safe for him to creep in beside me and share my
> warmth     (*LF*, 8; *R*, 82)

her language is made to echo that of *Ecclesiastes* (4:11), one of the
frequent occasions on which the play echoes the wording of that book.
Adopting a quite different linguistic register, she tells us that she "too
can play games" (*LF*, 9; *R*, 83), and she and her lover are soon exchanging pleasantries in the appropriate terminology for their own particular
games:

| | |
|---|---|
| EPI | Stale, mate? |
| GUPPY | Dead heat!     (*LF*, 10; *R*, 84) |

Epigyne tells us later that

> the silver fox is on heat only eight days a year     (*LF*, 18; *R*, 92)

so we may presume that it is spared the tribulations of a jaded sexual
appetite, or, indeed, of staleness. Where Epigyne and Guppy are concerned, we might well apply to them Chalone's observation "You have
mated unchecked" (*KT*, 14; *R*, 138) and they would presumably share
with Phagocyte the sense that "we are the pawns of night manoeuvres"
(*KT*, 15; *R*, 139). It is characteristic of the cynical Guppy that one of
his gambits in the game of sexual chess should be the use of inverted
Biblical quotation:

> The flesh is willing but the spirit is weak.     (*LF*, 10; *R*, 84)

Epigyne can play this particular middle game too:

> Look, fetch me an apple and some water, will you? I'm sick of love.
>       (*LF*, 11; *R*, 85)

Guppy inverts words from *Mathew* 26, Verse 41, words in which Peter
is forewarned that he will deny Christ. The original context provides a
damning judgement upon Guppy's misuse of the text. Epigyne, on the
other hand, perverts a text from the *Song of Solomon*:

> Stay me with flagons, comfort me with apples: for I am sick of love.
>       (2:5)

The idiom of Epigyne's travesty, and the context in which it is spoken, contrast vividly with the original and *its* context. The lyrical beauty of the *Song of Songs* passes eloquent comment upon Epigyne and her 'imaginings':

> I've got to the stage where I can't see a wood without thinking 'that would be a good place to take down my pants'. (*LF*, 11; *R*, 85)

She is condemned by the allusion to the *Song of Songs* as fully as all concerned are damned by the allusions made to the same text in *The Merchant's Tale*. It is hardly surprising that Epigyne's apple should contain a maggot. (*LF*, 11; *R*, 85)

As Guppy and Epigyne play out their adulterous games we realise that this is not the only kind of 'playing' which is going on. Guppy sees his job as an undertaker in the terms of play-acting:

> We in our profession are actors. Yes, actors. That would be a good word to describe it. We adopt a special tone to convey our condolences to those who remain behind . . . (*LF*, 11; *R*, 85)

We are reminded of Laz's earlier words:

> The undertaking was we should be re-hearsed. (*LF*, 3; *R*, 77)

The ambiguous realities of actor and part, as explored, for example, in *Lumen*, begin to reassert themselves. In a world where living actors play corpses which spring up and down like children's toys, and where hearses and rehearsals, undertakers and undertakings, are all too readily confused, how can we be sure what is 'real', what is 'true'? Reality turns out to be inaccessible to human reason, one of the central tenets of *Ecclesiastes*, be it noted. Guppy cannot get beyond the self-defeating limitations of reason in his attempt to understand Epigyne:

> You're a bundle of contradictions! Your back tells me your front is false, and your false front confirms that your back is telling the truth. If it's wrong, its right, and if it's right, it's wrong.
> (*LF*, 10–11; *R*, 84–85)

We have entered the realms of the Cretan Liar, of Eubulides and Epimenides or Tarski and Russell. The world of paradox achieves a kind of visual expression when Epigyne turns to leave the stage later in the scene (*LF*, 13; *R*, 87). When reason is defeated in *The Phoenix and the Turtle*, the poet can assert that if "Reason, in itself" is "confounded" then at least "Love hath reason". However, as Act Two of *Lying Figures* has shown us all too vividly, the world inhabited by Epigyne and Guppy is a loveless world. Its occupants have no alternative but to accept as real that to which their baffled reason and their confused senses give them access. Only Gonad learns, at a much later stage of the play, that

> The invisible, the moments of happiness, are more real, however dreamlike, than the visible world of time.　(*LF*, 37; *R*, 111)

Lacking any sense of reality Epigyne and Guppy operate in a moral mist. Epigyne announces "I love the world" to be suitably described by Guppy as "my worldly love" (*LF*, 12; *R*, 86). Guppy, in his turn, loves death, or rather, the apparatus of death and the dead. He indulges his necropolitan imagination with a fervour the equal of Sir Thomas Browne's:

> To go wreck-hunting off Hawaii . . . To voyage across the seas! (*Extravagant gestures*) Seek out the burial customs of the Incas. Investigate the pyramids, annotate the catacombs, gather fossils, resurrect dinosaurs, excavate mounds, relive the Coliseum! Burn with Rome, flame with Troy, drown with Sodom, get stoned with Gomorrah, find souvenirs from Passchendaele, hear the Last Post bugled through the Menin Gate, and return in time to visit the tomb of the unknown warrior in St. Paul's.　(*LF*, 12–13; *R*, 86–87)

Indeed his fervour runs ahead of his accuracy. He translates the unknown warrior from Westminster Abbey. Sir Thomas Browne appears to have been in Warner's mind at the time that he was composing *Lying Figures*,[4] so we are surely justified in borrowing some words of Browne's, addressed to those given to the excessive love of things funerary:

> Pyramids, arches, obelisks, were but the irregularities of vain-glory, and wild enormities of ancient magnanimity. But the most magnanimous resolution rests in the Christian religion, which trampleth upon pride, and sits on the neck of ambition, humbly pursuing that infallible perpetuity, unto which all others must diminish their diameters, and be poorly seen in angles of contingency.[5]

The words might well be addressed to Guppy and are eloquent affirmation of all that is absent from Guppy's vision.

Having shown us the gambits of adultery Warner removes Epigyne from the stage and replaces her by Xyster, without her husband Guppy's awareness that the change has taken place. The audience are given visual confirmation of the complementary nature of the two women:

> *Exit* EPIGYNE *upstage right. As she turns upstage to go, the audience suddenly see that she is naked from neck to heels, as the bridal dress has no back to it . . . Enter* XYSTER *downstage right as full-frontal nude.* (*LF*, 13; *R*, 87)

The two make one whole. Believing he has his mistress with him, Guppy can tackle with gusto the seduction of his wife, with accompanying fantasies, naturally enough. The irony is compounded when Epigyne returns and chastises him in the vocabulary and manner of a betrayed wife:

> Don't mind me! (*Furious*) You goat! Who was that woman? If you don't give me her name I'll rip out your false teeth . . . Am I your moral spittoon? Your sponge? The vomitory of your fornicatorium? Have you no respect for adultery? (*LF*, 14; *R*, 88)

In this carnal world of mirror paradoxes it is only to be expected that the husband in sexual pursuit of his wife should be accused of committing "unnatural acts" (*LF*, 14; *R*, 88). The scene dissolves into a dreamlike tableau. Guppy's moral blindness is made literal by the mask he dons, and Epigyne's bondage to the carnal is made similarly explicit by the revelation that beneath her black wedding-dress she is "*dressed only in belts, around neck, breasts, wrists, loins and ankles*" (*LF*, 14; *R*, 88). Further metamorphoses follow: Guppy into Death the Reaper and Epigyne into the Owl, "foul precurrer of the fiend" and Hermetic bird of death and night. The trio of Guppy and Xyster, spotlit, and Epigyne in darkness, close the scene, static against the fierce menace of Guppy's metronomic scythe. The brooding presence of the Owl, the insistent sound of the metronome, the motion of the scythe, hour-glass in shape, all combine in a powerful vision of human mortality, a vision indebted equally to Surrealism and to the Emblem Books.

The first two Acts having presented us with such powerful emblems of human carnality, Act Three presents us with a kind of account of the reasons for what we have seen, since it constitutes what is virtually a Warnerian version of the original and recurrent Fall of Man. Act Three is more than twice as long as any of the other Acts, and this length is used to present material of considerable complexity, in terms of both theme and plot.

Gonad is here first encountered imprisoned

*in the vulva of a hollow tree-trunk, the oval opening of which faces*
*the audience. This tree-trunk is pierced by sharpened metal stakes,*
*the points of which all enter to about the same depth. Within the*
*trunk, four stones hang from just above his head on a wheel, one*
*before, one behind, and one on each side of his head, so that each*
*time he moves he runs the risk either of being impaled or of being*
*severely bruised.*   (*LF*, 16;*R*, 90)

As Paul Hewison has pointed out, the stage image is derived from an
engraving in Jacques Lacarrière's *The God-Possessed*, an engraving
which represents one of the Desert Fathers, St. Maron.[6] It is an
emblem of contemplative withdrawal − or at least it would be, were
not the tree so evidently a vulva, and, just as evidently, a prison. Yet
the tradition of the Desert Fathers does have a relevance here. Some
words of Helen Waddell's will perhaps help to define the nature of that
relevance:

> These men, by the very exaggeration of their lives, stamped infinity
> on the imagination of the West. They saw the life of the body as
> Paulinus saw it, '*occidui temporis umbra*', a shadow at sunset. "The
> spaces of our human life set over against eternity" − it is the under-
> current of all Antony's thought − "are most brief and poor".
>    Think you the bargain's hard, to have exchanged
>    The transient for the eternal, to have sold
>    Earth to buy heaven?[7]

Gonad does have some capacity for experiencing the eternal. As we
have seen it is he who can perceive the greater reality of "the invisible"
(*LF*, 37; *R*, 111). It is he, in that moment, who can see the shadows in
the cave for what they are. He tells us he is meditating, tells us, indeed,
that he is praying not to die an atheist (*LF*, 17;*R*, 91) and he has qualities
which Epigyne, not surprisingly, can perceive only as "religiosity" (*LF*,
28; *R*, 102). However, his spiritual awareness is far too weak to with-
stand the pressures of the worldly. Well might he ask Epigyne to "Leave
me to pray" (*LF*, 18; *R*, 92), for she is clear enough as to the likely
sequence of events:

> Coming out of your shell today, crablouse, are you? Exchanging
> God for a crust of mammon?   (*LF*, 17;*R*, 91)

The answer to that second question, unfortunately, is yes.
   In his tree of contemplation Gonad, ironically, is doing no more

than guaranteeing his bondage to the transient. Meditation, as the nature of the tree might suggest, may do no more than allow his mind to explore its sexual imaginings:

| | |
|---|---|
| EPI | Look, misery; it would pay you to make a success of life. |
| GONAD | Oh, I don't know, I'm not a lesbian; that's something. |
| EPI | If you were you might get some gardening done, instead of sitting all day in that tree. Does impotence confine you to barracks? |
| GONAD | Leave me to my thoughts. |
| EPI | What's your erotoravenous imagination playing with now? |
| GONAD | You. |
| EPI | A likely tale! |
| GONAD | Was there ever a time when yours wasn't? (*Pause*) Give her her head, we used to say, give her her head and she'll give you her tail.  (*LF*, 17; *R*, 91) |

Epigyne may want to persuade Gonad to exchange the contemplative for the active life, but the direction taken by his "thoughts" tells us clearly enough why the tree, or rather what it symbolises, will continue to imprison him, whether or not he steps out of it. Like Spenser's Fradubio he is imprisoned in the tree both because he too has chosen Duessa and because he has then seen her for what she is. Like Ariel, imprisoned in the "rift" of the "cloven pine" he is required to perform the "earthy and abhorr'd commands" of his particular Sycorax. Unlike Ariel, however, he cannot be said to be "a spirit too delicate" to enact them, as the conclusion of Act Three will show us. Epigyne's first words of the Act tell us why, in applying the name "crablouse" to him. The word is not used here simply as a vague term of insult. One of OED's citations makes clear its very specific relevance:

The Pubic Louse . . . which is known by the common name of 'Crab Louse', attaches itself to the hairs of the sexual organs, the arm pits, and even of the eyebrows.[8]

It is a cruel, but distressingly accurate, description of Gonad, seen in terms of Epigyne's vision of humanity as

lascivious insects, lovingly stinging each other to death during their little stay.  (*LF*, 18; *R*, 92)

Gonad is parasitical, he does take such strength as he has from Epigyne's
sexuality, and from her ability to manipulate his. Like Macbeth, any
spiritual potential he has is readily nullified by his wife's appeal to his
sexuality; indeed he is as malleable as Macbeth himself, and Epigyne's
incitement to murder

> Prove your manhood, my tender love     (*LF*, 38; *R*, 112)

has a horrid familiarity about it.

At the end of Act Two we saw Epigyne in the fetters which bind her
and so thoroughly cripple her notion of the spiritual:

> You've got to have lovers. It's part of your spiritual growth.
>                                                        (*LF*, 22; *R*, 96)

Act Three shows how those fetters simultaneously hold Gonad in
bondage, through all "the grotesquerie of sexual politics" (*LF*, 22;
*R*, 96). Gonad can at best be said to be only a half-unwilling prisoner.
When Epigyne reads out Gonad's letter it only confirms our sense of
that predisposition of his for which his residence in the arboreal vulva
has been earlier evidence:

> I will sacrifice anything, my pride (as you must see reading this) my
> future, anything whatsoever, to earn you and win your love once
> more.  (*LF*, 27; *R*, 101)

Not only does Gonad give up God for a crust of mammon, he provides
Epigyne with the means for sophisticated and exquisite torture. The
torture in Act Three of *Lying Figures* is as gruesome as any that we see
in *Killing Time*. Epigyne has a fitting contempt for her victim:

> Your laugh is like the crackling of thorns under a pot.  (*LF*, 23; *R*, 97)

Phrasing her contempt in this particular fashion she does, of course,
adapt a famous verse from *Ecclesiastes*:

> For as the crackling of thorns under a pot, so is the laughter of the
> fool: this also is vanity.   (7:6)

Echoes of *Ecclesiastes* are so frequent in the play that even when Laz
and Sapphira are at their most squalidly bawdy

SAPPH          (*Excited*) Have you a candle for me, for when my
               fridge is off?
LAZ            In your vanity bag.
SAPPH          That's where you always push it   (*LF*, 42; *R*, 116)

the vulva's latest metamorphosis takes particular force from the phrase's
echo of that word which is at the centre of *Ecclesiastes*:

Vanity of vanities, saith the Preacher, vanity of vanities; all is vanity.
                                                              (1:2)

The whole of *Lying Figures*' fourth Act might be provided with a verse
from *Ecclesiastes* as epigraph:

As he came forth of his mother's womb, naked shall he return to go as
he came, and shall take nothing of his labour, which he may carry
away in his hand    (5:15)

and Act Three perhaps owes an even greater debt to *Ecclesiastes*. There
appears in Act Three a sermon glass (*LF*, 25; *R*, 99) and if this profoundly moral play has a text, then that text is Chapter Seven of
*Ecclesiastes*. A few verses from that chapter should make clear how
much it has contributed to both the verbal and visual texture of the
play in general, and Act Three in particular:

1.    A good name is better than precious ointment; and the day of
death than the day of one's birth.
2.    It is better to go to the house of mourning, than to go to the
house of feasting: for that is the end of all men; and the living will
lay it to his heart.
3.    Sorrow is better than laughter: for by the sadness of the
countenance the heart is made better.
4.    The heart of the wise is in the house of mourning; but the
heart of fools is in the house of mirth.
. . .
16.    Be not righteous over much; neither make thyself over wise:
why shouldest thou destroy thyself?
17.    Be not over much wicked, neither be thou foolish: why
shouldest thou die before thy time?
. . .
25.    I applied mine heart to know, and to search, and seek out
wisdom, and the reason of things, and to know the wickedness of
folly, even of foolishness and madness.

26.    And I find more bitter than death the woman whose heart
is snares and nets, and her hands as bands: whoso pleaseth God shall
escape from her; but the sinner shall be taken by her.

27.    Behold, this have I found, saith the preacher, counting one by
one, to find out the account:

28.    Which yet my soul seeketh, but I find not: one man among a
thousand have I found; but a woman among all those have I not found.

There in verse 26 is the relationship of Epigyne and Gonad stated with
bare and painful clarity. There in verse 28 is that Old Testament view
of Woman, the perennial Eve, which *Lying Figures* presents so forcefully, indeed savagely. Beyond the matter of verbal echoes there is a
deep sympathy of temper between *Lying Figures* and *Ecclesiastes*.
Like the Biblical book this first play of the *Requiem* trilogy presents
teachings which are largely, though not exclusively, negative. One
Biblical scholar has written of

> Koheleth's aim as being to induce a desire for and participation in
> the better life by exposing in no uncertain terms the vacuity and
> unreality of man's ordinary life in the world.[9]

The imagery of *Lying Figures* is as obsessed with death and the grave
as is that of *Ecclesiastes* — and, indeed, that of *The Atheist's Tragedy*.
Koheleth's work is devoid of any hope of salvation, and his repeated
confrontation with the facts of mortality serves only to stress

> the need for the hope realised only in the gospel of Christ

and

> testifies to the bankruptcy of an intellectual quest which is limited
> to material ends.[10]

Chapter 7 of *Ecclesiastes* is very specifically concerned with the question
of how the fact of death can be integrated within a vision of life as not
devoid of meaning. Time and again, characters in *Lying Figures* are
given words which, though they themselves are unconscious of it, do
seem to hint at one solution to the play's central obsession with human
mortality.

At the very beginning of Act Three we find Gonad amending a verse
from St. Luke's Gospel:

A fine sunny day, peace on earth, goodwill towards your husband.
(LF, 16; R, 90)

The verse which he 'edits' is taken from St. Luke's account of the vision given to the shepherds before the birth of Christ:

> For unto you is born this day in the City of David a Saviour, which is Christ the Lord.
> And this shall be a sign unto you; Ye shall find the babe wrapped in swaddling clothes, lying in a manger.
> And suddenly there was with the angel a multitude of the heavenly host praising God, and saying,
> Glory to God in the highest, and on earth peace, good will toward men.   (*Luke*, 2:11–14)

Gonad's version omits the Glory of God, and selfishly impoverishes the final clause. Most noticeably the birth of Christ is not explicitly mentioned in Gonad's version. Later in the same Act there is an equally telling elusion of an expected reference to the Crucifixion.

GUPPY       When am I supposed to come? Dinner next Friday?
GONAD      Actually it was last Friday.
GUPPY       Good . . .   (*LF*, 32, *R*, 106)

Guppy's phrase is not allowed to reach its logical conclusion; the nearest we come to 'Good Friday' is Guppy's cynical remark soon afterwards:

> Without Judas you cannot have heroism. Just the old patterns of affliction, dear boy.   (*LF*, 33; *R*, 107)

The materials are there for the inhabitants of this dramatic world to work upon. None of them, however, can sustain any sense of how the eternal might impinge upon the transient, how the one might give significance to the other. When they quote Christ's parable of the Kingdom of Heaven, from *Matthew* 13, it is only in a debased context, as when Guppy describes Epigyne:

> You are indeed my pearl of great prize   (*LF*, 27; *R*, 101)

and it remains for Epigyne herself to correct the quotation:

> Prize? Shouldn't it be 'price'?   (*LF*, 27; *R*, 101)

The attention thus drawn to the word 'price' serves to remind us of Gonad's earlier "The price of love is death" (*LF*, 20; *R*, 94) and to link it to Sapphira's "The price of life is death" (*LF*, 41, *R*, 115) in Act Four.

The ironies are less complex in the case of some other Biblical echoes set off by Warner's endlessly allusive technique. Gonad combines his knowledge gained as *Pediculus Pubis* with a certain rudimentary familiarity with Biblical story when he responds to Epigyne's lubricious gossip:

EPI                   I've just changed to a new Gynie, he's such a lamb.
GONAD            Don't you mean a ram, caught in that thicket?
                             (*LF*, 18; *R*, 92)

and he is bitterly ironic when Epigyne tells him one of her savage zoological fables and he comments

'And underneath the everlasting arms'.[11]   (*LF*, 19; *R*, 93)

Animals abound in this garden — as much a mental landscape as the text tells us Act Two's setting was. Epigyne's imaginings are particularly fertile in this respect:

Animals are not bestial. The silver fox is on heat only eight days a year. And those are in February . . . And the female praying mantis during copulation bites off the head of her love; who, all the same, still continues to thrust away with undiminished fervour.
                             (*LF*, 18; *R*, 92)

Epigyne's general attitude to the garden is made perfectly clear by the way we find her occupied at the very beginning of Act Three:

EPIGYNE, *in brief, blood-red, two-piece bathing costume, sits stage left in hanging basket chair. Her feet do not touch the ground. The chair swings gently. With a pair of scissors she snips off the heads of the tulips she is holding. The heads fall on the ground beneath her dangling feet.*   (*LF*, 16; *R*, 90)

The image is glossed later by Sapphira and Laz:

SAPPH            High wispy clouds, autumn blaze of splendour, the
                           October leaves, green, then lemon-yellow deepening
                           to brown, fully biscuit and off they fall!

LAZ      Acres, no, an Eden of beheaded blooms.

         (*LF*, 45; *R*, 119)

In her own "Eden of beheaded blooms" Epigyne weaves "a net of malice" (*LF*, 21) throughout Act Three; Gonad, Guppy and Xyster all contribute their own strands to the same net, but it is Epigyne who is the most powerful figure. Through all the twists and turns of the plot she contrives to keep the whip-hand (in *Meeting Ends* Wrasse will do so quite literally; the two women have much in common), recovering quickly from any temporary setbacks in the twists and turns of sexual politics. It is she who insists that Gonad assert his masculinity by doing the gardening, though the episode also reveals the ambiguities of her own role. She wants to be pampered, but she wants to assert her independence too. It is she who controls the hour-glass. It is the presence and pressure of the repetitively transient, of purely human time, which do much to put her in a position of power. In this garden the sundial is imaginary and is mentioned only in passing. Again we must wait until *Meeting Ends* before the sundial will become both literal and dominant, embodying the possibility of a different sense of time, a different encounter between eternal and temporal.

Gardening is not, of course, the only proof of virility which Gonad is called upon to provide. Even before Act Three's chilling conclusion, Epigyne tests Gonad's manhood in a copulatory moment of darkness. The garden is still dark, the sundial quite useless, when Epigyne lights up a cigarette after their intercourse. The moment is linked to an earlier remark of hers:

     Light my cigarette. Go on. You are irresistible to women. Know that?

         (*LF*, 19; *R*, 93)

and even more tellingly to the very beginning and end of the play. In the opening moments in the mortuary Gonad's actions are described thus:

*From stage left enter* GONAD, *the janitor of the mortuary, pushing trolley on which lies a corpse covered with a sheet. He stops centre-stage.*
*Walks round to downstage side of trolley and pauses to sit on stomach of corpse and light cigarette. After a few puffs, sure now that cigarette is alight, climbs down . . . Pinches open corpse's mouth, taps ash in.* (*LF*, 1; *R*, 75)

The lighting of the cigarette is thus used to link the moment at which

lust has been satiated with the facts of death. By way of contrast it is
the candle which is lit at the end of the play. For the moment, however,
let us concentrate on this symbolic identification of lust and death.
The next logical stage is to make a similar identification between the
act of lust and the act of murder. Such an identification is, of course,
a commonplace of Jacobean tragedy. Once again *The Atheist's Tragedy*
will provide a valuable illustration. D'Amville confronts a death's head
in Act IV Scene III:

> Why dost thou stare upon me? Thou art not
> The skull of him I murdered. What hast thou
> To do to vex my conscience? Sure thou wert
> The head of a most dogged usurer,
> Th'art so uncharitable. And that bawd,
> The sky there, she could shut the windows and
> The doors of this great chamber of the world,
> And draw the curtains of the clouds between
> Those lights and me about this bed of earth,
> When that same strumpet, Murder, and myself
> Committed sin together. Then she could
> Leave us i'th' dark till the close deed
> Was done, but now that I begin to feel
> The loathsome horror of my sin and, like
> A lecher emptied of his lust, desire
> To bury my face under my eyebrows and
> Would steal from my shame unseen, she meets me
> I'th'face with all her light corrupted eyes
> To challenge payment o'me.[12]

For D'Amville the moment at which a victim is slaughtered is a moment
of intercourse with "that same strumpet, Murder". Metaphorically for
Tourneur, and literally for Warner, Lust and Murder are both "deeds of
darkness". The stage lights went out while "the close deed was done"
between Epigyne and Gonad. They next go out at the spectacular conclusion of Act Three when Epigyne encourages Gonad to

> Prove your manhood, my tender love    (*LF*, 38; *R*, 112)

by an act which belongs simultaneously to the repertoires of Lust and
Murder — the bizarre castration of Xyster. Ostensibly she is punished as
the source of the syphilis which has ravaged this claustrophobically
mirrored society of wife-swappers. Guppy exits screaming at the

appearance of the mirror cyclorama, as well as at Epigyne's apt summary of events:

> Each man has two women, each woman two men. All eight of us
> poisoned by delight. (*LF*, 37; *R*, 111)

Of course the mirrors serve also to incorporate the audience more completely in the play's denunciation. The savagery which closes Act Three is couched in tones of tenderness, since it is also an act of 'love', but remains the most violent indictment we have yet had of a society which is "spiritually tone deaf" (*LF*, 35; *R*, 109). The stage direction which closes Act Three, "No scream" (*LF*, 38; *R*, 112), makes the brutality all the more chilling, and the potent silence which ensues constitutes an effective transition to the lyricism of Act Four's opening.

Act Four opens with an aubade, or tagelied. Act Three had plunged us into darkness. Moral darkness was seemingly universal and the Act ended in the literal darkness of an unlit stage. The prospect of dawn ought to be an attractive one. However our experience in *Maquettes* should have made us suspicious, for false dawns are by no means unknown in those plays. The aubade is certainly beautiful, but its beauty is not that of an easy optimism. The love it celebrates is adulterous:

> Are you foolhardy? Reckless of all . . . ? Hark!
>   He moves in the next room: there'll be no pardon
> (*LF*, 39; *R*, 113)

and an aubade, after all, marks an ending as well as a beginning:

> Tenderest safety ends, the East grows light,
>   Dress and depart;
> Dally no more, but vanish with the night,
>   Stay not to risk the terrors of the dawn.
> (*LF*, 39–40; *R*, 113–4)

Still, it *is* a poem of dawn. Its light is not only that of morning, but of love:

> Ah Love, since love has lit through miles and darkness to you.
> (*LF*, 39; *R*, 113)

The lark is startled by the light of love rather than by daylight. This mixture of continuing darkness, and nascent light, sets the tone for the last Act. Act Four does move us towards the light, but only a little and only hesitantly.

Indeed, once the exquisite aubade has been completed we are plunged into a veritable fire-work display of trivial jest:

| | |
|---|---|
| SAPPH | I first fell in love with you when you were an amateur brain-surgeon. |
| LAZ | And you a one-legged ballerina. |
| SAPPH | And you asked if you might split my infinitude. |
| LAZ | But you wanted to set up house. |
| SAPPH | You wanted the house upset. |
| LAZ | Wouldn't re-lease your free hold until we both reached morgue-age. |
| SAPPH | Remember the delirious way you would fumble with the bedclothes? Carphology, you used to call it. |
| LAZ | A modest talent will be buried with me. |
| SAPPH | You were always firm. (*Resigned pleasure*) The upright shall have dominion.   (*LF*, 40; *R*, 114) |

The bawdy fails to conceal the beginning of another pattern of Biblical allusion which maintains throughout Act Four an undercurrent of movement towards the light, offering a presence which ensures that the light is not wholly extinguished even if the characters on stage are largely blind to its existence. Laz, for instance, uses a revealing phrase when indulging in a piece of mild self-congratulation: "a modest talent will be buried with me". His words, inescapably, identify him with one of the three figures in Christ's Parable of the Talents, to be found in *Matthew*, Chapter 25. Lazarus corresponds to the 'slothful servant' who buries in the earth the money given him by his lord. We may remember what his fate was:

Cast ye the unprofitable servant into outer darkness: there shall be weeping and gnashing of teeth.   (*Matthew*, 25:30)

Remembering what has happened to the "unprofitable servant" (and Laz has reaped profit neither for himself nor for the Lord he has failed to recognise) we may simultaneously remember the other two servants and their rather more pleasant destinies.

The smugness of Sapphira's reply is similarly double-edged. Her contented memory of Laz's sexual prowess (doubtless the raising of Lazarus to which she attaches greatest importance) is expressed in words taken from one of the most important of the Psalms:

Like sheep they are laid in the grave; death shall feed on them; and
the upright shall have dominion over them in the morning; and their
beauty shall consume in the grave from their dwelling.

But God will redeem my soul from the power of the grave: for
he shall receive me.  (*Psalms*, 49:14—15)

Psalm 49 is concerned with the inevitable death of the worldly, and the
immortality of the righteous, a theme which has an obviously ironic
relevance here.

When Laz, in turn, echoes the language of the Psalms a moment or
two later, the pattern is extended. Watching the nun they offer their
comments:

| | |
|---|---|
| LAZ | She's praying that celibacy may prove a cheat before she's old enough to accept it. |
| SAPPH | Her buds should be stroked to feed children. |
| LAZ | Her children would be taken by the ankles and dashed against a wall. |
| SAPPH | It's the Lord's will. |
| LAZ | It's the law of the land.  (*LF*, 41; *R*, 115) |

Laz's central observation here takes its force from the final verse of
Psalm 137:

How shall we sing the Lord's song in a strange land?
If I forget thee, O Jerusalem, let my right hand forget her cunning.
If I do not remember thee, let my tongue cleave to the roof of
my mouth; if I prefer not Jerusalem above my chief joy.
Remember, O lord, the children of Edom in the day of Jerusalem;
who said, Rase it, rase it, even to the foundation thereof.
O daughter of Babylon, who art to be destroyed; happy shall he
be that rewardeth thee as thou hast served us.
Happy shall he be, that taketh and dasheth thy little ones against
the stones.  (*Psalms*, 137:4—9)

Laz is observing a world where man is, indeed, in exile; in a land where
the "Lord's song" goes largely unsung; where the Lord is not remem-
bered, where 'joys' (chief or otherwise) are preferred 'above' Jerusalem.
The enemy in this land becomes, not Babylon, but those such as the
nun who have some awareness of the eternal, some comprehension of
moral and spiritual values. *Their* children *will* be slaughtered, not, as
Sapphira wrongly asserts, because "It's the Lord's will" but, as Laz
more correctly insists, because "It's the law of the land". In the

"strange land" in which man chooses to live such, indeed, is the law.
We shall see that law in operation in *Killing Time*, the next play in the
sequence. If light is to come, then it must be light which will lead man
out of this "strange land". The possibility of such a light is hinted at in
a later remark of Laz's which belongs to the same pattern of Biblical
allusion:

> Off with your grass skirt of flesh. It's only real.   (*LF*, 45; *R*, 119)

The phrase contains echoes of the Psalms once more:

> For they shall be cut down like the grass, and wither as the green
> herb.   (*Psalms*, 37:2)

Even more forcefully Laz's words remind us of some verses from
*Isaiah*:

> The voice said, Cry. And he said, What shall I cry? "All flesh
> is grass, and all the goodliness thereof is as the flower of the field:
> The grass withereth, the flower fadeth: because the spirit of the
> Lord bloweth upon it: surely the people is grass.
> The grass withereth, the flower fadeth: but the word of our
> God shall stand for ever.   (*Isaiah*, 40:6—8)

*Isaiah* Chapter 40 is a prophecy announcing the end of exile and the
fall of Babylon. It is linked, thus, with the allusion to Psalm 137 which
we have just noted. Slowly the materials accumulate which might offer
a path out of the "strange land". "The word of our God shall stand
for ever": if we bear in mind the characteristic Warnerian preoccupation with those verses from St. John's Gospel which proclaim the
Johannine doctrine of the incarnation, we shall be on the alert for
evidence of the Nativity.

Act Four is centrally concerned with birth. In a land which inverts
so many Christian values we shall not be surprised to find that if death
is a kind of birth then this mirror world will show us birth as a kind of
death. Laz and Sapphira tell us that Gonad is not at work in the mortuary today. He has exchanged the house of death for that of birth,
but the language of the two turns out to be interchangeable:

| | |
|---|---|
| SAPPH | . . . . today his mind, like ours, is elsewhere. |
| LAZ | By the bedside of his breeding wife. |
| SAPPH | What a sweet girl! How thoughtful of her to let him be in at the kill.   (*LF*, 41; *R*, 115) |

The equivocation is a characteristically Baroque one:

> Birth is a kind of Resurrection;
> For Man is buried ere he be brought forth.
> Th' membrane that veiles the tender Embrion
> Is first its winding sheet, then swadling cloath.
>> Death ushers in mans life, so that the wombe
>> Is both his genethliack Inne and Tombe.
>
> Birth is a kind of Goal delivery.
> A Prisoner ere he knowes what's to be free
> Man is. Thrice three Moneths doth he cloystered lie
> In a maturnall Dungeon, after, he
>> Lives halfe in nights; whom *Lucine* forth doth let
>> Leaves not his darknesse, but exchanges it.
>
> Gods Commissary Nature doth bestow
> The inborn Principalls and Physicall
> Dictates of Reason on him, this yee don't know.
> And thus alone he proves he's rationall,
>> He wailes with cries which no salt teares do want
>> The Ignorance of which he's Ignorant.
>
> His lives twilight, or dawning of the Day
> In this same wheel or circular is spent,
> He sucks, sleeps, cries, *Tria sunt omnia*.
> As if he deem'd Death gain, Life punishment.
>> He's quiet but sleeping when in jeast he dies,
>> But when he wakes, and finds he lives, he cries.
>
> He is beholding to (though he's by Birth
> The Monarch of the whole creation)
> Brute Animals and hospitable earth
> Both for his vestments and nutrition.
>> Being cloath'd he's lulled asleep by his own cry,
>> So, ere he 'gins to live, he learns to die.[13]

In Act Four of *Lying Figures* birth is viewed in the context of such traditional patterns of thought. The nun who takes Gonad's place is the only character in the play who appears not to be the captive of her own sensuality. Not that there is any doubting her femininity. She is bare-breasted throughout and her only words of the play are a lullaby to an imaginary child:

(*Sings, cradling imaginary child to her bare breasts*)

Come my little tiny child,
   There's nothing now to fear,
And though outside the wind is wild
   Your warm content is here.   (*LF*, 42; *R*, 116)

The sentiments, and the simple texture of the verse, are in marked contrast to Gonad's poem which follows immediately upon it. The nun's words measure that range of experience from which Epigyne and Gonad have cut themselves off by their carnality. Yet, the nun's child *can* only be imaginary: celibacy is not, of itself, an adequate answer to the problems of human sensuality in a fallen world — that way there beckons another variety of suicide for mankind. The possibility of a middle way remains to be explored. It is hinted at in Laz's injunction: "Be a lustful stoic" and Sapphira's reply:

The old mistake. To suppose you can do always what you can do sometimes.   (*LF*, 44; *R*, 118)

The sentiments echo very closely the thoughts of another Baroque figure, Pascal. It is Pascal who is adapted in Sapphira's comments:

What the Stoics propose is so difficult and so vain! . . . . They conclude that what has been done once can be done always.[14]

Indeed the pages of Pascal seem to stand behind much in the closing moments of *Lying Figures*. I have discovered only this one verbal echo, but there is plenty of common ground intellectually. A full analysis of the relationship would be out of place here, but quotation of a few passages from Pascal should be enough to establish the analogy:

The Stoics say: 'Withdraw into yourselves; it is there you will find your repose'. But that is not true.
The others say: 'Go out of yourselves; seek happiness in distraction'. But that is not true. Sickness comes.
Happiness is neither without nor within us. It is in God, both without and within us.[15]

The nature of happiness is obviously a central theme of Warner's plays, and like Pascal, Warner finds Stoicism both attractive and absurd. The pattern of antithetical reasoning, moving towards a kind of *via media* is also of obvious relevance to the 'Requiem' plays. Warner's belief that a recognition of the limitations of human knowledge is a necessary prelude to spiritual development is similarly stated in Pascal; indeed, it is there stated in relation to much the same question as that which confronts us in *Lying Figures*:

> But will you say What is good? Chastity? I say no, for the world would come to an end. Marriage? No — continence is better. Not to kill? No; for the resulting lawlessness would be dreadful, and the wicked would kill all the good. To kill? No; for that destroys nature. We possess truth and goodness only in part, mingled with evil and falsehood.[16]

Pascal insists that any adequate religious philosophy must account for the simultaneous "greatness and misery of man", for the presence in him of "these astonishing contrarieties."[17]

His analysis is both succinct and logically formulated:

> Knowledge of God without knowledge of man's
>    wretchedness begets pride.
> Knowledge of man's wretchedness without
>    knowledge of God begets despair.
> Knowledge of Jesus Christ constitutes the
>    middle way, because in him we find both
>    God and our wretchedness.[18]

As *Lying Figures* moves to its conclusion we find more and more explicit allusion to Pascal's "middle way". Having listened to the full horror of Gonad's elegy for his dead child, Laz comments, in wordplay which enacts a complex of dignified emotions too grave to move us to laughter:

> The blighted star of mourning.   (*LF*, 43; *R*, 117)

Let us remind ourselves of the Biblical original for Laz's words:

> Blessed are they that do his commandments, that they might have right to the tree of life, and may enter in through the gates of the city.
> For without are dogs, and sorcerers, and whoremongers, and murderers, and idolaters, and whosoever loveth and maketh a lie.
> I Jesus have sent mine angel to testify unto you these things in the churches. I am the root and the offspring of David, and the bright and morning star.   (*Revelation*, 22, 14—16)

The "strange land", full of those who love, and make, lies, has brought forth only Epigyne's stillbirth. The star of morning (let us not forget that Act Four began with an aubade) has proved only a "star of mourning". The dawn has, indeed, proved a false dawn, its brightness turned to blight. Yet the path is still there. With a logic which is characteristically Baroque, and characteristic also of Warner's dramatic imagination, the Nativity and the Crucifixion are poetically fused. In their fusion exists an affirmation of the central importance of both events in any attempt to understand and give significance to Pascal's *via media*:

> LAZ        Restore my failing faith with vinegar. (*Pause*) Lend
>                me your napkin and let me sever the cord.
> SAPPH     Holy innocents! what a bloodbath childbirth is.
>
> (*LF*, 45; *R*, 119)

The allusions here to St. Veronica, the massacre of the Holy Innocents, and the Crucifixion are rapidly followed by a return to the language of *Isaiah*, Chapter 40:

> We must comfort those that are with young.

The original is to be found in Verse 11 of the relevant chapter, and comes from a passage which is often used in the Christmas Service. However, the optimism which lies implicit in these allusions exists in a precarious balance with the surrounding and preceding pessimism. Gonad may have learnt something:

> Let me reach out across the darkening lake!
> Oh little children, yet the briefest while
> We live to grieve our bearers, till the rake
> Claws out our wisdom with our bloody tears    (*LF*, 43; *R*, 117)

but the knowledge has been gained at enormous expense, and we see no sign that Gonad can put the knowledge to profitable use. Laz and Sapphira have learned something too. They see now the simultaneous grandeur and misery of man:

> LAZ        So with joy, tenderness and delight we transform
>                ourselves into beasts.
> SAPPH     What a wonderful and tiny thing a newborn baby is!
>
> (*LF*, 45; *R*, 119)

Yet they can still enjoy fond memories of their vices, reminiscing about the "faded glories of military splendour" and their attendant "good-time girls" (*LF*, 43; *R*, 117), a memory which looks ahead, as it were, to *Killing Time*. We are a long way from any final resolution which will make possible a vision of the relationship between the temporal and the eternal.

The ritual which Gonad performs with gentle dignity over the skeletal corpse of his child maintains the delicate balance. One candle is snuffed, but one stays alight. When Gonad finally leaves the stage the candle goes with him. We may be left in darkness, but Gonad takes illumination with him. The light is not overcome. Before he leaves the stage it falls to Gonad to speak the play's final words, words which take on an extra force from the long silence which has preceded them:

> I had hoped so much for you. (*Pause*) Emptiness enfolds. Darkness encroaches on the light, and in lightness we dare not comprehend.
>
> (*LF*, 47; *R*, 121)

Gonad's assessment seems to sum up the dominant mood of the play. Though the light is not extinguished, there can be no doubt that darkness has the upper hand. Still, we have seen hints, especially in the last Act, of seeds from which a greater light might grow. Even in Gonad's final words there is at least a recognition of human folly. That profound theologian Sir Topas asserts that "there is no darkness but ignorance" and for all its darkness *Lying Figures* does not deny the possibility that in the recognition of human foolishness there might exist a basis for the development of some greater wisdom. Epigyne, all unknowingly, goes near to the heart of the matter when, amidst her giggles, she tells us that

> There's many a true word broken in jest.   (*LF*, 30; *R*, 104)

In Gonad's realisation that their 'lightness' confines them to 'darkness' lies the possibility that he will similarly come to recognize the truth of some of those "true words" which he and his fellows have "broken in jest". The play's extensive scheme of Biblical allusion can be seen to serve both as a judgement upon those who pervert and invert its texts and an obvious source of that which might liberate them. That liberation has certainly not been found when this first play of the trilogy ends. Examination of the world of this first play leads one to a conclusion which might most relevantly be expressed, once more, in some words taken from *Ecclesiastes*:

> Lo, this only have I found, that God hath made man upright; but they have sought out many inventions. (*Ecclesiastes*, 5:29)

## Notes

1 E. H. Langlois, *Essai historique, philosophique et pittoresque sur les danses des morts*, Rouen, 1852, p. 191.

2 *Francis Warner: Poet and Dramatist*, ed. T. Prentki, Knotting, 1977, p. 97. To his list should be added the *Lying Figure in a Mirror* of 1971, a picture which has particularly close affinities with *Lying Figures*.

3 David Sylvester, *Interviews with Francis Bacon*, 1975, p. 78.

4 *Lying Figures* contains at least one phrase which must surely be an unconscious memory of Browne, when Laz observes of Sapphira "Your limbs and trunk were in angles of contingency". The final phrase here occurs in the passage from Browne quoted in this chapter.

5 Sir Thomas Browne, 'Hydrotaphia: Urn Burial', in *Religio Medici, Urn Burial, Christian Morals and Other Essays*, ed. J. A. Symonds, 1886, p. 169.

6 In Prentki, *Francis Warner: Poet and Dramatist*, p. 53.

7 Helen Waddell, *The Desert Fathers*, (Orig. Publ. 1936), 1965, p. 33. Her two quotations are from the *Vita B. Antonii* and Paulinus of Nola.

8 H. B. A. Moquin-Tandon, *Elements of medical zoology*, trans. R. T. Hulme (1861), II, VI, 1, p. 296.

9 H. Odeberg, *Qohaeleth*, 1929, paraphrased thus in *Peake's Commentary on the Bible*, ed. M. Black, 1962, p. 459.

10 *Ibid.*, p. 459.

11 It is worth noting that this version of *Deuteronomy*, Chapter 33, Verse 27 is placed in inverted commas, presumably as a way of indicating that Gonad's use of this quotation is entirely conscious and deliberately ironic, where so many of the other Biblical allusions in the play operate *at the expense* of the character who utters them.

12 Tourneur, *The Atheist's Tragedy*, IV, iii, ll. 212–230.

13 Robert Baron *Pocula Castalia*, 1650.

14 Pascal, *Pensées*, ed. L. Lafuma, trans. J. Warrington, (Everyman), 1967, p. 77.

15 *Ibid.*, p. 78.

16 *Ibid.*, p. 80.

17 *Ibid.*, p. 83.

18 *Ibid.*, p. 103.

# VII

## *Killing Time*: Pits and Snares

*Killing Time* was written after the other two plays in the *Requiem* trilogy, although it is the central play of the sequence. It is perhaps because of its composition after completion of the other two plays that it carries to a further extreme all that is most individual in their method of composition. In discontinuity of narrative it does not, perhaps, go very far beyond its companion pieces. In what one might call discontinuity of characterisation it certainly does. Psychological consistency of the individual is here largely jettisoned in favour of an adaptability of *dramatis personae* almost as fluid as that of Actor and Actress in *Lumen*. As dramatic need arises so one of the 'characters' is made to meet that need. As one of the 'characters' adopts a new role, so a new dramatic situation arises. The resulting kaleidoscope is both colourful and stimulating, but can present a reader or viewer with greater difficulties than confront him in any of the accompanying plays. He is here asked to survive with fewer of his normal assumptions than he is allowed to retain in encountering the other plays. One consequence of this intensification of Warner's characteristic dramatic method is that in *Killing Time* much of the thematic weight is carried by a network of images more intricate and more individual, than that to be found in any of the other works in the sequence.

Much of the play's pattern of imagery appears to be derived from a single source. This is Picasso's painting of 1910/11 *Le pigeon aux petits pois* (Plate 2). In this quintessentially Cubist work representation is strictly subordinated to questions of structure, rather as Warner's play subordinates psychological realism to thematic development.

Still, recognisable realistic 'clues' are to be found in the painting. Amongst other objects, one can discern the claw and (upturned) head of a pigeon, five peas, near the centre of the picture surface, and the flame of a candle, all of them, it would appear, seen in a mirror. The mirror and the candle have extensive roles to play throughout the *Requiem* cycle and indeed, they are not irrelevant in *Killing Time*. It is, however, with the pigeon and the peas of the painting's title that we should be most concerned, for it is upon these that much of the play's imagery, and therefore much of its dramatic weight, is made to depend.

As used in *Killing Time* the pigeon and the pea are the central terms in a sequence of related images. Several items in the sequence are brought together by Squaloid near the end of the play:

> I suppose your pea and your cherry are only inferior olives; just as the common pigeon's only a dirty dove, if you think about it.
> (*KT*, 64; *R*, 188)

One item from that sequence is introduced in the opening speech of the play, and another is forcefully implied in that same speech. Chalone's opening sentences make mention of the olive. In identifying it as the olive of peace which has been "burned up" in the "crematorium of war", and in telling us that "there are no birds in the sky", the particular olive borne by the dove to Noah is clearly suggested:

> The crematorium of war is here. Death creeps in our homes, our streets, our kitchens, disfigures the children in their beds. Even the animals have fled. There are no birds in the sky. The proud oaf man is pinned by his arrow of time, and our eggshell peace blown like thistledown in a whirlwind, (*Throws away scales*) the olive burned up like petrol.   (*KT*, 1; *R*, 125)

In *Genesis* the dove brought an olive leaf to Noah as evidence that God had made his peace with mankind. Here all is negative. There is no dove, no olive branch. No peace, that is, between man and God, and, therefore, no peace between man and man.

In Chalone's next speech the olive recurs. This speech is Chalone's lecture on the structure of the human brain, which constitutes Act One Scene Two. Its second paragraph includes the following:

> We know the seven nerves of the cortex. First, climbing fibres for comedy; second, mossy fibres for tragedy. As tragedy is the higher mode, the mossy fibres stimulate the largest number of cells and

Picasso                                    *Pigeon petits pois* 1911

provoke negative feedback. Comedy, on the other hand reasserts balance and peace, so the climbing fibres spring naturally from the two inferior olives of the brain stem. (*KT*, 9; *R*, 133)

The moral and scientific ambiguity of "higher" and "lower" here need not distract us from the clear identification of the olive with peace, an identification already made in Chalone's opening speech.

Since Squaloid describes the pea and the cherry as "inferior olives" we should expect them, within the play, to be identified with 'inferior' kinds of peace — and so they are. The pea first appears as an image in Act One Scene Five. That scene begins with Phagocyte making confession (to Chalone, appearing this time as a priest) of a sin which was simultaneously sexual and military in nature; in Scene Four we have seen him kill an anonymous military figure and then discover his victim to be feminine. He sees his crime as a punishment for his earlier callousness:

Curses return. They do! We took a good-looking girl, used her for a few days, then killed her because we were bored and satiated, and she complained and coughed too much. (*KT*, 13; *R*, 137)

Chalone enquires

You have mated unchecked? (*KT*, 14; *R*, 138)

and tells Phagocyte that

The peace of this world is no more than the peace in each one of us; in you, in me: the love that refuses to hate. (*KT*, 14; *R*, 138)

Chalone exits, and Phagocyte moves over into the priest's compartment and is thus able to hear confession made by Quark. He believes himself still talking to her when, in fact, Squaloid has taken her place in the confessional, in an echo of the earlier switch-over of roles. Imagining himself talking to Quark, Phagocyte sees the situation as one ripe for the exercise of a little sexual opportunism. In doing so he mimics Chalone's vocabulary: he talks of peace, and he talks of chess. Both terms of the discourse are sadly debased by him, however. He can conceive of peace only as the outcome of sexual gratification. It is at this point that he introduces the image of the pea:

Delight is eternal while tragedy passes. The mystery of sex was dispelled in a monastery garden when our bishop Gregor Mendel crossed a garden pea with green seeds with one with yellow seeds, and the seeds of all the daughter plants were yellow. So it is with humans. The seven chromosomes of his pea match the seven nerves of our cortex. We are the pawns of night manoeuvres. Be reassured, my dear, as the light is dark. Some genes are dominant and some recessive. I will simply place my hand on your lap, and give you peace. (*Screams*) A Man!　(*KT*, 15; *R*, 139)

His appeal to genetics, and his use of terms from Chalone's earlier discourse on the human brain, amount to little more than a pseudo-scientific attempt to evade moral responsibility for his actions. If the hand in the lap is the kind of peace it stands for, then the pea is indeed a distinctly inferior olive.

Elsewhere the text reinforces the association of the pea with sexuality. Telling Quark of her sexual encounter with Phagocyte (immediately after the funeral ceremony), Kuru tells Quark:

He gave me these peas I'm podding! Said it was our secret code, what he'd like to do to me. I was so low, and sick of all this death and depression and destruction and mourning and anyway it was a warm day and my most randy time of the month and I just felt I had to affirm life at once then and there. Anyway, Phagocyte's always attracted me.　(*KT*, 52; *R*, 176)

The words she uses echo two important moments earlier in the play. When placing Quark in the guillotine, Kuru had looked closely at her neck:

KURU　　　　　　. . . Now that's interesting. The stalk's beak-mark usually fades during the first week of life — just above bridge of nose and back of neck at hair line — but it's especially noticeable when baby cries. It proves baby comes on a stalk, doesn't it? Like a pod of peas!

QUARK　　　　　(*Whimpering*) What are you doing to me?

KURU　　　　　　(*Going behind guillotine to begin undressing QUARK*) Bestiality is one thing, dear, but bedding plants really is a little beyond the pale.

　　　　　　　　　　　　　　　　　　　　(*KT*, 30; *R*, 154)

(The pun here on stalk/stork adds a further twist). At the same time, and perhaps even more importantly, her later words to Quark pick up an important sentence of Chalone's, and in doing so they expand the significance of this image of the pea. When she tells Quark that she and Phagocyte share a "secret code" which relates to peas in the pod, Kuru employs almost precisely the words which Chalone had used earlier. At the opening of Act Two Scene Three Chalone questions Squaloid:

| | |
|---|---|
| CHALONE | Where's Phagocyte? |
| SQUALOID | He's alive somewhere. |
| CHALONE | We don't trust him. He has not been told the code, but we believe he may know it. If he knows it he's with the suborned wing. See if you can find out, when the chance comes. The code is Peas in Pod. |
| SQUALOID | Urine and pregnancy. |
| CHALONE | Yes. No more, now. In war, as in marriage, never tell more than the other person needs to know. |

(KT, 39; R, 163)

When he talks of a "code" he reminds us unmistakeably of his own speech at the beginning of the play when he had contrasted the 'bestial' behaviour of man, killing for pleasure, with that of other animals (save the fox, similarly "deformed"). Chalone comments that

Even wolves have a code for killing their kind.  (*KT*, 2; *R*, 126)

Here, in his later exchange with Squaloid, Chalone treats marriage and war as synonymous fields of activity. *Killing Time* both follows on from, and parallels, *Lying Figures*. The pea, as emblem of the battlefields of sex and war, stands in opposition to the olive of peace. Quark and Phagocyte are identified as victims by their unknowing declaration of the code:

I love the smell of freshly split peas in pod

they both say.  (*KT*, 53, 64; *R*, 177, 188)

The cherry plays a simpler role in the play. Its first appearance is innocent enough, or almost so. Squaloid's account of the filthy horrors of life in the trenches ends with an incongruous touch of brightness:

Oh, if you slept on the top level, just underneath the ground, that's where the rats 'ud run. You'd wake up and find rat-shit all over you. One bit my nose when I was asleep. It swelled up like a cherry.

(KT, 7; R, 131)

Elsewhere the cherry is a straightforward sexual symbol. When the whores Kuru and Quark, in corsets, stockings and wide-brimmed hats (and entering on stilts) observe their potential customers, Squaloid and Phagocyte (loud suits, large bow-ties, and pogo-sticks), the greeting they offer them is appropriately coarse and to the point:

KURU          No great sheiks. Cherry ripe?    (*KT*, 25; *R*, 149)

Elsewhere a slightly wiser Kuru, in a somewhat more reflective mood, advises the younger Quark that

The pearl of sex is not in your cherry but in the mind.
(*KT*, 48; *R*, 172)

The olive in the mind is quite distinct from the sexual cherry.

Squaloid's formulation, with which we began consideration of this cluster of images, is in two parts. The first suggests that the cherry and the pea are inferior olives. The second observes that " the common pigeon's only a dirty dove" (*KT*, 64; *R*, 188). The dove and the olive are similar emblems of peace. We should, therefore, expect the "common pigeon" to stand in the same relationship to the dove as the cherry and the pea stand to the olive. Indeed, Phagocyte, in the long passage immediately preceding Squaloid's observation, has associated the pigeon and the pea in some detail. He talks of the birds' destructiveness:

They eat three times a day, and when there's snow on the ground or a hard frost they'll pick the heart out of the middle of a Brussel sprout — you know, where it's nice and whitish when you've pulled the outer leaves off. When you get a flock of them on a nice field of Brussel sprouts you can imagine the damage they do

and then comes to a particular instance of their behaviour:

I can watch them for hours. Swing with all their weight on a pod of peas to bring it off the stalk on to the ground. Then, when it's fallen, peck it open. I cut a pigeon open once and found one hundred and twenty peas in its crop. That's counting every pea, the small ones as well. Now, if there's a thousand pigeons, you can see, they do no end of damage. (*Pause*) They sometimes go over a crop of clover and do it good. They bite the heads off the young plants, and two or three will grow in their place. Same as when the wheat crop is gathering well. From one kernel of corn, five or six on the stalk, if your land's in good condition.    (*KT*, 64; *R*, 188)

The first section here draws an implicit parallel between the pigeon's activity and the activity of men at war. Man too is a destroyer of plants, as Phagocyte and Squaloid have earlier made clear:

PHAGOCYTE    The harvest's over and ungathered.
SQUALOID     Burned with flame throwers. (*KT*, 35; *R*, 159)

In time of war the harvest meets the same fate as the olive of peace. The identification of pigeon and pea with destruction is made even more explicit in the next phase of Phagocyte's account: his cutting open of the pigeon. The destroyer is thereby destroyed. It is akin to his account, immediately before, of what he presumably regards as the 'study' of nature, since he speaks in response to remarks by Squaloid which are couched in such terms:

SQUALOID      In order to study the nature of man you must study nature.
PHAGOCYTE     Nature? We saw a lot of foxes. They'd go on a killing spree, but the fox would always come back later to collect more of his kill. We'd go out when the wind was right and spread a ring of traps, six or eight gins — they're illegal now — round where he'd been killing. He usually came back the next night, unless he sniffed us; and once one leg was caught, his pawing the ground all round to get free would sometimes catch all four legs and the muzzle. (*KT*, 64; *R*, 188)

The speech is an elaboration of sentences from the play's Prologue:

man and the fox are deformed . . . The fox kills far beyond his need for food, for pleasure, until exhausted. (*KT*, 2; *R*, 126)

Yet, if the fox kills for pleasure, why do Phagocyte and his friends kill the fox? There is no suggestion of any useful purpose served by the hunting; they too kill for pleasure. If violence is an ascending spiral man is at the top of that spiral. His choice of means reveals his 'superiority' over the animals — which means merely that he is able to employ more elaborate and more ruthless resources. When Squaloid and Phagocyte prepare for the apparent torture of Chalone the piece of equipment they choose to use is "the claw" (*KT*, 60 *ff*; *R*, 184 *ff*). The allusion is simultaneously to a piece of electrical equipment used by the torturers of more than one modern power, and to the pigeon's claw, the claw poised threateningly (if beautifully) in Picasso's *Le pigeon aux petits pois.*

Phagocyte's 'study' of the fox and the pigeon seems to have encouraged his propensity for violence, a propensity which develops and intensifies as the play proceeds. He seems oblivious to the hint of something creative which might dwell within the pigeon's destructiveness. In "going over" the clover, "cropping the heads off the young plants" (*KT*, 64; *R*, 188) the pigeons may actually aid and increase the growth of the clover. The hint is in line with other such suggestions made elsewhere in the play that human violence might contain the seed of something paradoxically positive. It echoes, indirectly, Chalone's tentative query (soon dismissed) in the prologue:

> Perhaps there is a greatness in man only brought out in war. What a frail hope    (*KT*, 1; *R*, 125)

and is related to Kuru's assertion (not borne out by the play as a whole) that

> Strength is a beauty only known in grief:
>     Like men at war
> Who find true comradeship in cruelty,
>     And bravery.   (*KT*, 32; *R*, 156)

If studying the fox and the pigeon have encouraged Phagocyte's tendency to violence, then his related reminiscences of eels suggest a source, or any rate an encouragement, of his sexual appetites:

PHAGOCYTE    If you get a nice Indian summer, you'll get pigeons nesting again for the second time. I saw some a month ago.

SQUALOID    Did you fish in the fens?

PHAGOCYTE    Often. Eels . . . I love eels . . . We get big ones; five and six pounds. Now abroad, congers go up to a hundred pounds. Serpents! Thick as you are.

SQUALOID    Eh?

PHAGOCYTE    Round the waist. Get eels in a fossil pit and they grow pretty big in England, too. I've one in a drainpipe in a pond in my garden. Feed him lob worms. All those worms, lying about on the lawn when the

sun's down. They may have no eyes, those worms,
but they've sensitive skin.   (*KT*, 65; *R*, 189)

As the rest of his account of his eels makes all too clear, Phagocyte
takes pleasure from their violence. It is also clear that the eel has a
definite sexual significance for him. This is a development of an earlier
remark of Kuru's addressed to Squaloid:

> Do you know what my secret and pet name for
> your penis is? Your eel. I've never told anyone
> before. That's what I think of when I stroke it.
> (*KT*, 42; *R*, 166)

Where Kuru uses the word eel as a 'pet name', Phagocyte actually keeps
eels as pets. The eel which grows pretty big and the pit which encourages its growth have an obvious enough sexual significance. The
worms with the "sensitive skin" are surely related to the "worm"
invoked by Shango when he announces his intention of castrating
Ensoff:

> The Cretans kept snakes as household gods...
> Let's get the worm.   (*ME*, 46; *R*, 242)

The pigeon of violence and the eel (or serpent) of sexuality are adroitly
united — extending thus the chain of related images — not only by
Phagocyte's lengthy reminiscences in Act Two Scene Nine, but with
startling economy, in a pun of Kuru's when she exclaims upon the
way her man stares at her:

> Ooo! His eyes are serpiginous, creeping from one
> part to the other!   (*KT*, 26; *R*, 150)

(Typically of *Killing Time* it is not a matter of characterisation or plot
which gives rise to this pun. It is justified by considerations of imagery,
and given its point by the manner in which imagery here sustains and
clarifies the play's argument). There is a similar moment when Squaloid
mocks Chalone (or pretends to):

> Better than having your skin peeled off, innit?
> (*KT*, 61; *R*, 185)

where "peeled" unites "pea" and "eel" in a single word.
   At the beginning of the play, as we have seen, the dove is not named,

but by the placing of other details, we are forcefully reminded of its specific absence. The bird of peace can have no place in the theatre of war. Though it, in turn, is not named, the pigeon plays a very important part in the play's curiously poignant conclusion. Chalone and Squaloid busy themselves hanging up the bodies of Phagocyte and Kuru (the scene is, of course, a precise echo of the two slabs of meat in *Lumen*), and then come downstage for the final passage of dialogue in the play, which opens as follows:

SQUALOID     Have you ever heard the sound of birds in Trafalgar Square late at night, when it's floodlit and there's not a soul around? Unnatural. (*Pause*) I've always imagined that as the only sound left at the end of the world.

CHALONE      Birds are divine remembrancers.

SQUALOID     What shall we do with his suitcase?

CHALONE      Use his clothes to mop up his blood, then burn the lot.
             *Cockcrow offstage*

SQUALOID     That's odd. (*Lights begin to fade*) We don't usually hear cockerels in towns. I was right out in the middle of no-man's land, and dark had just begun to hint the feeling of dawn, when far in the distance, right on the edge of silence, there was the crow of a cock. Then a long moment later, almost as far away, another answered. Nothing but that. (*Pause*) Then right beside me! Coarse, raucous, jumping me out of my skin.

CHALONE      The musical equivalent of first light.
                                          (*KT*, 70; *R*, 194)

The birds in Trafalgar Square can only be pigeons, and for the sort of end to which a professional soldier like Squaloid might reasonably expect the world to come, their presence, the dirty doves of war, is apt enough. Chalone's "Birds are divine remembrancers" is part of an important thread of imagery in the plays. Only moments earlier he had been suddenly reminded of Quark's continued loving presence, and, moved, had described her as

                a feather dropped from the plumage of heaven!
                                          (*KT*, 69; *R*, 193)

At the same time his remark serves to introduce the cockcrow heard offstage. On the one hand the sound is a kind of 'failed' remembrancer of the divine; it was after all the sound which heralded rather than prevented Peter's betrayal of the divine. As such it is a fitting symbol of that almost universal betrayal of divine love which we have witnessed in *Killing Time*. Simultaneously the cockcrow is, as Chalone points out, a harbinger of light. Might its presence now indicate a movement towards some kind of dawn? Is there in sight an end to this dark night of brutality? Does it look forward to that cock which appears in Ensoff's prologue to *Meeting Ends*, the cock of spiritual vigilance? The question remains unanswered, the ambiguities unresolved. This is a point of balance. *Lying Figures* ended with darkness encroaching on the light; Gonad took the candle with him when he left the stage. *Meeting Ends* closes with the brightness of a ring of candles. Here in *Killing Time* the lights dim during the dialogue we have been considering; but the dialogue itself makes a kind of equivalence between dusk and dawn:

> dark had just begun to hint the feeling of dawn

and the talk of dawn, above all Chalone's ringing phrase "the musical equivalent of first light", offers a movement which goes some way towards balancing the dimming of the stage lights. Even here, one feels, the light is not absolutely extinguished.

It is clear, then, that much of the play's argument is sustained by its images. In fulfilling this role the images are supported by a particularly forceful pattern of Biblical quotation and allusion. Such a pattern begins with the play's epigraph:

> The strength of sin is the law.    (*I Corinthians* 15:56)

It occurs in St. Paul's discussion of Christian belief in the resurrection, perhaps the very first such discussion:

> Behold, I shew you a mystery; we shall not all sleep, but we shall all be changed,
>
> In a moment, in the twinkling of an eye, at the last trump: for the trumpet shall sound, and the dead shall be raised incorruptible, and we shall be changed.
>
> For this corruptible must put on incorruption, and this mortal must put on immortality.
>
> So when this corruptible shall have put on incorruption, and this mortal shall have put on immortality, then shall be brought to pass the saying that is written, Death is swallowed up in victory.

O death, where is thy sting? O grave, where is thy victory?
The sting of death is sin; and the strength of sin is the law.
But thanks be to God, which giveth us the victory through our Lord Jesus Christ.
Therefore, my beloved brethren, be ye stedfast, unmovable, always abounding in the work of the Lord, forasmuch as ye know that your labour is not in vain in the Lord.   (*I Corinthians* 15:51—8)

It is important to note that Warner's epigraph omits the first part of the relevant verse, and that, in any case, verse 56 is a kind of parenthesis (concerned with the Mosaic law and its capacity to stimulate sin) within an optimistic context. The context of the play's epigraph thus provides a kind of 'solution' missing from most of the suceeding play itself. Paul's argument here is related to a passage in the *Epistle to the Romans* (7:7—11) where he explains that knowledge of the moral laws, designed for the governance of man, merely prompted in him a desire to perform whatever was forbidden: a paradox not to be escaped without faith in Christ. There is a clue here as to how we might interpret the role of Chalone in *Killing Time*, and the inevitable consequences of his behaviour.

*Killing Time*, in the funeral ceremonies which constitute Act Two Scene Five, is more explicit in its acknowledgement of its Biblical sources than any other of Warner's plays. Chalone, in that scene, reads passages from *Kings*, *Lamentations*, *Ecclesiastes* and, centrally, from *Jeremiah*. If *Ecclesiastes* played a governing role in determining the tone and direction of *Lying Figures*, it is *Jeremiah* which makes the greatest similar contribution to *Killing Time*. In Chalone's funeral address the longest paragraph runs as follows:

From Jeremiah forty-eight and forty-nine. Fear, and the pit, and the snare shall be upon thee. He that fleeth from the fear shall fall into the pit; and he that getteth up out of the pit shall be taken in the snare. If the grape gatherers come to thee, would they not leave some gleaning grapes? If thieves by night, they will destroy till they have enough. But I have made Esau bare: his seed is spoiled. All the cities thereof shall be perpetual wastes. Howl and cry; tell ye it in Arnon, that Moab is spoiled.   (*KT*, 44; *R*, 168)

The speech is a kind of cento of material taken from two chapters of *Jeremiah*. Its main sources are: 48:43—44; 49:9—10; 48:9; 48:20. One verse from *Jeremiah* which is not used here might, however, serve as a key to much of what we see in *Killing Time*:

And Moab shall be destroyed from being a people, because he hath magnified himself against the Lord.   (48:42)

That is a characteristic sentiment where Jeremiah is concerned. John Paterson, writing of Jeremiah, uses words which not only throw light on *Killing Time*, but are also recognisable as a source for one of that play's most important phrases:

> As with Hosea there is only one sin here, the sin of infidelity that has spat in the face of God and done despite to his grace . . . The human heart he knew well from his own encounters with the High and Holy One: 'It is desperately corrupt' (17:9) . . . Birds also he notes in their coming and going, and what a pathos lies in these words:
>> 'I looked — and, behold, no man was there, And all the birds of heaven were flown' (4:25).
> A world without birds was as 'the abomination of desolation' to Jeremiah. For these birds were the divine remembrancers.[1]

Elsewhere allusions to, and quotations from, *Jeremiah* abound throughout the play. A few examples will suffice; two verses from Jeremiah:

> For death is come up into our windows, and is entered into our palaces, to cut off the children from without, and the young men from the streets.
> Speak, Thus saith the Lord, Even the carcasses of men shall fall as dung upon the open field, and as the handful after the harvestman, and none shall gather them   (9:21—22)

receive at least four distinct echoes in *Killing Time*:

> Death creeps in our homes, our streets, our kitchens, disfigures the children in their beds.   (*KT*, 1; *R*, 125)

> The harvest's over and ungathered.   (*KT*, 35; *R*, 159)[2]

> It's not dung on that field, it's a pile of dead.   (*KT*, 36; *R*, 160)

> I've seen no children in the streets since we came. The squares are empty.   (*KT*, 37; *R*, 161)

Squaloid's "Every man's a brute underneath" (*KT*, 4; *R*, 128) adapts Jeremiah's "Every man is brutish in his knowledge" (10:14) and

Chalone's "All the proud men" (*KT*, 14; *R*, 148) quotes from Jeremiah
43:2 (a verse which contains Jeremiah's prophecy "Go not into Egypt,
to sojourn there" — advice ignored, to their cost, by the characters in
*Killing Time*). The debt to *Jeremiah* (and perhaps especially to Chapters
48 and 49) extends, though, beyond details of phrasing. The play's
central situation of the besieged city also derives in part from *Jeremiah*,
though influenced by other Biblical presentations of the same motif —
a motif which had a similar importance in the analogous play *Troat*.
When for example, Quark reminisces about her adventures in a male
brothel, the language in which she couches her memories:

> It was like being lodged in a garden of cucumbers     (*KT*, 16; *R*, 140)

is more than a piece of outrageous phallic symbolism. Her words are
taken from a passage in Isaiah which evokes the whole world of *Killing
Time*:

> Your country is desolate, your cities are burned with fire, your
> land, strangers devour it in your presence, and it is desolate, as
> overthrown by strangers.
> And the daughter of Zion is left as a cottage in a vineyard, as a
> lodge in a garden of cucumbers, as a besieged city.   (*Isaiah* 1:7—8)

The fall of a great city is a recurrent motif in the play, culminating in
Squaloid's "We'll repair the waste cities" (*KT*, 70; *R*, 194) at the
play's conclusion. The destruction of so-called civilisation, implicit in
this motif, is ascribed to a number of causes in the play's analysis
of war. On one level it is seen as prompted by narrow notions of
patriotism and nationalism. Kuru and Quark worry about people who
are "Overners" (*KT*, 17; *R*, 141) and "Kabloonas" (*KT*, 27; *R*, 151),
and Quark propounds the dangerous doctrine that

> An outside enemy heals family factions.   (*KT*, 17; *R*, 141)

Elsewhere war is seen as merely an aspect and function of the human
capacity for fear:

> Oh, fear is the womb of war, which a little violence will awake
> $\qquad\qquad\qquad\qquad\qquad\qquad\qquad\qquad$ (*KT*, 70; *R*, 194)

says Squaloid, and he has earlier suggested that

> It's not war you should fear. It's fear     (*KT*, 4; *R*, 128)

echoing, amongst others, Lord Bacon. To Kuru fear is at the heart of both social order and disorder:

> It's so like men. They make a society based on fear; fear of breakdown of law and of outside enemies. Create an army with a rigid hierarchy that cultivates death as a means of enforcement. This leads to war, and so to the collapse of the very society that had created it for its own protection! . . . . The sexual urge forces us to mate, so the next generation will be born. This is straight-jacketed into marriage, society's tolerance of sex in a limited context. But you can't damn up natural forces like that, so what happens? Sex outside becomes disruptive and illegal, divorced from society, this leads to exploitation, and violence, and so the police, then the army come in. . . . That's why I'm guilty.    (*KT*, 51–2; *R*, 175–6)

Once more the link is forged between the sexual malaise of *Lying Figures* and the violent world of *Killing Time*. In both worlds power is most attractive to precisely those who are least fitted to exercise it. Kuru observes that

> Power should go to people who don't particularly want it
>
> (*KT*, 23; *R*, 147)

but here in *Killing Time* power resides in the hands of such as Squaloid and Phagocyte. When Phagocyte produces the red-hot branding iron, to be used in the 'torture' of Chalone, Squaloid comments "Now this really is power" (*KT*, 60; *R*, 184); eventually it is the 'claw' which is used, the claw which is, apparently, inserted in Chalone's anus. The action, recalling the murder of Edward the Second in Marlowe's play, is simultaneously an act with sexual significance and a particularly brutal act of war.

Chalone's earlier lecture has previously implied that human violence is a function of the structure of the brain. Yet his account of the cerebellum might be thought to present a 'balanced' account

> If the cerebellum is split down the middle, the folds form a pattern which resembles a tree. This has been called from time immemorial the tree of life. Unfortunately, it is also the tree of death.
>
> (*KT*, 9; *R*, 133)

We are told that there is

> finally, an overall judge, with checks and balances, serving as sole master of the system . . . Purkinje    (*KT*, 9; *R*, 133)

and that

> Chalone is the stopping agent that prevents the brain growing too
> large for its skull, as bone grows at a different rate . . . The only
> moral direction of the entire unit is towards survival. This it has,
> of course, in common with animals. What distinguishes man from
> animals is not speech, writing and such, for which there are many
> analogues, but his ability to commit suicide. Even lemmings don't do
> this intentionally. They swim madly, hoping to get to the other
> side. (*Pause*) But you can argue that this ability of man also implies
> its opposite, and that — may — save us from the holocaust. On the
> answer to this question hangs the future of the world. Goodnight.
> (*Exit*)                                        (*KT*, 10; *R*, 134)

What, in fact, Chalone asserts is the human freedom to choose. It is
the precise opposite of Phagocyte's insistence that "we are the pawns
of night manoeuvres" (*KT*, 15; *R*, 139), or of the attitude that underlies Squaloid's use of scientific language to avoid facing up to the 'truth'
of the savagery he is about to perform (*KT*, 59; *R*, 183). Chalone
delivers his speech

> *wearing half-cut glasses, full-bottomed wig and codpiece, black gown*
> *open down the front.*   (*KT*, 9; *R*, 133)

He is the play's judge-figure, its figure of authority who appears in a
variety of guises. In the prologue he is executioner, soldier and judge.
Later he is father and priest. His is a voice of stern authoritarianism:

> The judge is condemned when the guilty are acquitted
> (*KT*, 11; *R*, 135)

he says in justification of his strictness,[3] and quotes *Ecclesiastes*, "A
gift destroys the heart" (*Ecclesiastes*, 7:7; *KT*, 11; *R*, 135) as part
of a morality of austere and loveless rigidity. The scene in which he
does so, however, demonstrates vividly his consequent distance as both
father and husband. His words as priest, when hearing Phagocyte's
confession, are wise and important, but he fails to live up to them
himself:

> The peace of this world is no more than the peace in each one of us;
> in you, in me: the love that refuses to hate. It's the withdrawal of
> imagination we must study; in marriage, in torture, or a mercenary.
> (*KT*, 14; *R*, 138)

The complete withdrawal of his own imagination is evident in his treatment of his wife in Act One Scene Three and, above all, in the cruel deception practised upon Phagocyte in Act Two Scene Nine. Though he may tell Squaloid after the deception:

> Pretending is extraordinarily exhausting. It's terribly hard work. Sympathy is innocence  (*KT*, 67; *R*, 191)

it is surely Squaloid's reply which comes closer to telling the truth about Chalone's behaviour:

> No. Sympathy is impotence. Withdrawal of sympathy is essential if one is to get anything done, let alone interrogation.
> (*KT*, 67; *R*, 191)

Chalone, as judge, is marked out as the god-like figure within the hierarchy of the play. As *Killing Time* occupies the middle place in the *Requiem* trilogy, so Chalone marks only a mid-point on a scale whose extremes are the godless world of *Lying Figures* and the loving figure of Ensoff. Squaloid seeks to get from Phagocyte a 'denial' of Chalone which evidently parallels the larger denial of God which is a major theme of the sequence as a whole:

SQUALOID      Now, what about Chalone?
PHAGOCYTE   He's a ruler who can't bear the sight of his own shadow.
SQUALOID      Good. More. Deny your master.
PHAGOCYTE   He became a general by default.  (*KT*, 22; *R*, 146)

Within the play, this must be seen as the equivalent of Squaloid's attempt to extract a denial from Quark:

SQUALOID      (*Good-humouredly, a whim*) Would you deny there's a God?
QUARK          I can't say I've given it much thought. (*Pause*) But I'm sure He's there!
SQUALOID      Will you say there's no such thing as God if we let you go?
QUARK          (*Pause*) I can't.
SQUALOID      Even with pain facing you?
QUARK          My birthday's February 2nd, Candlemas. Snowdrops are emblems of the Feast of Lights.
(*KT*, 55–6; *R*, 179–80)

Squaloid's pressure produces only a ringing affirmation, expressed in language which looks forward to the culmination of the trilogy and which, in doing so, offers a yardstick by which we can measure how far Chalone falls short of Ensoff. When, for example, Phagocyte has made his 'denial', there follows what is presumably designed as a kind of grotesque burlesque of the revelation of the Unknown God, to be presented more 'seriously' in *Meeting Ends*:

> PHAGOCYTE  It's unfair.
>
> SQUALOID  It's an unfair world, Phagocyte. Remember what you've said about your leader? Now look who's here. Isn't that strange?
> (CHALONE *moves coat-stand to one side to reveal his presence.* PHAGOCYTE *falls to the ground at the shock and remains motionless until end of scene*).   (*KT*, 22; *R*, 146)

It is, however, in his 'passion' that Chalone's inadequacies and his moral ambivalence are seen at their clearest. In the final scene of the play, we see Squaloid and Phagocyte apparently torturing Chalone. While he 'suffers' Squaloid tells him

> Just think of yourself as the suffering servant.   (*KT*, 62; *R*, 186)

Chalone prays:

> Keep me as the apple of an eye, under the shadow of thy wing.
> (*KT*, 63; *R*, 187)

His words are taken from *Psalms* (17:8). Squaloid has already made what sounds like a covert allusion to the trinity:

> That which is one is one . . . That which is not one is also one.
> (*KT*, 62; *R*, 186)

It is not merely Phagocyte who is mocked, then, when Chalone leaps up unharmed, the whole episode having been an elaborate charade designed to deceive Phagocyte, and to lead him on to a damning confession. If Chalone *is* a kind of God-figure, then he is certainly a God who sets pits and snares in the way of humanity. Phagocyte chatters blithely about setting traps for foxes, while the snare is set and sprung for him. The love which might "lighten" (*KT*, 69; *R*, 193) human "wraths and sorrows" will not come from Chalone. Within *Killing Time*

Quark appears to be the only vehicle of such a love. There are hints within the play of Christ's passion. In the very first passage of dialogue in the play Phagocyte invites Squaloid:

> Share any bread? Something to drink? . . . Local wine?
>
> (*KT*, 3; *R*, 127)

thus hinting at the possibility of a communion more durable than the uneasy truce they have just established. My quotation, however, is not complete. The full text is crucially different. Phagocyte's invitation is to

> Share any bread? Something to drink? Whisky? Local wine?

to which Squaloid replies "Cheese". We in the audience may perceive the symbolic potential of Phagocyte's collocation of bread and wine, but for the characters on stage these are but two items in a list, items which have no greater sacramental value than the whisky and the cheese. Chalone's name is quite close to the Greek τὸ καλόν; the morally beautiful, the *summum bonum*. It is only, however, a profoundly flawed moral beauty which he can be imagined to represent. His name has another, more pressing, significance, revealed, as we have seen, in his own lecture on the cerebellum.

Chalone is "the stopping agent" (*KT*, 10; *R*, 134) within the human brain. The opening stage direction of the play tells us that *"The stage is a giant human brain"* (*KT*, 1; *R*, 125). The 'family' breakfast of Act One Scene Three takes place over and around *"a table in shape of human brain"* (*KT*, 10; *R*, 134). The stage-direction of Act One Scene Five tells us that

> *centrestage is revealed a large brain out of which is hollowed a confessional box.* (*KT*, 13; *R*, 137)

Act Two Scene Eight is introduced as follows:

> *Lighting should now emphasise the fact that the full stage is and has throughout the play been a human brain in which and in front of which the action takes place.* (*KT*, 54; *R*, 178)

The interrogation, or torture, seat in the final scene is *"an upstage centre part of the brain"* (*KT*, 59; *R*, 183). The whole of *Killing Time*, in fact, makes literal that suspicion we had in our discussion of *Troat* — that all the action was a representation of the Old Man's mental activity. At the same time this later play is a quite literal rendering of the tradition of the psychomachia. The human mind is, indeed, a battlefield in *Killing Time*. This is confirmed by the names of some of the other characters, for Chalone is not alone in bearing a name from biochemistry. Kuru's name is, rather clumsily, explicated within the text:

QUARK        What was your name?

KURU         Kuru.

QUARK        . . . Kuru. That's an unusual name, dear. Isn't it a spreading disease caused by eating live brains? . . . Impaired mental and motor functions, presenile dementia, usually followed by death. *Very* raised eyebrowish. I'm surprised the priest baptised you!   (*KT*, 17; *R*, 141) [4]

Phagocyte takes his name from a leucocyte which, under certain limited conditions, has the power to defend the system against infection by absorbing pathogenic microbes. Clearly the conditions are not met here. Phagocyte has a certain 'innocence' at the beginning of the play. Squaloid finds him "soft" (*KT*, 4; *R*, 128). He is shocked by the "terrible wrong" he did when he

stabbed a woman, thinking it was a man.  (*KT*, 13; *R*, 137)

He is soon, however, attempting a cynical seduction of Quark, which fails when he discovers he has, as it were, made advances to a man, thinking it was a woman. Soon he announces that "vice is the only pleasure" (*KT*, 28; *R*, 152). When he observes that

Technology's given us the power of gods, yet turned us into beasts
(*KT*, 35; *R*, 159)

the suggestion is little more than an abdication of his own moral responsibility for his actions. Though his behaviour in the final scene marks him out as retaining some kind of moral sense, at least as compared with his companion Squaloid, there can be no doubting that the 'infection' has taken, where Phagocyte is concerned. Kuru, on the other hand, though she and Quark appear to be "interchangeable women" (*KT*, 26; *R*, 150) in Act One Scene Six, does not succeed in infecting her young partner with her degenerative disease. Quark retains her innocence, through whoredom, betrayal and a horrible blinding. She can still assert, however naively, the importance and permanence of love as the play moves towards its close:

> I am full of love for my teddy-bear. And my Mummy and Daddy, and my grandparents. God bless everyone!   (*KT*, 69;*R*, 193)

Squaloid dismisses her suffering, and her enduring love, in terms which are coldly clinical:

> That was an error. We all make these inaccuracies at times. If we survive, there's plenty of time to repent.  (*KT*, 69;*R*, 193)

For all his powers of physical endurance, for all that he is "a born survivor" (*KT*, 36;*R*, 160), Squaloid is a much fitter emblem of despair than Quark is, accused of that sin by Kuru. Phagocyte tells him that the situation is "Desperate, but not serious" (*KT*, 3;*R*, 127) and the phrase sums up, unfortunately, all too much in the two men's attitudes to the moral situation in which they find themselves.

"Time and chance happen to all" (*KT*, 19;*R*, 143) observes Kuru, adapting *Ecclesiastes* (9:11). Yet in Quark's selfless love (and to a lesser extent in the love for her which is one aspect of Kuru's relationship with her) there exists a suggestion of a worthwhile response to those eventualities. Quark's lyric and Kuru's responding poem constitute a kind of thematic hinge for the play. Indeed, occurring where they do, at the mid-point of the middle play, it is clear that we should see them as a kind of turning point in the trilogy as a whole. The vision of life and love which Quark's lyric celebrates, embodied in a revelation of that firm "shaft" on which the "universe spins", asserts the existence of something permanent beneath the often bewildering and changeful surface of life:

> The universe spins on a shaft of light
> Whose name is love.   (*KT*, 31;*R*, 155)

In that apprehension there resides a truth which might enable man to escape both the pit and the snare. It is a hope for which no cosy fulfilment is offered in these plays, however. For the dramatis personae "the raw wound of the mind" (*KT*, 1; *R*, 125) and the "pageant of futility" (*KT*, 38;*R*, 162) are more common experiences. In life lived and viewed as such a pageant the names of those who have invested it with greater meaning are too trivial to merit more than the most flippant of punning. The theologians get short shrift:

| | |
|---|---|
| PHAGOCYTE | Bath, Karl? |
| SQUALOID | I don't bath till I itch, Paul. |

. . . .

| | |
|---|---|
| PHAGOCYTE | Très bonne affaire! Peace! |
| SQUALOID | Nice piece.  (*KT*, 25; *R*, 149) |

The life (and death) of Bonhoeffer, grimly relevant to this of all plays, is a matter of jesting for these two soldiers. Naturally the word "peace" is appropriately debased in their usage. Composers and writers have even less significance for them:

| | |
|---|---|
| PHAGOCYTE | Are you welshing on me? |
| SQUALOID | (*Affably*) Pure music, bach. I hide an idea you handled that Mozartfully. |
| PHAGOCYTE | Do you see evil in war? |
| SQUALOID | Only vile bodies.  (*KT*, 40; *R*, 164) |

The title of Waugh's novel serves further to condemn Squaloid; he can see no evil in war.

Chalone, the moral inhibitor, can do nothing to encourage moral insight. Legislation offers only

Just riddles for life. Law's contradictions.  (*KT*, 63; *R*, 187)

While his is the voice of authority then it will remain the case that

Peace is the breathing space between two wars; when we lick our wounds, mourn our dead, and prepare our defences.

(*KT*, 68; *R*, 192)

The violence of *Killing Time* can only be transcended by understandings capable of seeing that "defeats ... should count as victories" (*ME*, 44; *R*, 240). A possible path to such an understanding is traced in *Meeting Ends*.

## Notes

1  J. Paterson, in *Peake's Commentary on the Bible*, ed. M. Black, 1962, pp. 539–40. Warner's reading in this commentary is evident elsewhere in *Killing Time*. Another speech of Chalone's is clearly derived (how consciously is not clear) from the same source. In Act One Scene Five Chalone tells Phagocyte that

> Even in the choicest spirits the gold must be passed through
> fire to purge it of dross, and man's spirit must be stabbed
> broad awake. (*KT*, 13; *R*, 137)

His words are clearly derived from Paterson:

> Even in the choicest spirits the gold must be passed through the
> fire to smelt away the dross and man's spirit must be 'stabbed
> broad awake.' (*Peake*, *op. cit.*, p. 539)

Incidentally, Paterson's inverted commas around his last phrase here acknowledge that phrase as a quotation (unattributed) from Robert Louis Stevenson's poem 'The Celestial Surgeon'.

2   cf. also *Jeremiah*, 8:20.

3   He quotes Publilius Syrus; *cf. Sententiae*, No. 296.

4   Abundant information on the disease can be found in the fascinating volume *Kuru. Early Letters and Field-Notes from the Collection of D. Carleton Gajdusek*, edited by Judith Farquhar and D. Carleton Gajdusek, New York, 1981. Warner's own source of information may have been J. J. Holland's article "Slow, Inapparent and Recurrent Viruses" in *Scientific American*, Feb. 1974, pp. 33–40, since its date of publication falls precisely in the period when Warner was most probably engaged on the composition of *Killing Time*. Similarly, R. R. Llinas' article "The Cortex of the Cerebellum" in *Scientific American*, Jan. 1975, pp. 56–71, may well have been a source for the details of cerebellar anatomy used in the play.

# VIII

## *Meeting Ends:* Lux umbra dei

*Meeting Ends* begins with Agappy's Last Post (as, mirror-like, it will close with her Reveille), and then we see Ensoff, that 'chancellor of the mind' (*ME*, 27; *R*, 223), as he brings the world of the play into being:

> A sunshaft strikes the steeple by my room,
> Flares the high cock that crowns created day . . .

It seems reasonable to take this as the first of the play's many allusions to that tradition of Hermeticism which, as we have seen in our consideration of his earlier plays, has exerted a powerful influence on Warner's work as a dramatist. The influence is one he shares with some of the figures in whom he has shown himself most interested — Pico della Mirandola, Ficino, Cornelius Agrippa, Samuel Palmer and Yeats, for example. The particular image in these lines may be familiar to us from Vaughan's 'Cock-Crowing'. In Hermetic symbolism the cock is an emblem of vigilance — vigilance understood in a special sense as a

> tendency towards eternity and taking care to grant first place to the things of the spirit, to be wakeful and to greet the Sun — Christ — even before it rises in the East.[1]

A passage from Ficino's *Commentary on the Symposium* is helpful here. Ficino compares God and the sun. He explains that

> [Plato] says that the light of the mind for understanding everything is the same God Himself by whom everything was created

152

and he makes a comparison between God and the sun insofar as God
stands in the same relation to minds as the sun does to eyes:

> The sun generates eyes and it bestows upon them the power to see
> . . . In the same way, God creates the soul and to it gives mind, the
> power of understanding. The mind would be empty and dark if it
> did not have the light of God, in which to see the principles of
> everything . . . . Thus, we understand everything through the light
> of God, but the pure light itself and its source, we cannot see in
> this life.[2]

The very name of the speaker of Warner's lines reassures us that it
is not fanciful to read these lines in terms of this Hermetic and
neo-Platonic tradition. The name Ensoff is clearly a version of the
Cabbalistic 'Ensoph' — 'the one without end' — whose relevance to
the play's argument we must later consider. Warner's early poem
*Perennia* bears as its epigraph sentences from Edgar Wind's remarkable
book *Pagan Mysteries in the Renaissance*:

> Only by looking towards the Beyond as the true goal of ecstasy
> can man become balanced in the present. Balance depends on
> ecstasy.

Professor Wind's work has continued to influence Warner. Ensoph,
indeed, is the subject of another chapter in this same volume, a chapter
entitled 'The Concealed God'. Does Ensoff, then, represent the *deus
absconditus*, that

> pure light itself and its source, [which] we cannot see in this life

of Renaissance neo-Platonism? The terms in which Warner's stage
directions introduce him might indicate some support for this suggestion:

> *Light on* ENSOFF, *who is dressed throughout the play in the robe
> of the Chancellor of Oxford University. He stands high up on a
> raised platform, downstage left, that is quite separate from the
> main, circular acting area. Stage itself dark.*   (ME, 1; R, 197)

The emphasis on the separateness of Ensoff's platform is suggestive,
as is his position looking down upon a circular stage upon which poor
players are to strut and fret. But equally suggestive, in a different
way, are his robes. The designated robes suggest, initially, that we

have here a character who embodies learning. However, in the light of what we have considered already, we probably need to be more specific than this, and think of Ensoff as a figure representative rather of the Renaissance idea of wisdom — a notion intimately bound up with that of the Contemplative Life (as well as with the Hermetic tradition). Let us take some evidence from the text. Callisterne tells us that

> he has a kind of chaotic majesty    (*ME*, 4; *R*, 200)

and the cosmological pun suggests the Cabbala's creator figure. In Act One Scene Seven Ensoff is in dialogue with Agappy:

| | |
|---|---|
| AGAPPY | I suppose when you are executed your head will dance up and down on the ground like a moonbeam. |
| ENSOFF | Lose my head? |
| AGAPPY | Those robes give you away. You're out of the ordinary. *You* can't last long! |
| ENSOFF | A Chancellor of the mind? |
| AGAPPY | That won't save you. |
| ENSOFF | The towns I have called into being and peopled with my imagination.  (*ME*, 27; *R*, 223) |

After the revelation of the sundial which closes Act Two Scene Four, Ensoff tells Wrasse and Callisterne

> It's an unknown God who's come. If you love him, stay with him.
> (*ME*, 46; *R*, 242)

By the end of the play Ensoff has left his raised platform (to be replaced by Agappy) and utters the unmistakably human sentiments:

> The silent stars play havoc with our toys
> But we have kingdoms that they cannot touch.  (*ME*, 47; *R*, 243)

Ensoff, then, is at one point in the play a "Chancellor of the mind" who talks of the creative force of his imagination. Taken against the background of Renaissance neo-Platonism all this suggests that, from one angle at least, Ensoff is best viewed as a kind of Renaissance magus. He belongs, that is to say, in the tradition of *magia* developed out of the alleged writings of Hermes Trismegistus by such figures as Pico and Ficino and given its most complete expression by Cornelius Agrippa

in his *De occulta philosophia* — of which work Warner has an edition
in preparation. We may take the hint to see Ensoff as magus from some
other lines in his prologue which glance at the magi:

> But higher than the not yet risen lark
> Three wise men from the west reach for the moon.
>
> (*ME*, 2; *R*, 198)

As magus he will necessarily be a man apart:

> The wise man, who has knowledge of the secrets of nature, is secret
> and spiritual. He lives alone, far from the common mob. Placed high
> above other men, he is unique, free, absolute, tranquil, pacific,
> immobile, simple, collected, one. He needs no one.[3]

That, at any rate, is the theory. Ensoff assumes initially that the contemplative life is a sufficient end in itself, that it is enough for his lamp
to be seen at midnight hour in some high lonely tower. The working
out of the play suggests, however, that this is an end which will not
meet his needs.

Ensoff as magus is both God-figure (the magus, as theurgist, controls
both self and nature) and, by an analogy common and natural to neo-
Platonism, a poet. It is a central tenet of Renaissance neo-Platonism
that where God creates in the world by means of His thought, the poet
conceives within himself the intellectual species (forms which are the
definition of a plurality of objects of the same class) and expresses
them by making a copy in earthly materials — the work of art. *Meeting
Ends* may be about Ensoff's "chaotic majesty", but it is also about the
imagination's attempt to turn chaos into coherent symbolic language.
It presents to us an imagination which can only know itself by suffering
at the hands of that which it has created.

The first of Ensoff's creations, within the play at any rate, is that
revealed to us by the dawning light which opens scene one:

> *three women, each with her head and hands in a pillory.* AGAPPY
> *downstage right* . . . . WRASSE *upstage* . . . . CALLISTERNE . . .
> *downstage left.*   (*ME*, 2; *R*, 198)

To them there enters Shango, nude save for his bull's head. After paus-
ing at the edge of the circular acting area he walks over to Callisterne.
He kisses her chastely in the middle of the forehead. He walks to
Wrasse:

*with one movement rips off her bathing costume and throws it*
*offstage leaving her naked . . . . Walks downstage to* AGAPPY.
*Pause . Slowly kneels on one knee before her, takes off the bull's*
*head mask and lays it at her feet, bowing his own head in homage.*

(*ME*, 3; *R*, 199)

What we see is an act of choice made by this mysterious nude man. As
yet we know nothing of him, though the bull's head may offer some
suggestions. Purely as a stage spectacle the scene is resonant but enig-
matic. It is only in the light of what we shall see and hear later that we
shall be able to offer some kind of elucidation. The characters' names
offer a convenient point of departure.

Agappy is clearly a version of 'agape'. In pre-Biblical Greek *eros* denotes ecstatic passion while the verb *agapan* denotes a cooler emotion,
a love based on rational preference. This is also the sense of the noun
*agapesis*. The form *agape* is, I believe, unknown before the Septuagint.
As used there it denotes a love whose definition would have to find
room for the doctrine of fidelity. *Agape* as used in the Gospels, and
above all in the Pauline and Johannine Epistles, refers to beneficent
love, love which is unselfish and seeks only the good of others. It is
theocentric, since it is a reproduction of God's own 'outgoing' love.
It is frequently translated by the Fathers as *caritas*. *Eros*, on the other
hand, is egocentric, love directed to the pursuit of some object to be
acquired for the self, love which seeks to possess or control. If we are
right to see Agappy as Warner's version of *agape*, then we should
expect these distinctions to operate in discriminating between this
character and the other two women who share the stage with her.
This the text confirms. Agappy tells Wrasse:

(*Gently*) If you accept something as good, then you choose it
(*ME*, 13; *R*, 209)

and at the close of the three-part polyphony which constitutes Act
One Scene Two she has the final words:

We are the unknown ones whom all men know. When we please
we are fulfilled. In our birth, sorrow is our deepest joy. We are
beaten but not killed. Poor, we bring wealth to others; inheritors
of nothing but the world. (*ME*, 13; *R*, 209)

Both her sentiments and her phrasing set up distinctly Pauline echoes.
Elsewhere her compassion is much in evidence. She addresses Callisterne:

Let me wipe away all tears from your eyes    (*ME*, 6; *R*, 202)

in language which echoes both Old and New Testaments — in *Isaiah*
25, the promise is that the Lord

> will swallow up death in victory; and the Lord God will wipe away
> tears from off all faces; and the rebuke of his people shall he take
> away from off all the earth: for the Lord hath spoken it.[4]

In *Revelation* 7, those who have suffered "great tribulation" are described before the throne of God, and we are told that

> They shall hunger no more, neither thirst any more; neither
> shall the sun light on them, nor any heat.
> For the Lamb which is in the midst of the throne shall feed
> them, and shall lead them unto living fountains of waters: and God
> shall wipe away all tears from their eyes.[5]

The contrast with Wrasse is vividly clear. Wrasse can evoke the tears of
Christ only as a way of complaining about her period:

> *Damn* the menstrual clock! You're sorry when it comes and you're
> sorry when it doesn't. Oh Jesus wept!    (*ME*, 42; *R*, 238)

It may be worth noticing too that she, perhaps unconsciously, cites
a Biblical text: the laconic verse 35 of Chapter Eleven of St. John's
Gospel. Where Agappy's sentiments are entirely in harmony with her
Biblical originals, the verse from St. John has only a harshly ironic
relevance to Wrasse and her situation. Agappy makes a similar use of
Biblical allusion elsewhere. She tells us that her mother "bound up the
broken-hearted" (*ME*, 29; *R*, 225) and here again she adopts a Biblical
phrase which tells us much about her own role in the play:

> The Spirit of the Lord God is upon me; because the Lord hath
> anointed me to preach good tidings unto the meek; he hath sent me
> to bind up the brokenhearted, to proclaim liberty to the captives,
> and the opening of the prison to them that are bound.[6]

We know that Agappy is unmarried and childless and we may remember
that in the early days of the Church the Agapetae were Virgins dedicated
to God. Agappy has given some thought to purifying and punishing
the sinful:

> I cupped my hands full of coals from the fire and put them in my handbag to scatter over the city.　(*ME*, 7; *R*, 203)

The scheme has obvious Biblical precedents, as well as being an echo of the Old Man's activities in *Troat*; but Ensoff is surely right when he tells her that she "lacks the grimmer virtues" (*ME*, 27; *R*, 223). Her injunction is to

> prove your power by throwing it away　(*ME*, 28; *R*, 224)

a piece of advice which is offered after a long scene in which we have seen Wrasse endeavouring to prove *her* power by exercising it over Shango. Agappy's long soliloquy which constitutes Act One Scene Ten makes her role even clearer:

> I made a man's love the centre of my life. My own selfish passion of universal importance! When it failed, chaos came. Ah well! Love comes and goes, but friendship stays . . . He said 'Nice to take you to the theatre this evening. I didn't think I'd shave as I had onions for lunch' . . . 'Be charitable,' he said. Well, I thought, chastity stirs the passion it's supposed to restrain! But an act of faith is an act of love.　(*ME*, 32–3; *R*, 228–9)

It is not, then, surprising to find Agappy telling us

> I was never a good hater.　(*ME*, 44; *R*, 240)

She displays a happy certainty about some characteristically Christian paradoxes. She prays

> In all my guilt remember my innocency　(*ME*, 44; *R*, 240)

and her

> My defeats I should count as victories?　(*ME*, 44; *R*, 240)

is surely as much assertion as it is question. She can recognise, as the play moves towards its conclusion, "The infinite serene of no defeat!" (*ME* 45; *R*, 241). Her vision is at its clearest when she tells Ensoff

> I long ago became aware that a life lived solely for human rewards was shallow.　(*ME*, 45; *R*, 241)

Standing in most direct opposition to Agappy, morally and thematically, is Wrasse. Again the name helps us. The Wrasse is a cleaner-fish, that is, it eats parasites from the skin and inside the gills and mouths of other fish. Wrasses are territorial creatures, living in well-defined groups of eight to ten individuals. Within each group there is only one male, the rest of the group consisting of a harem of mature females, and a number of immature females. The male is the dominant force of the group, and there is a hierarchy of dominance among the females. What is remarkable, though, is what happens in the event of the dominant male's death. Within an hour or two the leader of the female hierarchy begins to take over the male role, and simultaneously she begins to change sex. In behavioural terms she does this quite quickly. A physiological change follows. The female wrasse is, in fact, a kind of hermaphrodite. In their female state they have small quantities of testicular material in their ovaries. Once the behavioural change has triggered the physiological change the gonad is taken over by the testicular material, and the egg-producing elements degenerate. Within a matter of weeks the new male is producing sperm. One particularly interesting feature of Wrasse society follows from all this. The male usually directs the greater part of his aggression towards the female(s) he imagines to be most likely to change sex in this way. It is scarcely surprising that Warner should find in this fish an apposite point of reference for that theme of the conflict of sexual roles which runs all the way through the *Requiem* trilogy. The theme is perhaps seen at its clearest in *Lying Figures*, where Gonad actually appears as a character. Within *Meeting Ends* it is in the relationship of Wrasse and Shango that we see this theme treated most fully. Wrasse's opening word of the play is a simple "Men" (*ME*, 3; *R*, 199) and her preoccupation with the power game of gender is rapidly made clear:

Let alone, men are literally inconceivable.   (*ME*, 3; *R*, 199)

It is she who talks of the "post-marital bloodbath" (*ME*, 4; *R*, 200) and she who sees marriage purely in terms of dominance and submission:

Maternity. Forced labour and endless penal servitude.
(*ME*, 5; *R*, 201)

Still, she is far from simply submitting to the "penal servitude" (the pun is a favourite Joycean one). She has other ideas:

Any woman can get control over a man, simply by flattering his ego and placing a hand on his genitals.   (*ME*, 5; *R*, 201)

Dominance, it seems, comes naturally to her: "I was a bully at school" (*ME*, 7; *R*, 203). As the dominant female in a school of cleaner-fish Wrasse's remark has the ring of truth about it. As that dominant female she can be expected, as we have seen, to be eager to take the final step to the top of the hierarchy. The idea is already present in her mind:

> I love the idea of a ruthless brute of a husband eating and drinking all those things that will ultimately put his wife in his place.
>
> (*ME*, 7; *R*, 203)

Even so, she is aware that the battle can only be won at the cost of losing those pleasures which are produced by the tensions of the conflict itself:

> I don't want to lose my new man, neither do I want to whine after him. Anyway, if I could control him I'd lose interest . . . . I've got to have him   (*ME*, 10–11; *R*, 206–7)

When we first see this particular battle of wills and wits, in Act One Scene Three, it is Shango who appears to have the upper hand. His fatuous flattery delights the shallow Wrasse. He sees the long-range telephonic courtship of Wrasse and the completion of the *Times* crossword as analogous problems. He succeeds in both:

> A kiss (*Fills in clue on crossword. To audience*) Won across.
>
> (*ME*, 18; *R*, 214)

But we are aware that for all his apparent dominance, he speaks from a seat within a mousetrap. When the next scene opens the trap has been sprung, the mouse has been caught and given his mouse's wheel on which to play, a wheel which imprisons and tortures him in a grotesque parody of Vitruvian man. Wrasse has achieved the transfer of power, and has, in the terms of the cleaner-fish, completed her sex-change. She enters dressed as a ring*master*, in top hat, morning dress coat and tights. She carries the doubly appropriate whip. When she asks Shango

> (*Indicating* CALLISTERNE) Do you want another crack?
>
> (*ME*, 20; *R*, 216)

the crack of the whip and the crack of the vagina are fused in a peculiarly savage fashion. Well might she add

What is a crack regiment but one that's been brutalized out of its first compassion!   (*ME*, 20; *R*, 216)

Shango's response of "Amazon!" (*ME*, 20; *R*, 216) somewhat understates the case. Wrasse is wholeheartedly committed to sensuality. She believes it to be her means to power:

I can always twist the boss round my finger by letting him have a little feel.  (*ME*, 19; *R*, 215)

However, the first two scenes of Act Two suggest how inadequate this is as a basis for power. She is characterised throughout as a woman of gaudy banality. When she asserts confidently:

I eat, and wipe my mouth, and say I've done no wickedness
(*ME*, 24; *R*, 220)

we need to remember the original Biblical context of her words, if we are to appreciate how fully she reveals herself. She has, significantly, omitted the first part of the verse she quotes from *Proverbs*:

Such is the way of an adulterous woman; she eateth, and wipeth her mouth, and saith, I have done no wickedness.[7]

An earlier exchange with Shango similarly works by significant omission. Again the original is from *Proverbs*:

WRASSE       I am a fair woman. (*Strokes her hair*)
SHANGO       As a jewel in a swine's snout.   (*ME*, 19; *R*, 215)

It ought not to escape our notice that Shango's quotation remains incomplete:

As a jewel of gold in a swine's snout, so is a fair woman which is without discretion.[8]

The full extent of Wrasse's sensuality is perhaps expressed most vividly in an altercation with Shango in Act Two Scene Two, where the bestial imagery is taken up in a rather different allusion:

WRASSE       You're inhuman.
SHANGO       Flattery! Sounds as corny as hell to anyone else, yet we always believe it about ourselves.

| WRASSE | Pacify. Overshake me. |
|---|---|
| . . . . | |
| SHANGO | . . . Anyway, when you've seen one woman penetrated you've seen them all. |
| WRASSE | Flyfisher. If I were disguised as a cow, I'd attain my end.   (*ME*, 40; *R*, 236) |

Wrasse's "If I were disguised as a cow" confirms what one had already suspected: that her "Pacify" was a punning allusion to the legend of Pasiphae. As such, of course, it gives a particular point to Shango's bull's head, which reappears several times after the opening tableau. The Pasiphae who entered Daedalus' hollow wooden cow, so that she might be mounted by the white bull of Poseidon serves as a forceful comment on Wrasse. Her speech does nothing to raise our opinion of her. Her dialogues with Shango (notably in Act One Scene Four) and her soliloquy in Act Two Scene One are couched in an idiolect of relentless triteness. She is well summed up by her dress of shocking pink and her addiction to bubble-gum. In the interwoven conversations of Act One Scene One she remarks:

> The trouble with the senses is not that they give pleasure but that it doesn't last.   (*ME*, 4; *R*, 200)

The remark takes us back, curiously enough, to neo-Platonism. It takes us back, indeed, to Ficino, via Professor Wind. Wind's fourth chapter reminds us that

> As Ficino was never tired of repeating, the trouble about the pleasures of the senses is not that they are pleasures but that they do not last.[9]

Clearly Ficino is not alone in finding the aphorism worthy of repetition. Ficino's most extended consideration of the aphorism's implications is to be found in his *De voluptate* and *Apologus de voluptate*. This latter work contains a fable narrating how True Pleasure, which originally dwelt on earth, has been translated to Heaven, and her place on earth has been taken by a deceptive imitation, False Pleasure. But properly understood, False Pleasure can be seen as a reflection of True Pleasure. The distinction corresponds roughly to that between Aphrodite Uranos and Aphrodite Pandemos. Wrasse is Warner's false, or earthly, *voluptas*.

We have in Agappy (Love) and Wrasse (Pleasure), two members of the Three Graces, so important a motif in Florentine neo-Platonism. The third member we should expect to be *pulchritudo*. The pattern is thus completed logically when the third figure in Ensoff's tableau is discovered to be Callisterne, or, in Greek, the 'beautiful-breasted one'. We can now see that the three women with whom the action of the play begins are a Warnerian version of the Three Graces. Callisterne is the central figure of the three, not in terms of stage position, but in respect of her role as intermediary between the chastity of Agappy and the sensuality of Wrasse. While Wrasse is naked when the dumb-show ends, and Agappy wears her "old-fashioned bloomer-style bathing costume" (*ME*, 2; *R*, 198), Callisterne wears the 'compromise' of the bikini. In character too she has elements of both the others. She is not without some of Agappy's spirituality — particularly towards the end of the play. She is the youngest of the three women and her character is not fully formed at the beginning of the play:

> I was sleeping with boyfriends at week-ends and working for 'A' levels during the week with the nuns at school and what with my mother and the pressure of two lives at once it was just too much, so I chucked it and ran away to Morocco for eight weeks with Fraise.
> (*ME*, 9; *R*, 205)

Her boyfriend's name, presumably, bears the weight of one of OED's definitions of the word "sb. 3. A tool used for enlarging a circular hole". From a career as a stripper, she moves to the role of ministrant in Ensoff's final ritual. Indeed, the characters and roles of all three women are best understood through consideration of their relations with, on the one hand, Ensoff, and on the other, Shango.

Agappy's relationship with Ensoff appears to be the most complete, at any rate when the play begins. It is to her that the others turn for information about him:

> CALLISTERNE    (*Brightly*) I always think when I see Ensoff 'He's so sweet he must do unspeakable things in bed'.
> WRASSE    (*To* AGAPPY) Does he?    (*ME*, 4; *R*, 200)

Agappy knows, like any good neo-Platonist or follower of Dionysius the Areopagite (or, indeed like any reader of Ensoff's 'own' book, the Cabbala), that the lesson is

> To be initiated, close your eyes.    (*ME*, 7; *R*, 203)

Her long soliloquy in Act One Scene Ten makes it clear that she has moved from *eros* to *agape*. She stands, that is to say, at the end of a journey which Callisterne must undertake during the course of the play.

The same possibility exists for Wrasse, but she shows only fleeting signs of ever making the journey. Ficinian argument insists that since sensual pleasures are transitory (but decidedly pleasurable), they should be viewed as images of less mutable delights. The sexual language used between Ensoff and Agappy recognizes this, as, indeed, does one of the central traditions of Christian mysticism. For Wrasse, however, sexual ecstasy is never an image of transcendence. It is rather, as we have seen, a means to mundane power of a very delusive kind, or, in an allusion to *The Shipman's Tale*, it becomes a currency, a means of social exchange:

> I had an overdraft of sixty-eight pounds on the housekeeping . . . .
> He said he'd pay it if I wrote out in my own hand a list of things
> I would do to him and let him do to me, and their various prices,
> so I could write off the debt. He pinned it above the bed and made
> me pay every penny.   (*ME*, 38–9; *R*, 234–5)

With Ensoff and Agappy we are in the world of, say, Richard of St. Victor's Spiritual Marriage. With Shango and Wrasse we are in the world of the *fabliau*. The possibility of exchanging one world for the other is offered to Wrasse during the course of the play. In Act Two Scene Three she is beginning to learn the limitations of sexual power. Unlike her fishy namesake the change of sex and sex-role cannot be complete. "Damn the menstrual clock" (*ME*, 42; *R*, 238) she is forced to exclaim. Her frustrations and depression are vented in jealous suspicions of Callisterne:

| CALLISTERNE | You are distraught. |
|---|---|
| WRASSE | Have you no feelings? |
| CALLISTERNE | For what? |
| WRASSE | For me. You've enough for my man. |

(ME, 43; R, 239)

Callisterne suggests

> Let's go and be with Ensoff. He's wise, and understanding.

(ME, 43; R, 239)

She is invited, in those words we saw used as the epigraph to *Perennia*, to look "towards the Beyond as the true goal of ecstasy". In Act Two Scene Five we find that Wrasse and Callisterne have, indeed, come to see Ensoff. Wrasse's sensual banality is at least partly hidden. She enters with a

*cloak of muted colour over her bright dress.*    (*ME*, 45; *R*, 241)

They enter immediately after Ensoff has, in his gesture of revelation, uncovered the sundial. Wrasse has reached the moment of choice, but is unable or unwilling to choose:

WRASSE        What shall I do, Ensoff?
ENSOFF        It's an unknown God who's come. If you love him,
              stay with him. (*Pause*) If you both wish.
WRASSE        I wish for both.    (*ME*, 46; *R*, 242)

It takes the violent intervention of Shango to force her choice:

SHANGO *leaps on* ENSOFF *and castrates him. Holds up trophy.*
*Leaps up and tries to drag the two women offstage with him.*
CALLISTERNE *tugs free, and is left weeping over the slumped*
*body. Exit right* SHANGO *and* WRASSE.    (*ME*, 46; *R*, 242)

Shango and Wrasse go off together into the darkness. Callisterne visibly and vigorously makes a choice at this point too, but, in a sense, her real choice was made much earlier. As early as Act One Scene Two she asserts:

It was Ensoff who changed my mind.    (*ME*, 4; *R*, 200)

In her weakness, isolation, and beauty, as we see it in Act One Scene Eight, she is vulnerable and seems momentarily to be in danger of choosing Shango, as represented by the bull's head. However, the very vulnerability and beauty which she possesses revive in Ensoff a new concern for her, as his beautiful lyric in Act One Scene Nine makes clear. Soon she can say (in her next appearance) that Ensoff is, indeed, "wise and understanding" (*ME*, 43; *R*, 239) and make the complementary assertion: "Shango's not had my bird's nest" (*ME*, 43; *R*, 239). Even before Shango's violence Callisterne has made her position clear, and Ensoff has accepted her:

CALLISTERNE  And me? I hardly dare speak to you, as I think
             of you as a father.
ENSOFF       I will not importune, nor yet desert you. I am
             your close friend and will never hurt you.
                                        (*ME*, 46; *R*, 242)

Callisterne has proved her fitness to minister to the castrated Ensoff, just as Agappy has demonstrated her fitness to blow the closing Reveille.

Of the dramatis personae only Shango remains undiscussed. How does he fit into these symbolic and thematic patterns? His name is that of a Yoruba God. He is the God of thunder and lightning, of hunting and pillage. His role as a thunder god explains the epithet "Shango Boanerges" (*ME*, 23; *R*, 219) applied to him by Wrasse in Act One Scene Five. He is said, in Yoruba mythology, to have had the power of invoking fire from the heavens, but with Promethean results. The fire destroyed every other member of his family and in agonies of self-reproach he hanged himself — a fitting end for the Judas of *Meeting Ends*. Other Promethean allusions are common in the *Requiem* plays and, notably, in *Lumen*, the corresponding play in *Maquettes*. We need not look far for the reason. Renaissance humanism makes much use of Prometheus as a symbol of all-embracing wisdom, and of the adventurous effort to possess it. For many humanists Prometheus is an entirely admirable figure. Budé, for example, writes:

> I believe that Prometheus is the philosophic intellect which, once it has mastered natural science, astronomy, and the other branches of philosophy, is able to rise with assurance to a knowledge of divine things.[10]

But for Agrippa in the *De vanitate* Prometheus seems better understood as a symbol of human presumption, of the failure of humanism. It is in such a context that Agrippa makes use of a pseudo-Pauline saying of much relevance to Warner's plays:

> The Ignorante arise, and take the Kingedome of Heaven: and we with our learning, fall headlonge into Hell.[11]

Shango's Promethean tortures produce the soliloquy which occupies the whole of Act One Scene Six. The torture brings him to his nearest approach to some kind of spiritual apprehension, but the approach is only tentative and flawed:

> Try prayer, they say it works. Jesus Christ save me, help me to bear it, see me through, you must have felt something like this on your cross, what did you do? Oh yes, say over the Psalms. I can't remember them.   (*ME*, 24; *R*, 220)

He has some fragmented notions both of Christian teachings in general and the Last Judgement in particular:

> I'm too superstitious. Mars Hill. The good shepherd bites off the balls of his lambs to make them good meat later. If they grow they're useless. Old smelly billy-goats. Sheep. Last judgement — aaah! Christ! Crushed soul weeping in penitence and terror! Bullied. No! I'm sorry, I didn't mean it, wasn't thinking.  (*ME*, 25; *R*, 221)

Here the allusions both to Mars Hill and to castration look forward to crucial events in the play's conclusion, but their significance finally escapes Shango: "Oh God why don't you exist?"  (*ME*, 25; *R*, 221) His anguished

> I'm treading this winepress alone    (*ME*, 26; *R*, 222)

takes on ironic force from the original context of the words in *Isaiah* 63:

> I have trodden the winepress alone; and of the people there was none with me: for I will tread them in mine anger, and trample them in my fury; and their blood shall be sprinkled upon my garments, and I will stain all my raiment.
> For the day of vengeance is in mine heart, and the year of my redeemed is come.[12]

The recognition that

> Man is but a thing of nought    (*ME*, 26; *R*, 222)

is simultaneously an Old Testament recognition of human mutability and an assertion of the human obsession with sexual pleasure, the word nought being a Shakesperean punning title for the female genitals.[13] Still, the pain does ease at this point, the torture ceases and Shango sees a kind of new day dawning:

> At least pain asserts the power of human pity, if only for oneself. First light of day — God I'm trembling — birds sleepily begin their duty. Streak of sun through the wineglass of water by my bed. The snare is broken and we are escaped.  (*ME*, 26; *R*, 222)

Even here he does not escape from his dominant egotism. There is no suggestion that he might learn to exercise his pity on more than just himself. Still, he can now quote the *Psalms*:

Blessed be the Lord, who hath not given us as a prey to their teeth.

Our soul is escaped as a bird out of the snare of the fowlers: the snare is broken, and we are escaped.

Our help is the name of the Lord, who made heaven and earth.[14]

The ambiguities of his position are not resolved by the punning ambivalence of the conclusion he draws:

If there is a God he lies in the teeth of pain.   (*ME*, 26; *R*, 222)

Well might Shango tell us, as he does in an earlier speech,

I am a man wracked by doubts but capable of glimpses of perfection.
(*ME*, 13; *R*, 209)

Such, then, are the characters who act out the play's spectacular conclusion. The final movement of the play can perhaps be said to begin with Act Two Scene Three. It is there that Callisterne responds to the jealousy of Wrasse by suggesting that they visit Ensoff:

CALLISTERNE  Gently, gently; you're wrong. Let's go and be with Ensoff. He's wise, and understanding.
WRASSE  An acropolis of an intellect. Broken, majestic, high.
CALLISTERNE  Shango's not had my bird's nest. You're overwrought.
WRASSE  Because of the present rain, and because of the cold.   (*ME*, 43; *R*, 239)

That Wrasse should talk of Ensoff in classical (and specifically Athenian) terms, rather than in Christian ones we shall learn to be significant; similarly her final words here are a beautifully timed and cadenced preparation for the vital act of revelation which will follow shortly. Her words are taken directly from *Acts* 28, where they follow the narrative of Paul's shipwreck:

And when they were escaped, then they knew that the island was called Melita.

And the barbarous people shewed us no little kindness: for they kindled a fire, and received us every one, because of the present rain, and because of the cold.

And when Paul had gathered a bundle of sticks, and laid them on
the fire, there came a viper out of the heat, and fastened on his
hand.

And when the barbarians saw the venomous beast hang on his
hand, they said among themselves, No doubt this man is a murderer,
whom, though he hath escaped the sea, yet vengeance suffereth not
to live.

And he shook off the beast into the fire, and felt no harm.

Howbeit they looked when he should have swollen, or fallen
down dead suddenly: but after they had looked a great while, and
saw no harm come to him, they changed their minds, and said that
he was a god.[15]

The encounter of Paul with the venomous serpent is analogous to
Shango's attack upon Ensoff. Like Paul, Ensoff emerges strengthened
by the encounter. Before then, however, we see the last meeting of
Ensoff and Agappy in Act Two Scene Four. Ensoff's opening words
point us forward to the candle-lit conclusion of the play, and take up
more forcefully the allusion to *Isaiah* first made in Shango's soliloquy:

I will search out Edinburgh (*Or wherever play is being performed*)
with candles, and trample my fury through their houses. Not one
window in this city will remain, not one street swept clean of
ruins. No thrush tugging its worm, no snake about to swallow its
fledgling, no cat playing for hours with a minute, shivering, short-
sighted mouse, no widow speechless on her mutilated husband will
know the full terror to come. They will lie down in the evening and
tear their own cheeks from their faces.   (*ME*, 44; *R*, 240)

It also takes up the theme of the purification of the corrupted city
which has run right through the *Maquettes* and the *Requiem* plays,
and which has been particularly prominent in this last play of the
series. We noted earlier Agappy's plan to scatter burning coals over
the city (*ME*, 7; *R*, 203). The language used there appears to echo
*Ezekiel*, 10:2. A little later Wrasse and Callisterne evoke a different
Biblical image of the corrupt city:

| | |
|---|---|
| WRASSE | Even judges are evening wolves. |
| CALLISTERNE | Why? |
| WRASSE | They don't chew your bones until the following morning.   (*ME*, 12; *R*, 208) |

Their dialogue adapts a passage from *Zephaniah*:

> Woe to her that is filthy and polluted, to the oppressing city.
> She obeyed not the voice; she received not correction; she trusted not in the Lord; she drew not near to her God.
> Her princes within her are roaring lions; her judges are evening wolves; they gnaw not the bones till the morrow.[16]

Ensoff had earlier spoken of

> the towns I have called into being and peopled with my imagination    (*ME*, 27; *R*, 223)

and there is, indeed, something peculiarly urban about the whole texture of *Meeting Ends*.[17] Callisterne narrates her adventures at Selfridges, at El Paso, Miranda's and the Belle de Nuite    (*ME*, 9; *R*, 205), Wrasse and Shango conduct a seduction by telephone and their language in Act One Scene Five is very specifically that of the 'City':

| | |
|---|---|
| SHANGO | Gold-digger! |
| WRASSE | Marriage makes economic sense. It saves on whores. |
| SHANGO | Would you credit it! |
| WRASSE | By all means. I'm losing interest. |
| SHANGO | Don't be mean. |
| WRASSE | How do you account for that? |
| SHANGO | Virtue is largely self-interest. |
| WRASSE | Then your soul must be in mint condition. |
| SHANGO | I'd endorse that. |
| WRASSE | Your stock is rising! |
| SHANGO | (*Looking down*) Don't bank on it. |
| WRASSE | That's valuable advice, you asset-stripping golden fleece. |
| SHANGO | Wash my bonds! |
| WRASSE | Paid in your own coin? Overrated? Fine! Coming up for your nickel wedding. (*Cracks whip*) I reckon you want to be left with your guilt-edged, ungainly groans.   (*ME*, 22; *R*, 218) |

The play certainly shows us a city in need of purification, and here as it approaches its conclusion Ensoff's promised 'searching out' with candles is announced in terms which are once more adapted from Zephaniah's account of divine vengeance:

> Howl, ye inhabitants of Maktesh, for all the merchant people are cut down; all they that bear silver are cut off.
> And it shall come to pass at that time, that I will search Jerusalem with candles, and punish the men that are settled on their lees: that say in their heart, The Lord will not do good, neither will he do evil.[18]

We do not see such acts of purificatory violence, however. As this scene develops Ensoff and Agappy move towards a harmonious understanding:

| AGAPPY | My defeats I should count as victories? |
|---|---|
| ENSOFF | Unchain a ray of light. |
| AGAPPY | The wind! |
| ENSOFF | Dark words upon a zither. |
| AGAPPY | I long ago became aware that a life lived solely for human rewards was shallow. |

(ME, 44−5; R, 240−1)

The recurrent shaft of light, one of Warner's most potent symbols, here makes an effective appearance as part of a vision of the interaction of human and eternal. Ensoff's other words evoke and explain Agappy's apprehension of the divine spirit. His "dark words upon a zither" are an adaptation of some beautiful verses from the *Psalms*:

> Hear this all ye people; give ear, all ye inhabitants of the world:
> Both low and high, rich and poor, together.
> My mouth shall speak of wisdom; and the meditation of my heart shall be of understanding.
> I will incline mine ear to a parable: I will open my dark saying upon the harp.[19]

His second allusion to the *Psalms*, later in the scene, similarly indicates a modulation from violence to compassionate faith:

> Then now is the time to be generous. Our bones are scattered at the grave's mouth.　(*ME*, 45; *R*, 241)

His words incorporate words taken directly from *Psalms*:

Our bones are scattered at the grave's mouth, as when one cutteth and cleaveth wood upon the earth.

But mine eyes are unto thee, O God the Lord: in thee is my trust; leave not my soul destitute.[20]

Ensoff's 'Passion' approaches. We are told that he is

*thinking of his coming agony.* (*ME*, 45; *R*, 241)

The affirmation of resurrection is, though, only partial and tentative. Agappy still quotes pagan poets on burial. Her remark:

But such as we are, the unwise ones, sleep deep in the hollow earth
(*ME*, 45; *R*, 241)

is surely a version of lines from Moschus' *Lament for Bion*:

Ay me! When the mallows and the fresh green parsley and the springing crumpled anise perish in the garden, they live yet again and grow another year; but we men that are so tall and strong and wise, soon as ever we be dead, unhearing there in a hole of the earth sleep we both sound and long a sleep that is without end or waking.[21]

Agappy may make the adjective a negative, and thereby perhaps imply that for the truly wise there is something different, and she doesn't, after all, complete the quotation. Still, there is no easy confidence in her words. The ambivalence is sustained when Ensoff's

The dead shall be razed

(which, of course, the audience hears as 'raised') is completed by

to the ground. (*ME*, 45; *R*, 241)

In between comes Agappy's more confident

The infinite serene of no defeat! (*ME*, 45; *R*, 241)

What kind of awakening there might be is the subject of their final exchange:

| AGAPPY | Can dead people have babies? |
|---|---|
| ENSOFF | (*Grimly; thinking of his coming agony*) Preconceived. |
| AGAPPY | Like a spring of well-water in a graveyard. |
| ENSOFF | Only thought lives. |

AGAPPY          What is right is what is left.
ENSOFF          Only the human remains.  (*ME*, 45; *R*, 241)

The lines are richly ambiguous. Ensoff's "Preconceived" answers
Agappy's question on two levels. A dead man may, indeed, have a
posthumous child. (Though her question spoke of "people", not men.)
But the word he uses directs us to another kind of creativity. Ideas,
or, indeed, works of art can be "conceived" too, and can outlive the
life-span of those who conceived them. Perhaps this is the only form of
immortality available to humanity: "Only thought lives". The two final
lines punningly expand the idea, and the qualified optimism of Ensoff's
final line reasserts some kind of dignity in the face of earlier passages
in the trilogy. Phagocyte has quoted Jeremiah to describe what he sees
through his telescope:

It's not dung on that field, it's a pile of dead    (*KT*, 36; *R*, 160)

and Chalone has prayed

Lord, let something remain.  (*KT*, 43; *R*, 167)

This final movement of *Meeting Ends* at least allows the possibility of
that prayer being met.

After Agappy's exit there follows Ensoff's revelation of the sundial
beneath the stage-cloth. The symbolic significance of the sundial has
been discussed earlier,[22] and little need be added here save perhaps
to note how, along with the circle of candles, shortly to be lit, it
completes a pattern of circles within this final play of the *Requiem*
cycle. The unbroken circle offers suggestive support to the play's tentative affirmation of continuity. Wrasse, at her nearest approach to
redemption, enters with Callisterne, and they are greeted by Ensoff
in what seem at first to be somewhat puzzling phrases:

It is a light thing for the shadow on the sundial to go down ten
degrees, but you ask me to let the shadow return back as much.
(*ME*, 45–6; *R*, 241–2)

The punning on 'light' introduces talk of the miraculous. His words,
in fact, come from *2 Kings* Chapter 20. They are part of the narrative
of Hezekiah's sickness. Isaiah hears the voice of the Lord promising
a cure for Hezekiah, but Hezekiah requires a sign before he will believe
the message:

And Hezekiah said unto Isaiah, What shall be the sign that the
Lord will heal me, and that I shall go up into the house of the Lord
the third day?

And Isaiah said, This sign shalt thou have of the Lord, that the Lord will do the thing that he hath spoken: shall the shadow go forward ten degrees, or go back ten degrees?

And Hezekiah answered, It is a light thing for the shadow to go down ten degrees: nay, but let the shadow return backward ten degrees.

And Isaiah the prophet cried unto the Lord: and he brought the shadow ten degrees backward, by which it had gone down in the dial of Ahaz.[23]

Hezekiah's words are transferred to Ensoff, from petitioner to petitioned, as it were. Ensoff performs no miracle, offers no spectacular sign for Callisterne and Wrasse. If they are to believe in what he represents, their faith must be founded on a less obvious sign. For Callisterne, Ensoff's humanity is a sufficient sign:

I think of you as a father.   (*ME*, 46; *R*, 242)

Of the choice which Callisterne will make there can be little doubt. Wrasse's position is a good deal more problematical. Her uncertain "What shall I do, Ensoff?" is answered firmly:

It's an unknown God who's come. If you love him, stay with him.
(*ME*, 46; *R*, 242)

The earlier allusions to St. Paul fall into place. Ensoff here paraphrases part of St. Paul's speech on Mars Hill, during his visit to Athens. Mars Hill has already been named in Shango's soliloquy (*ME*, 25; *R*, 221). His first phrase is in itself an allusion to the Biblical account of the Mars Hill speech, to be found in *Acts*, Chapter 17. It is in the context of Paul's meeting with Stoics, Epicureans and other philosophers — a central thread of the later *Light Shadows*. In *Acts* it is related how

Paul stood in the midst of Mars hill, and said, Ye men of Athens, I perceive that in all things ye are too superstitious.

For as I passed by, and beheld your devotions, I found an altar with this inscription, TO THE UNKNOWN GOD. Whom therefore ye ignorantly worship, him declare I unto you.[24]

There follows an eloquent statement of some central Christian doctrines, ending with an affirmation of the resurrection of the dead:

And when they heard of the resurrection of the dead, some mocked: and others said, We will hear thee again of this matter.[25]

Shango's reaction is more savagely violent. He enters, nude and bearing an open razor, incapable of seeing the relationship of Wrasse and Ensoff as anything other than sexual, and therefore a focus for his jealousy.

Shango's castration of Ensoff marks the jealous failure of Promethean aspirations, of materialistic and sensual presumption. We may observe how the keynote of jealousy has been sustained throughout the play by a sequence of allusions to *Othello*. When Shango, *"desperate, against the bars of his cage"* pleads with Wrasse

I did the state some service, did I not?     (*ME*, 20; *R*, 216)

there is a very clear echo of Othello's penultimate speech in Act Five Scene Two. Hardly less clear-cut is the correspondence between Agappy's

I made a man's love the centre of my life. My own selfish passion of universal importance! When it failed, chaos came
(*ME*, 32; *R*, 228)

and Othello's

Perdition catch my soul
But I do love thee; and when I love thee not
Chaos is come again.[26]

The actual castration of Ensoff (perhaps there is intended a macabre pun in his name?) has evident Christian overtones, and insofar as Ensoff is at least a type of Christ it constitutes a kind of crucifixion. The neo-Platonic dimension of the play will not, however, allow us to leave it at that. There is in this castration an implicit allusion to the castration of Uranus. In Hesiod's *Theogony* the legend is related that the heavenly Aphrodite (Aphrodite Urania) arose from the foam of the sea produced by the castration of Uranus. Once more Professor Wind's masterly exegesis of neo-Platonic thought is of great assistance here:

The castration of Uranus is of one type with the dismemberment of Osiris, Attis, Dionysus, all of which signify the same mystery to the neo-Orphic theologians: for whenever the supreme One descends to the Many, this act of creation is imagined as a sacrificial agony, as if the One were cut to pieces and scattered. Creation is conceived in this way as a cosmogonic death, by which the concentrated power of one deity is offered up and dispersed: but the descent and diffusion of the divine power are followed by its resurrection, when the Many are 'recollected' into the One.[27]

We cannot be sure that this sacrificed Creator *will* be resurrected. The castration of Uranus may have produced Aphrodite Urania, but it also produced the Furies and a brood of monstrous giants. Both the status and the value of Ensoff's castration remain ambivalent.

Shango's "household god" (*ME*, 46; *R*, 242) is evidently the penis. In getting the "worm" he imagines himself to have destroyed Ensoff. Wrasse's choice is now simpler. She exits with Shango. Far from destroying Ensoff, however, Shango, in castrating him, has left him free to comfort Callisterne with a compassion and purity which are unsullied by the least taint of desire.

The play's epigraph ought not to be forgotten. It is taken from *Job* — "Yet in my flesh shall I see God". The passage reads thus:

> For I know that my redeemer liveth, and that he shall stand at the latter day upon the earth.
> And though after my skin worms destroy this body, yet in my flesh shall I see God.[28]

Ensoff, after his castration, seems an entirely human figure, confirmed in a faith which puts him above both passion and suffering. His careful lines to Callisterne are eloquent:

> Rest, while the masters of our waking joys
> Rule over us and stretch the oceans' clutch:
> The silent stars play havoc with our toys
> But we have kingdoms that they cannot touch.  (*ME*, 47; *R*, 243)

The lines sound like Christian Stoicism. They may remind us of Seneca:

> Mens bona regnum possidet[29]

or of the  Elizabethan lines sometimes attributed to Sir Edward Dyer:

> My mind to me a kingdom is;
>     Such perfect joy therein I find
> As far exceeds all earthly bliss
>     That God or Nature hath assigned[30]

or even of our old friend Francis Quarles:

> My mind's my kingdom.[31]

Within the plays it constitutes a kind of answer to the invocation of
Aeschylus by the Old Man in *Troat*. Ministered to by Callisterne in a
fashion which betrays debts both to Lear and Cordelia and to Oedipus
and Antigone, Ensoff acts out a conclusion of great dignity and serenity.
He takes the stick proferred by Callisterne, but rejects the bull's head.
He can reject it because what Shango would regard as a defeat is, for
Ensoff, a victory. Ensoff is at the centre now of two circles, the sundial
beneath his feet, the circle of lighted candles above his head. The effect
of a halo is unmistakeable and the theatrical vision has obvious echoes
of *Revelation*. The sundial beneath his feet is that globe upon which
the light of God casts its shadows. The candles above his head figure
forth an image of eternity and possible redemption. Ensoff steps
forward to deliver the epilogue. His opening words

> But in the blue . . .

are better taken as a riposte to his own prologue than as any kind of
answer to the virtual lullaby he has just spoken to Callisterne. The
prologue had ended:

> . . . And yet Earth looks so small, so blue,
> So lovely an oasis, that a spark
> Of heaven might once have touched some one-celled life:
> But mastadon, or grain of wheat, or shark —
> Gross fantasy; and for man to be true?
> Reason rejects such lunacy run rife.  (*ME*, 2; *R*, 198)

The continuity is clear when Ensoff begins his Epilogue:

> But in the blue of that light space oasis . . .

In stepping forward to deliver the Epilogue, that is, in stepping outside
the acting area, Ensoff does, as it were, step outside time, at least as
it can be understood in relation to the dramatic world that he has
created. As such, all that has happened to him there seems a mere
interlude, an interruption of a monologue composed of the play's
Prologue and Epilogue. The Epilogue picks up his own question.
If there is an answer to be found, it is hinted at in his final stanza:

> Yet at my feet a snowdrop breaks moon's winter
> Its secret yellow trussed up in green gauze
> Traced round and rimmed with white, and all enfolded
> By three white lips that shield it out of doors,
> Weighing down like a bell from a sheathed splinter
> This surge of life the icy dust has moulded.

The single flower of spring appears at his feet. The central play of the trilogy had already prepared us for its appearance. Callisterne's nearest counterpart in *Killing Time* is Quark. In Act Two Scene Eight Squaloid seeks to trap her into one of the sequence's many denials of God:

| | |
|---|---|
| SQUALOID | (*Good-humouredly, a whim*) Would you deny there's a God? |
| QUARK | I can't say I've given it much thought. (*Pause*) But I'm sure He's there! |
| SQUALOID | Will you say there's no such thing as God if we let you go. |
| QUARK | (*Pause*) I can't. |
| SQUALOID | Even with pain facing you? |
| QUARK | My birthday's February 2nd, Candlemas. Snowdrops are emblems of the Feast of Lights! |
| SQUALOID | She's nuts. Come on, help me give her the treatment. |
| QUARK | The infant daisies in January down by the river are so small in the grass they look like the remains of frost. (*KT*, 55–6; *R*, 179–80) |

It is Candlemas we are invited to witness at the end of *Meeting Ends*. Ensoff's single snowdrop is, indeed, an emblem of the Feast of Lights. At Candlemas, candles are carried in procession, in celebration of the spiritual light which is Christ. In the frozen world which Ensoff describes it is, indeed, difficult to be sure whether one sees the flowers of hope or the frost of immobility. The ambivalence of Ensoff's Passion is maintained. When Agappy blows Reveille we cannot feel sure what kind of response it will produce. It is an expression of hope rather than of expectation.

The candles do continue to burn, though. While ever they do, there remains the possibility of other kinds of illumination. After the trilogy's ruthless examination of human viciousness and frailty it would be dishonest if we were offered a conclusion any more comforting than this.

## Notes

1  M. M. Davy, *Essai sur la symbolique romane*, Paris, 1955, quoted thus in J. E. Cirlot, *A Dictionary of Symbols*, transl. J. Sage, 1971, p. 51.

2  Sears R. Jayne, *Marsilio Ficino's Commentary on Plato's Symposium. The Text and a Translation, with an Introduction*, Univ. of Missouri Studies, XIX, 1944, pp. 206–7.

3  Carolus Bovillus, *Metaphisicum introductorum cum alio quodam opusculo distinctionis nonnullorum omnibus communium quae ad metaphisicam spectant*. Paris 1503/4; I quote, slightly adapted, the translation by E. F. Rice Jr. in his *The Renaissance Idea of Wisdom* (Orig. publ. 1958), Westport, 1973, pp. 117–8.

4  *Isaiah*, 25:8.

5  *Revelation*, 7:16–17.

6  *Isaiah*, 61:1.

7  *Proverbs*, 30:20.

8  *Proverbs*, 11:22.

9  Edgar Wind, *Pagan Mysteries in the Renaissance*, 1967, p. 55.

10  Budé, *De Studio literarum recte et commode instituendo*, Paris, 1532, XVII, v.

11  Henry Cornelius Agrippa, *Of the Vanitie and Uncertaintie of Artes and Sciences*, transl. J. Sandford (1569) ed. Catherine M. Dunn, Northridge (Cal.), 1974, p. 15.

12  *Isaiah*, 63:3–4.

13  See T. Pyles, 'Ophelia's Nothing', *Modern Language Notes*, 44, 1949.

14  *Psalms*, 124:6–8.

15  *Acts*, 28:1–6.

16  *Zephaniah*, 3:1–3.

17  Here men are "let alone" and dealt with by "contract" and "rent letter" (*ME*, 3; *R*, 199); the motif is one that has been earlier introduced by Laz and Sapphira:

> LAZ        . . . you wanted to set up house.
> SAPPH    You wanted the house upset.
> LAZ        Wouldn't re-lease your free hold until we both reached morgue age.   (*LF*, 40; *R*, 114)

18  *Zephaniah*, 1:11–12.

19  *Psalms*, 49:1–4.

20  *Psalms*, 141:7–8.

21  *The Greek Bucolic Poets*, with an English translation, J. M. Edmonds, (Loeb), 1919, p. 453. Agappy's allusion may simultaneously be to the *nox est perpetua una dormienda* of Catullus.

22  See Chapter II.

23  *II Kings*, 20:8–11.

24  *Acts*, 17:22–3.

25  *Acts*, 17:32.

26 *Othello*, III, iii, 91–3.
27 Wind, *op. cit.*, p. 133.
28 *Job*, 19:25–6.
29 Seneca, *Thyestes*, II, 380.
30 E. K. Chambers, *Oxford Book of Sixteenth Century Verse*, 1961, p. 195.
31 'School of the Heart', Ode 4 st. 3.

# IX

## *A Conception of Love:*
## The Curious Knotted Garden

In Act I Scene XII of *A Conception of Love* Amatrix tells Koinonia about one of her supervisions at Cambridge on a hot summer's afternoon:

> I sat in the garden surrounded by neat yew-hedges staring into the pool wishing it were tea-time, while my Supervisor droned on about Sir Walter Raleigh and the School of Night in the sunshine ... I'd forgotten all about *Love's Labour's Lost.* (*CL*, 36)

The reader of *A Conception of Love* would be well advised not to forget *Love's Labour's Lost*, for Warner's play is a comedy of love which has definite affinities with Shakesperean comedy in general and with *Love's Labour's Lost* in particular. This, however, is a comedy in which love's labours are *not* lost, in which news of a death does not prevent the comic conclusion of dance and marriage. This analogy should not, however, blind us to the continued presence in *A Conception of Love* of themes and motifs first brought to our attention in the *Requiem* plays and their *Maquettes.*

*A Conception of Love* is set in an Oxford College garden — *Love's Labour's Lost* takes place in the King of Navarre's park. There the King is determined that

> Our court shall be a little academe,
> Still and contemplative in living art.[1]

The king and his attendant princes "have sworn for three years term"

181

to study — vowing themselves, at the same time, to certain accompanying austerities, notably "not to see a woman in that term".[2] In Warner's college garden the young men *and* women act out their three years' term. This is a decidedly heterosexual world — evidently the play takes place at a date after the introduction of co-educational colleges in the University. The Master talks of two of the female students to Mara, the non-University girl:

| | |
|---|---|
| GRIOT | They are girls with strong boarding-school ties, trying to adapt to the heterosexual world of Oxbridge. There's a real feeling of failure if they do not get their man during their three years . . . |
| MARA | And a real feeling of relief for the young men if they escape their three years unscathed. |

(CL, 42)

In common with the young men of Navarre, the young men of this anonymous College are moved to write poetry by love. Berowne's confession "By heaven, I do love; and it hath taught me to rhyme"[3] is one that might be shared by both Thalassios and Gan. The formally composed poems of the young lords of Navarre are performed only to a mocking audience of unsympathetic hearers.[4] So in *A Conception of Love* there is nothing surprising about the way in which the first poetic efforts of the two young men are presented to us:

| | |
|---|---|
| FASHSHAR | Amatrix's main jealousy is not that Koinonia has Thalassios but that Thalassios has Koinonia. |
| THALASSIOS | But I haven't! I've brought a poem along about her, but Amatrix suits the metre better. |
| GAN | So have I, but Amatrix is too short for mine. |
| FASHSHAR | I suppose you're going to ask the girls if they want their lines endstopped! |
| THALASSIOS | (*Holds up hand for silence. Reads*) |
| | Better far the lazy eyes |
| | Closed in languor at sunrise |
| | Effortlessly lost in sleep |
| | Where the scythe can never reap, |
| | Than the chromium day's despair |
| | Swept grotesquely here and there. |
| | Best of all, where joy embalms — |
| | Soft Amatrix' sensual arms. |
| FASHSHAR | It's a ridiculous set of lines — but Amatrix fits the last line better than Koinonia. |

| | |
|---|---|
| THALASSIOS | And her arms are more obviously sensual. I can't think of Koinonia as sensual. |
| FASHSHAR | I hope yours is better. |
| GAN | Light-eyed Koinonia's<br>Faun-touched hair<br>Never so soft<br>Never so fair<br>Brightness enhances<br>Evening and dawn<br>Happiness dances<br>Rapture is born. |
| FASHSHAR | Vile! Vile! There's nothing in it. Nothing! Either in your poem or choice of whose name. Ah well! Così fan tutte, they're all the same.  (*CL*, 49–50) |

The shallowness of Fashshar's observations on women ("They're all the same" and the remark about Amatrix being jealous over Koinonia) and the vulgarity of his manner, do not entirely convince us that there is no truth in his judgement of the two poems. They are not "vile" or "ridiculous" lines, but they certainly fall far short of the other verses which occur in the play, all of them prompted by, as it were, the heightened emotions of the moment and functioning as part of the play's movement between formal and informal. As with the lords of Navarre, the inhabitants of this college garden are at their most poetic when at their least studied. It is a measure of this that their lyrics should be effectively interchangeable in their dedication — Thalassios's poem is addressed to Amatrix rather than Koinonia for, it would appear, purely metrical reasons (with the proviso that the phrase "sensual arms" also fits Amatrix more than Koinonia). As *A Conception of Love* moves towards its closing moments the echoes of *Love's Labour's Lost* are very evident, though the two plays are moving towards radically different conclusions. When Griot instructs and invites:

Let the music start and the engagements be announced. Koinonia, will you take your Gan? Amatrix, your Thalassios? The seasons must turn, and three years come to an end.  (*CL*, 74)

his final sentence alludes to, and effectively invokes, the songs of Spring and Winter which close *Love's Labour's Lost* and that cycle of the seasons which they embody and represent. But Armado's words there[5] insist "You that way: we this". Ladies retire one way, lords the other. Berowne observes that

these ladies' courtesy
Might well have made our sport a comedy.[6]

In *A Conception of Love* the ladies are courteous — the comic pattern is completed, the form fulfilled. The marriage and the dance can follow. Griot's request that the music begin and the engagements be announced has no parallel in *Love's Labour's Lost*. If we want a Shakespearean analogy we shall have to turn to the more conventional comic conclusions such as those of *As You Like It*:

Play, music, and you brides and bridegrooms all,
With measure heaped in joy, to th'measures fall.[7]

or *Much Ado About Nothing*:

Let's have a dance ere we are married, that we may lighten our own hearts and our wives' heels . . . therefore play, music.[8]

In *Love's Labour's Lost* the comic pattern remains incomplete for a number of reasons. One reason merits consideration here. Within the Arcadia of the King of Navarre's park there are no serpents, no scheming, or even sceptical, characters, no warning notes of destruction, no Don Johns or even Malvolios. The impact, theatrically and thematically, is therefore stunning when the messenger Marcade arrives unheralded with his news of death. It is a hammer blow too savage for the fragile rhetorical Arcadia of Navarre to bear. The pieces are by no means put together in the moments which follow, though most of the characters come to some sort of preliminary realisation of how they might be. *A Conception of Love* adopts this device of the news of a death arriving just as the pattern of courtship moves towards a conclusion, but uses it in a significantly different manner.

*A Conception of Love* offers only a milder, less startling, version of Marcade's arrival. Theatrically this makes sense because the earlier garden/park scenes have established different dramatic modes. The college garden of *A Conception* is no serpentless Arcadia — a reading of Warner's earlier plays would not encourage us to expect it to be so. Fashshar and Mara represent forces of destruction (in potential at any rate) which the comic world must either assimilate or exclude. Here the pattern is to exclude one (Fashshar) and to assimilate the other (Mara). There is here no Arcadia to be marred by the arrival of a Marcade. News of the death — and it is no longer news of the death of an offstage character — is now entrusted to the play's guardian figure,

Griot, who offers means whereby Broomy's death might be understood and seen as part of the larger comic pattern. If we agree with Northrop Frye that tragedy is a kind of uncompleted comedy, and that comedy always contains within itself a potential tragedy,[9] then this is entirely to be expected.

By considering the play's main characters we can observe how the comic pattern is worked out. Griot stands at the apex of the play's dramatic pyramid, as Master of the College. The significance of his name is introduced in the opening exchange of the play:

| | |
|---|---|
| BROOMY | Morning, Master of the College. |
| GRIOT | Morning, Broomy. After all these years you still never use my name. |
| BROOMY | Funny French one; can't get my mouth round it. If you don't mind me asking, sir: what does it mean? |
| GRIOT | Griot? Oh, it's probably African originally, though remains of the French occupation still cling round it. The griot is the story-teller of the tribe; he perpetuates its beliefs and customs — though that's going back a long way. |
| BROOMY | Sort of priest, you might say?   (*CL*, 1) |

Griot's role as a custodian of tradition is thus rapidly established. He is no mere antiquarian; rather he sees his role as being to uphold and affirm values which might readily be lost or ignored. So we find him, later, expressing to Amatrix and Koinonia his conviction that

> The values of courtesy and honour are good. In the First World War they were misused, and now they're under attack. But that doesn't make them wrong.  (*CL*, 22)

It is in the same scene that he juxtaposes the moral concern of the sermon and the triviality of modern journalism:

> The press is interested in what is urgent, not in what is important. Why does no Sunday paper carry a column analysing contemporary sermons? Yet the Oxford Professors review rubbish weekly for their own self-aggrandizement.  (*CL*, 22)

At the centre of *his* conception of love is the University and his vision of that institution as an intermediary between past and present, custodian of a living tradition which facilitates the full appreciation of moral values:

> What do you think a University is? I'll tell you. It's no more nor less than this: a family of people who love their subjects gathered round those who live their subjects.   (*CL*, 63)

It is he who acts as a kind of judge passing sentence on Fashshar in the long scene from which this last quotation was taken, Act 2 Scene VII. Fashshar's irresponsibility as a University tutor and lecturer is part of a larger failure of love. In acting as the play's judge figure and custodian of moral values, Griot becomes a comic version of the figure familiar to us previously in such characters from the earlier plays as Chalone, Ensoff, and even the Old Man in *Troat*. This role is sustained by some of the epithets applied to him by other characters. Mara tells him "You have an iron gentleness" (*CL*, 41) and later calls him "an unseen king" (*CL*, 75), thereby evoking the whole tradition out of which Ensoff grows. In the opening scene, in which the characters are identified with their emblematic trees, Griot's tree is the ailanthus. As Broomy says:

> Look at that Tree of Heaven there, the ailanthus, reaching up to the sky like a hand in a glove! Oh, my back! It fair hurts to look to the top sudden-like.   (*CL*, 2)

The source of Griot's strength of spirit is made very clear in the allusion to his "father" which closes this opening scene of the play. Broomy talks about fishing and then adds:

> By the way, what happened to your father? He was taken abroad wasn't he? Was it in France?   (*CL*, 4)

We ought to be reminded of the Old Man's words in *Troat*: "Christ was a fisher" (*M*, 32; *R*, 52); if we are so reminded then the transition will appear less arbitrary. Griot's reply brings out its significance:

> A trumped-up charge. A howling mob. A magistrate frightened of a power-ridden administration. Dying alone, his closest friends leaving him. One can't be sentimental about such a death. (*Pause*) He was a good man.   (*CL*, 4)

The sentence "Dying alone, his closest friends leaving him" reminds us of the characteristic Warnerian motif of love or friendship betrayed. We have met this motif in the earlier plays and it will occur again in *Light Shadows*.

Griot is the senior member of the play's hierarchy (as Master of the College) and next to Broomy he is the senior figure in age too. As such he is able to speak out of emotional experiences which are as yet beyond the understanding or scope of the students. His beautiful soliloquy on winter (preparing us for news of Broomy's death) which opens the final scene encompasses emotions (and appropriate cadences) not yet accessible to the young people. It is he, too, who, with calm certainty, can say of the newly dead Broomy "He became his garden" (*CL*, 74) and who can put into words a fundamental principle of the comic view of things:

> If we lament a death, life for us must have meaning. We must pick up the fragments of order left behind.  (*CL*, 74)

Fittingly he has the last words of the play — sentiments which 'place' both the departed Fashshar and the dance which follows:

> The shadow in the brook. Let him go; each of you pooling two unique and individual lives.  (*CL*, 75)

It is a repeated feature of *A Conception of Love* that its characters are clarified by inset anecdotes, most often concerned with their own past. Some of these insets constitute quite lengthy set pieces. In the case of Griot the main example is his long story, told to Thalassios and Gan in Act One, Scene Two, of the Lebanese Sputnik. The story is amusing enough in itself, but it serves an important function too. In being a story of space and the heavens, it repeats, at length, Broomy's earlier identification of Griot with the ailanthus, reaching towards the sky. At the end of the scene Griot is giving advice, and reminiscing about his experiences as a pilot. His affinities with the air have been very positively established. That this identification is part of a structural design one is entitled to suspect from the way the scene closes:

GRIOT    I had an instructor who used to make me try to land on a cloud. You'd feel the kite begin to spin like a sycamore. One's instinctive reaction is to pull back the stick. That's why many pilots die in the early stages. They don't realize that when you start the spin, and see the ground going round and round towards you, you should continue down to gather speed enough to enable you to fly out of the spin on the far side.

GAN      It's not only what you know, it's who you learned

it from. That information may one day save my
life.

GRIOT      But *you* know the land. You know it as well as a
poacher.

GAN        Wind and the stars are the poacher's guide. It's the
fog that leads him astray.   (*CL*, 8–9)

Griot himself establishes the polarity. If he is a creature of the air, it is
with the earth that Gan has a special affinity — though needing guidance
from the element of air if he is successfully to explore the land.

Gan's name is straightforward enough. It is Biblical Hebrew meaning
'garden'. It is the word used for the garden in Eden. He is repeatedly
identified with activities of the land and the earth. He is a rock-climber
(*CL*, 7) and an explorer of the jungle (*CL*, 7) and, indeed, one of his
set-piece anecdotes is a long narration about the jungle (*CL*, 53–4).
He even recommends it to Amatrix: "You should try the jungle"
(*CL*, 51). In the opening scene's identifications and introductions Gan,
sitting in the audience, is identified as the hornbeam:

GRIOT      What's that young, neat, unbroken one?

BROOMY     That's the hard hornbeam. Like the chestnut girl,
he has both male and female seeds and pollinates
himself. Dapper, with clean branches. That sort
will coppice well, and make a good hedge.

GRIOT      Not here, though.   (*CL*, 3)

Implicit here is recognition of Gan as a character in quest of both personal and sexual identity. As yet "unbroken" there is no real doubt
that Gan will, eventually, "coppice well", though as Griot implies, he
will have to look beyond the confines of the University, beyond the
walls of that enclosed park which his name signifies, before he will be
able to do so. The characterisation thus sketched in by Broomy and
Griot prepares us for our first meeting with Gan in the immediately
succeeding scene. The setting is a pub:

THALASSIOS Don't sit there! That's where the homosexuals
sit!

GAN        How do you define a homosexual? Like most
people here fresh from school, I still prefer the
company of my own sex, men rather than women,
anyway. Does that make me one?   (*CL*, 5)

His uncertainty as to his sexual identity is nicely (and not at all unkindly)

mocked in the episode in which he dresses up as a girl to woo Amatrix
— whom he imagines to be a lesbian! His disguising neatly inverts the
usual disguises (female to male) of Shaksperean comedy and is thematically balanced against Mara's later appearance in men's clothing. A neat
twist is given to the theme of homosexual love during his exchange with
Amatrix before she realises who he is. Content, for the moment, to
believe that she is talking to Gan's sister, Amatrix observes a further
resemblance:

| | |
|---|---|
| AMATRIX | You're like a girl I had a pash on at school. |
| GAN | They weren't allowed at mine. |
| AMATRIX | Did you have them all the same?     (*CL*, 28) |

Gan's "They weren't allowed at mine" is taken by Amatrix to refer to
"pashes"; actually, of course, it refers to girls not allowed at Gan's all-
male boarding school. The ambiguity extends, herself all unknowing,
to Amatrix's next question: "Did you have them all the same?" — to
which the answer would, presumably, be 'no'. This ambiguity of sexual
role is still present in Gan's later conversation with Fashshar:

| | |
|---|---|
| GAN | Any generation before now it would have been ridiculous to say this, but I think I would rather have been born a girl today than a boy. |
| FASHSHAR | Perhaps Amatrix should have dressed as a man to woo you? You'd get on fine with Mara.     (*CL*, 48) |

When Gan tells us that he did indeed take Mara out to dinner on one
occasion, it is no surprise to learn that she was the dominant partner
who "entirely controlled the decision" (*CL*, 48). The strange story he
tells to Amatrix is not without relation to this side of his character,
concerned as it is with another kind of 'incestuous' relationship, not,
this time, between members of the same sex, but between members of
the same family.

Gan's friend Thalassios — 'the dweller by the sea' — makes an obvious
contribution to that pattern of the elements which we have begun to
trace. Time and again the text insists upon his association with all that
is liquid:

I've been boating round Scotland, studying whisky     (*CL*, 7)

he tells us in the second scene of the play, and as soon as the four
students meet his opening words are "Let's all go punting" (*CL*, 12),
a somewhat hasty invitation which is politely spurned by Koinonia.

He wishes the sea were his life (*CL*, 17) and his long inset-narrative (*CL*, 51–3) is about swimming in the sea, and rescuing swimmers from the sea. Gan's remarks about the need for guidance from the stars when one crosses the land at night are precisely paralleled by words spoken by Thalassios:

> You realize how desperately important the stars are when you're sailing alone at sea on a night so dark you can only see the furrow of your boat, and blackness. (*Pause*) You might try to love me.
>
> (*CL*, 66)

For all his affinities with the liquid, Thalassios is also given an emblematic tree in the opening scene: he is the ilex, the "evergreen oak by the lake" (*CL*, 3). It is a measure of the precision of this play's composition that the tree should occupy that particular spot.

It will naturally be expected that our fourth male character will complete the pattern of the elements, and expectations are not here disappointed. The very first words to greet this fourth character's arrival on stage are Gan's "Here's fiery Fashshar" (*CL*, 13).[10] His name is taken from Arabic folk-literature where it designates a mischievous or scheming person.[11] Traditional comic form includes at least one figure of the kind which Frye describes as "blocking characters"[12]. Fashshar's role as the embodiment of dangerously destructive ideas is soon established. He too is identified with a tree. He and his tree are carefully and immediately juxtaposed with Griot and *his* tree:

| | |
|---|---|
| BROOMY | Now I love my trees here; naming them, talking to them winter and summer. The young come and go, but these don't wander. Look at that Tree of Heaven there, the ailanthus, reaching up to the sky like a hand in a glove! Oh, my back! It fair hurts to look to the top sudden-like. And this old devil of a cedar, making wolf hand-shadows with its branches. |
| GRIOT | The cedar of Lebanon. Egypt means 'black' and Lebanon means 'white'. Strange, isn't it? But it probably means 'the white mountain' where all these cedars originate. |
| BROOMY | Well, there you got me, I don't know; but they say some's as old as Solomon, and it's the wood that made the Cross. Damned old tree! |

(*CL*, 2)

The trees which don't wander embody eternal principles, and it is clear that the conflict of ailanthus and cedar, the conflict of Griot and Fashshar, echoes and embodies an eternal conflict. Fashshar's tree, and with it Fashshar himself, is an "old devil", a "damned old tree". As the wood which, legend has it, was used to make the Cross, it complements neatly that allusion to Griot's "father" which we have already discussed. Here the tree makes "wolf hand-shadows" and later in the play when Gan asks Broomy

> Have you ever seen a fox in this garden?

we can surely have no doubt when Broomy replies "All sorts" (*CL*, 27) that Fashshar is one form which the fox takes in this particular garden. He displays the characteristically devilish emotions of slander and envy. He is trivial and boastful:

> Well, you'll be glad to hear that I've just used my column in *Woman's Eternal* to attack a dozen of my colleagues who've published a book together. It didn't take me long, as I only skimmed and had read nothing of the person they were writing about.
>
> (*CL*, 46—7)

He seems unaware either of any real purpose in his work at the University or of the nature of that conception of love for which the students are searching. As a don he is well described by Griot as:

> One of the young executives who are now dons; bustling, inflated, leisureless and proud.   (*CL*, 41)

His long 'trial' scene with Griot effectively offers a condemnation of him on both main counts. His emotional shallowness is evidenced by the feeble jest with which he introduces himself:

> GRIOT       How are you feeling?
> FASHSHAR    I feel like a sixteen-year-old. (*Pause*) But I can never get one!   (*CL*, 60)

The audience are adroitly given the role of jury:

> GRIOT       I'm afraid there are complaints against you.
> FASHSHAR    Oh. I'm on public trial, am I?
> GRIOT       Public? The only people present are those you see.
>
> (*CL*, 61)

The charges against him boil down to a failure to engage his emotions in his teaching, a failure as marked as the absence of emotional commitment in his sexual relations. Both are failures of love. Earlier he has revealed the limitations of *his* conception of love:

FASHSHAR      ... Love is the mechanism for the perpetuation of the species.

MARA          You mean sex is.   (*CL*, 43)

Well might Mara tell him "You are a moral oaf" (*CL*, 47). Towards the male students he adopts an air of contemptuous superiority. The crudeness of his manner stands in contrast to their essential courtesy. Having listened to their attempts at love poetry — not great poetry but decidedly *love* poetry — his dismissal is couched in terms of repellent callousness:

Put away your warbling, you'll never snare chicks like that. I'll leave to shaft Mara.  (*CL*, 50)

That they are moved to wish him "Good luck" is merely evidence of his effectiveness as an agent of the morally unattractive. His own sexual dealings appear to be marked by a failure to see the woman he is with as an independent personality of any kind. His first long conversation with Griot (Act One Scene Nine) illustrates his failure to understand Mara. Griot's question "How is your new pupil surviving with you?" uses the language of education to ask a question about Fashshar's other failure of love. The word 'love' is noticeable by its absence from Fashshar's idiolect. He tells Griot:

We had one of the best week-ends ever ... Sex good, the sun shone, everything.  (*CL*, 24)

His boastful account, again to Griot, of his masterful handling of Mara, is given without any apparent awareness of its ironies. He is quite impervious to the absurdity of arrogantly announcing your dismissal of a girl whose company you still seek to share:

FASHSHAR      'Whether or not I've recovered,' I said, 'this is the end of our association.' She didn't speak a word from that moment on. I called a taxi, gave her some money for it, helped her into it. I meant it. I passed her a day or two later on my bicycle and I waved and smiled, and she blushed on the

|         |                                        |
|---------|----------------------------------------|
|         | pavement and looked sheepish. But I didn't stop. No ill feelings. I'd done the decent thing. |
| GRIOT   | And now you're back together.          |
| FASHSHAR | (*Abashed*) Eh? Oh. (*Pause*)          |
| GRIOT   | I know she was hurt.                    |
| FASHSHAR | My dear Master, so was I!     (*CL*, 25) |

The boasting is effectively punctured, but only momentarily. Even more significant is Griot's sympathy for Mara, a quality entirely absent from Fashshar. Earlier in the scene Griot has reacted to one of Fashshar's unkind descriptions of Mara by saying simply "She seems entirely different to me" (*CL*, 24). Here is preparation for one important strand in the play's resolution. Fashshar's arrogance, though, remains incurable. In the six-voice polyphony of Act Two Scene Six Mara complains, surely with justice, "You were aggressively sexual" (*CL*, 57) and Fashshar's answer, characteristically, is relentlessly self-absorbed:

> Would you have liked it if I were not? Don't be daft. I know your bodily rhythms and wants. And mental too. You want to be thought desirable. (*CL*, 58)

Real observation or understanding of Mara remains impossible while he continues to be certain of his all-knowingness in these matters.

The blocking characters of traditional comic form are usually either converted, cured of the errors of their ways and thereby reconciled to the community, or they are expelled, excluded from the final harmony as unacceptably discordant notes. It is clear which course will be followed with Fashshar. Incapable of learning, of evolving a worthwhile conception of love, he is necessarily excluded. Act Two Scene Eleven gives us his final rejection by Mara, and at the end of the play he can only comment, again with innocent irony:

> Student marriage? You're behaving like a group of irresponsible children! (*CL*, 75)

and stalk off before the final dance. It is hard to believe that he will ever be revenged on the whole pack of them. His bold threats of revenges to be taken against Groit after the 'trial' scene, have already been dissipated in his scene with Broomy (Act Two Scene Nine), where Broomy is engaged to try to win back the Master's favour. This is Broomy's last appearance in the play, and throughout the scene he is evidently in pain. His "I won't be playing bowls today" (*CL*, 71) picks up his earlier remark:

'Never shed a tear', said my old wife, God bless her, 'till you can't roll a bowl.' When I can't put a wood up the green (*Bowling gesture*) it's time to leave this world.   (*CL*, 27)

Broomy in this scene with Fashshar is visibly under the shadow of death, and when Gan says of his death "The dark angel has touched once more" (*CL*, 74) it is hard not to think of Fashshar as, at least metaphorically, that dark angel. Insofar as he is the play's spirit of evil his role is analogous to that of Shango in *Meeting Ends*. But where Shango castrates Ensoff and thus (in his own eyes at any rate) 'rescues' his woman, who leaves the stage with him, Fashshar has no scene to correspond to the castration and loses his woman to Griot. He may be "the shadow in the brook" (*CL*, 75), but as a threat he is as ephemeral as the most transient of shadows. As so often in Warner's plays the shadows are ultimately most important as proofs of the light.

When the play opens Mara is very much associated in our minds with Fashshar. She is his sexual partner — one hesitates to use the word lover. She seems to have no objection to the man or his manners:

| FASHSHAR | There are only two sorts of women; those that do and those that don't. And I don't want to waste time with the don'ts. Come on, Mara — shall we investigate? |
| MARA | Invaginate, you mean.   (*CL*, 20) |

Like the other characters we have been considering, she is allotted an emblematic tree in the opening scene:

| BROOMY | Thousands of greeny-white and yellow flowers on that tulip-tree all through June and July. Oh, she's a show off. Look at that trunk. Here, feel it, with all those well-filled bulges. |
| GRIOT | We need her brashness in this garden.   (*CL*, 2) |

This is lively enough as a character sketch (and Griot's remark looks forward to her presence in the garden at the play's close), while her name tells us most of what else we need to know in order to understand her role in the play's comic argument. The name is actually that of a masculine figure in Buddhist mythology, but most of his symbolic and metaphysical attributes are eminently in evidence in the person of this girl who bears his name. In Buddhist mythology

Mara embodies desire, the universal fetterer, the sensual life both here and in the other world.[13]

Mara is most famous for one incident in the life of Buddha.[14] When the Buddha Shakyamuni sat beneath the sacred fig-tree, determined to gain full enlightenment, Mara was naturally disturbed and afraid:

> Mara, the inveterate foe of the true Dharma, shook with fright. People address him gladly as the God of Love, the one who shoots with flower-arrows, and yet they dread this Mara as the one who rules events connected with a life of passion.[15]

Mara's three seductive daughters ('Discontent', 'Delight' and 'Thirst') attempted to divert Buddha from his intentions, singing and dancing as charmingly as they could. The Bodishattva remained quite unmoved however, and eventually Mara (after trying more violent means too) was forced to acknowledge defeat. It is the life of passion which Mara seems to represent in the earlier part of Warner's play. Fashshar calls her "a magnificent woman" (*CL*, 16) and only half mockingly assumes that she is out "scouting for boys" (*CL*, 15). She is scornful of Koinonia's chastity, and she is herself regarded as an expert on adultery. To Broomy, admirably choric as ever, she is "that older one who don't go back to her lodgings till the birds sing in the morning" (*CL*, 28). She enjoys shocking Koinonia with her scandalous stories and suggestions:

> Let's go and stand on the flyover with bright knickers on and watch the cars swerve as they look up.   (*CL*, 32)

There, in comic microcosm, is her role as destructive tempter. The girls are convinced that when she takes Thalassios offstage with her it is to "initiate" him. She is by no means happy to play the subordinate female — a role she assumes the students to be accepting too readily. The assumption is part of the air of superiority she adopts towards them:

THALASSIOS   I was going to meet Koinonia here. Don't talk sex to her, will you?

MARA   She's no one to point the finger, poor frustrated girl. Don't the real men prefer the challenge of a woman with personality, instead of a little wife who only wants peace, no tantrums, calm, order, no demands?   (*CL*, 19)

Her path in the play, however, follows a quite different course from that of the superficially similar Fashshar. Where he fails to learn and must therefore be excluded, she, and the threat she represents, are ultimately assimilated within the comic vision. For this to happen she must, necessarily, undergo a kind of comic moral conversion. The beginnings of such a conversion can, I think, be seen in the dialogue she has with Griot at the beginning of Act Two (Act Two Scene Two). Mara is dressed as a man, and Griot is seated with the roots of a fallen tree serving as his backrest. It is not entirely fanciful to see this scene as having a kind of parodic relationship with that episode from the life of the Buddha Shakyamuni which was discussed above. Griot is no Buddha, but he is, as we have seen, the most 'enlightened' character in the play. Prior to Mara's entry Griot tells us he is "alert in every sense" (*CL*, 40). He is able to recognize the full beauty of his surroundings:

> The dignity and formality of each tree, so different; even when distorted, so self-assured. Endlessly changing light through the branches on the water, in the hollows and humps and trunks and undergrowth. Music of peace. Sticky buds. A lungful of spiritual air with its oxygen of quiet.  (*CL*, 40)

In the context his arboreal observations are also human observations, and he is thus able to offer Mara a certain kind of moral guidance:

> Making happiness the goal instead of a by-product of living is like hunting for cream without milking the cow . . . We define ourselves by what we decline.  (*CL*, 41)

When Mara says "You'll help me" (*CL*, 41) she means that she hopes Griot will help her in her "sardonic" schemes. The sentiments, though, are truer than she knows or intends. It is from this point onwards that there are visible — though not consistently — signs of a transformation in Mara. Immediately after this scene we find her displaying an awareness of the distinction between sex and love which seems to be beyond Fashshar's emotional scope. Later she shows evidence of a developing conception of what love might mean. When she complains to Fashshar:

> You could only think of me as someone to go to bed with, not as a friend, as someone to share at least some of your life with  (*CL*, 57)

she displays a more mature understanding of emotional values than anything she had been able to offer previously. She can see why Fashshar's behaviour towards her has not been an expression of love:

You say you love me, but you only help me when it suits you.

(CL, 58)

In the lyric of separation which she shares with Fashshar, her sentiments are radically different from those she expressed at the play's
opening. Her comic conversion is complete. She can now leave Fashshar,
with an honest conviction that the action is not a selfish one:

> Our freshness has departed, and concern
> For you as much as me makes me depart.   (*CL*, 73)

She is now insistent that "adulteries must cease" (*CL*, 73) and declares
her choice of a passionless life:

> I'll live the College Master's new housekeeper.   (*CL*, 73)

The terms of her conversion may be surprising – but then surprising
conversions are not unknown in comic conclusions! Her final words
are resonantly poetic:

> We are in a game of chess, and I must mate with an unseen king.

(CL, 75)

In these words there are deliberate echoes of *Meeting Ends* which
ought to alert us to an important aspect of this later play's continuity
with the *Requiem* plays. I suggested earlier that Fashshar could be
seen as a comic version of Shango. It is natural, then, that we should
see Mara as similarly related to Wrasse. In their sensuality, in their
desire to take over masculine roles, in their weakness below a show
of assurance, they have much in common. The important difference,
though, is to be found in the parts they play within two triangular
relationships: Shango–Wrasse–Ensoff and Fashshar–Mara–Griot. When
Wrasse makes her journey to Ensoff he tells her

> It's an unknown God who's come. If you love him, stay with him.

(ME, 46; R, 242)

She chooses, however, to leave with Shango and his household god,
the phallic worm, rather than to stay with Ensoff. Mara's final words
announce her as, as it were, a Wrasse who chooses Ensoff. Fashshar,
unlike Shango, leaves alone. In their allusion to St. Paul, Mara's final
words also look forward to *Light Shadows*.

It was suggested earlier that the characters of the four main male figures constituted a version of the four elements. Recognition of Mara as analogous to Wrasse enables us to see that the three women in *A Conception of Love* all have prototypes in *Meeting Ends*. Koinonia corresponds to Agappy, and Amatrix to Callisterne. As such the three of them constitute another version of the three Graces, i.e. Koinonia (Castitas/Spiritual Love), Amatrix (Pulchritudo/Married Love) and Mara (Voluptas/Pleasure). Those, at any rate, are their starting points on the play's comic map.

Koinonia's Greek name means 'friendship' or 'sharing'. It is a constant reminder that her chastity is not that of frigidity or frustration. Rather it is the active virtue of Spenser's *Faerie Queene* or the "married chastity" celebrated in *The Phoenix and the Turtle*. Yet again the opening scene's catalogue of trees establishes her basic character beyond all doubt.

| | |
|---|---|
| BROOMY | . . . look at the lovely slender trunk of this maidenhair. Unmarked. Just a touch of moss for colour. Two branches perfectly balancing each other. |
| GRIOT | A living fossil, perhaps the oldest type of tree under the sky. It's called Chastity because it's so rare: unlikely to find a partner. |
| BROOMY | She's a darling.  (*CL*, 2) |

To the mocking Fashshar she is "the untouchable Koinonia" (*CL*, 13). Blind to the kind of virtue she possesses he can only see her as a "garden statue made not of stone but of concrete" (*CL*, 14). Griot calls her "very strict and perfect" (*CL*, 4) and certainly she is shocked by Mara's outrageous anecdotes, where Thalassios and Amatrix are both, in their different ways, fascinated and amused. She has a strong sense of family loyalty:

I would *always* return to my father to help him if he needed me
(*CL*, 31)

and experiences great difficulty in adjusting herself to the twin demands of family and College life. There is much that is still schoolgirlish in her. Her inset anecdote is the narrative of an 'adventure' with her friend Ianthe. Her confiding

It was a Perilous Quest, you see    (*CL*, 36)

seems to be offered quite without irony, and there is a delightful solemnity in her

We took the roses out of our hair, the symbols of our fading beauty
— we are both getting on, twenty now.   (*CL*, 37)

The innocence of her narrative of her only boyfriend (*CL*, 34–5)
contrasts with Amatrix's account of her love-life. It is clear that at
least during the first half of the play friendship is more important to
Koinonia than love is. She attaches paramount value to friendship
shared with her "best friend" (*CL*, 3) Amatrix. The two girls close Act
One with a double sonnet of friendship. Within the structure of the
play these lyrics counterpoise the heterosexual lyrics of Act Two.

Her friend Amatrix has similarily to develop a fuller understanding
of her emotions, to work towards a conception of love. For her the task
is, in some respects, harder. She was adopted as a child and has no
knowledge of her mother — save a certainty that she sees her in the
mirror. Not surprisingly she tells Koinonia

I'm all interested in ancestors. Do you know yours?   (*CL*, 9)

Gan's innocent question "Good journey?" prompts a revealing
anecdote:

| AMATRIX | There was a girl weeping at Oxford station saying good-bye to her mother. She was going back to boarding-school. 'I miss you too!' the mother was saying and got on the train, and then the poor girl had to console her weeping mother, and push her off! |
| KOINONIA | There are shadows of sun on the grass.   (*CL*, 12) |

Her loneliness is evident both in her unhappy

I'd give anything to find one person in the world who looks like me
(*CL*, 56)

and in her plea to Koinonia:

I've always wanted a sister; promise we'll be sisters always?
(*CL*, 38)

Koinonia makes no such promise. She has earlier (*CL*, 11) made it clear
that she appreciates the difference between friendship and the bonds of
family loyalty. For Amatrix the absence of family life means that she
has great difficulty in developing or sustaining a meaning for the word
love:

I don't really know what a relative is. Most people grow up loving their parents. It's so normal they don't even think about it. But I can't even imagine what it's like. I won't know till I have a baby. Is that bond different from just loving someone because you have been brought up by them? I don't know. It confuses me so much, the idea of brothers and sisters being more than friends.  (*CL*, 10)

Related to this difficulty, and paralleling the position of Gan, is her relative insecurity as to her sexual role. Fashshar calls her a gynandromorph (*CL*, 14), that is, suggests that she has both male and female characteristics, thus echoing a remark made earlier by Broomy which identifies the hornbeam of Gan and the chestnut of Amatrix:

That's the hard hornbeam. Like the chestnut girl, he has both male and female seeds.  (*CL*, 3)

Broomy has, just before this, described her, in describing her tree:

BROOMY     . . . this magnificent horse-chestnut, young sticky-
            buds bursting into leaves and candles.
GRIOT      What branches!
BROOMY     Including us all in her arms.  (*CL*, 2)

Griot, as we saw earlier, talks of the difficulty experienced by both girls in making the adjustment to a heterosexual world. Amatrix talks of the 'pashes' she had at school (*CL*, 28–9), and herself says, somewhat ruefully:

Funny how hard the transition to men is if you've spent all your life at a girls' boarding school.  (*CL*, 68)

Her whole nature, though, makes her more sensually inclined than Koinonia; indeed her stories of the loss of her virginity and of her "Business Arrangement" for "clumsy Sunday afternoons" (*CL*, 67) of sex appear to move her into territories more obviously occupied by Mara. The problem is to know whether we should believe her stories. The particular anecdotes are introduced as a 'test' of Thalassios. As Amatrix says:

Look! I'll test you, and tell you what I am.  (*CL*, 66)

She may be telling him of the truth of her imagination, but one wonders whether the story really corresponds to any kind of literal truth. Her earlier narrative begins:

> The man I really liked is called Straw     (*CL*, 35)

and he sounds suspiciously like a 'man of straw', a fictional creation. Amatrix's narratives are best understood as imaginative exercises in pursuit of a conception of love. The second Act of the play brings to both girls some experience of the thing itself. The many theoretical definitions of men, women and emotions which they offer in Act One can gradually be replaced by statements of experienced emotion. For them, as for Gan and Thalassios, the play is concerned with the conception of love in more than one sense of that phrase.

The garden, obviously enough, is the play's overriding symbol for comic harmony. In it the elements work together and are united — even fire, ultimately excluded as destructive, is not without its part to play. The women, as well as being, like the men, symbolically associated with certain trees, are constantly associated with flowers in the play's pattern of imagery. Mara is the tulip and in her lyric at parting from Fashshar she reminds us that

> Flowering time is brief,
> Girls cannot linger, waiting love's return.   (*CL*, 73)

Her phrasing here echoes that of Amatrix in her long scene with Thalassios:

> As women have a shorter flowering-time, they can suffer from decision-fatigue. (*CL*, 66)

Amatrix is more than once described as "budding" (*CL*, 2, 14, 39, 57). In the original production she wore a flower in her hair, as did Koinonia.[16] Koinonia's most important set-piece anecdote is about her adventure with her friend Ianthe (whose name derives from the Greek *ianthos* — a violet), an adventure for which they were dressed in white with white roses in their hair (*CL*, 36). Their ceremony of the roses has already been referred to. When Koinonia and Amatrix exchange sonnets to close Act One the imagery of flowers is again prominent, as it is in Koinonia's love lyric to Gan (*CL*, 72). Her final lines extend further the image of the garden:

> My sleeping breasts will rise for you alone.
> Your lips sealed up, my garden is your own.   (*CL*, 72)

The *Requiem* plays were much concerned with the conflict between social sanction and natural instinct. In comedy the two must be seen to be working in harmony. What more perfect emblem of nature and human order working together, of discipline and instinct in co-operation, than the garden? The garden both contains and is the comedy, a comedy of love and the elements. The King of Navarre's "Curious knotted garden"[17] here finds a fellow in which, as befits a comedy, many a knot is firmly tied. As also befits a comedy of love there are knots to be untied first. Gan begins by pursuing Amatrix, Thalassios sets out to woo Koinonia. Where there is a foursome of lovers there ought, in any self-respecting comedy, to be at least one change of partners before the final dance. In searching out their proper partners the characters of *A Conception of Love* are simultaneously defining, by action and choice, their own characters and the "half-defined potential" (*CL*, 45) they find there. There are other important themes in the play which I have left undiscussed: the relationships between individuals and communities for example. It is, though, as a play of love that it is most remarkable. Where the *Requiem* plays picture a bleak and predominantly loveless world, this successor, without ever settling for a merely facile optimism, affirms love's possibility and, indeed, love's realisation. With the chains and circles of the final dance, with the subtly differentiated movements and gestures of the three couples, the play fittingly closes in music.

## Notes

1 *Love's Labour's Lost*, I, i. 13—14.
2 *Ibid.*, I. i. 37.
3 *Ibid.*, IV. iii. 8—9.
4 cf. IV. iii.
5 *Ibid.*, V. ii. 918—9. The line appears only in the Folio text.
6 *Ibid.*, V. ii. 863—4.
7 *As You Like It*, V. iv. 172—3.
8 *Much Ado About Nothing*, V. iv. 113—115.
9 cf. 'The Argument of Comedy' in *English Institute Essays, 1948*, edited D. A. Robertson, New York, 1949.
10 It is ironic that he should find Mara "cold as a cinder" (*CL*, 57).
11 I am indebted to Miss Khairat Al-Saleh for this observation.
12 Northrop Frye, *Anatomy of Criticism* (Orig. publ. 1957), 1971, 165.
13 J. Hastings, *Encyclopaedia of Religion and Ethics*, 1915, Vol. VIII, 407.
14 The episode is included in the *Buddhacarita* of Ashvagosha. An abridged translation is contained in *Buddhist Scriptures*, selected and translated by Edward Conze (1960).
15 Conze, *Buddhist Scriptures*, 48.
16 See the photographs contained in the published text.
17 *Love's Labour's Lost*, I. i. 235.

# X

## *Light Shadows:* The Choir of Love

The two plays which Francis Warner has written since completing
the *Requiem* trilogy have both been composed in response to com-
missions. *A Conception of Love* was commissioned by the *Observer*
as part of the first *Observer* Oxford Festival of Theatre. *Light Shadows*
was commissioned by the Reverend Canon Peter Pilkington, on be-
half of the 1979 Kingsweek Festival Committee, for performance in
Canterbury Cathedral, where it duly received its first performance in
July 1979. In turning to Warner for a play about St. Paul that committee
showed a shrewd understanding of his earlier work. As I have sought to
demonstrate there is much that is Pauline in Warner's thinking in the
*Requiem* plays. Paul's visit to Rome, as recounted in *Acts*, plays, as
we have seen, a crucial role in the final statement made in *Meeting Ends*.
It was both natural and fitting then, that in writing a play explicitly
concerned with St. Paul, Warner should choose to give further consideration to the significance of that visit.

*Light Shadows* (possessor of a characteristically Warnerian punning
title) is in part an examination of the social and intellectual energies
brought to focus in Neronian Rome, energies from which the distinctive
theology we recognise as Pauline was to emerge, influenced but individual. The play is very much a play of ideas. Almost, indeed, a dramatic
debate, though not without its powerfully effective moments of theatre,
sufficient to ensure that it is more than merely a study in the history of
ideas. Like the *Requiem* plays (and to a lesser extent *A Conception of
Love*) it is much concerned with the nature of power and its expression
in a human context. Like those plays it finally asserts the creative
victory of apparent defeat.

Approach to the play's central concerns is best made through examination of the individual 'voices' which make up its larger polyphony. The analogy is not, it should be pointed out, merely a piece of critical impressionism. Scene Nine, for example, is organised upon a kind of permutational, fugal, structure as precisely thought out as that of, for example, Beckett's *Lessness*. The stage direction "Interwoven conversations" (*LS*, 35), gives no indication of how intricately that weaving is carried out to pattern. The scene is shared between six 'voices', plus a single speech by Paul. Perhaps the pattern may best be clarified diagramatically. If we represent the characters as follows (in the order in which they speak): Josephus 1, Luke 2, Seneca 3, Lucan 4, Thecla 5 and Philo 6, then the pattern is as follows:

121321432154321654321Paul654321654321543214321432132121.

The first two speeches of Josephus, for example, are separated by a single speech from Luke. Then his third speech appears after speeches by Luke and Seneca. The fourth follows speeches by Luke, Seneca and Lucan. The fifth, as by now one would expect, succeeds speeches by Luke, Seneca, Lucan and Thecla, while the sixth comes after speeches by all these plus Philo, and the seventh follows speeches by all the other characters on stage, including Paul's single intrusion into the sequence. Josephus' succeeding speeches repeat this sequence in exactly inverted form, so that the whole scene closes, as it began, with two speeches by Josephus separated by one from Luke. The speeches of each of the other five characters are disposed in a similar fashion, as examination of the above diagram will demonstrate. The rhythms thus established throw into relief Paul's single speech, itself expressed in a more formal idiom than any of those that surround it. The interweaving which is patterned so precisely in this scene constitutes a model in small of the polyphonic design of the play as a whole.

If Scene Nine offers a model of the play's form, it is perhaps Nero's remark to Philo "Philo, I've heard of your philosophical banquets" (*LS*, 33) which offers the best internal model of the play's content. Scene Ten actually shows such a symposium, and the play as a whole offers the same kind of debate on a larger scale. Apart from Paul himself, the main voices, each identified with a particular philosophical stance, are those of Petronius, Philo, Josephus, Lucan, and Seneca. Though we must also consider their views it would I think be to stretch terminology unacceptably if we were to call the stances of Nero, Poppaea and Tigellinus 'philosophical'. Warner has set his play in the Rome of the mid-sixties A.D. In fact a number of events are telescoped for dramatic purposes. Seneca talks of "last year's fire", and since he clearly refers to the Great Fire of Rome in 64 A.D. that would give us a date of 65 A.D. for the play's action. The enforced suicide of Petronius, referred to at the close of Scene Twelve, took place in 66 A.D.; the deaths of Seneca and Lucan (Scene Ten) in 65 A.D.; the death of Octavia (also Scene Ten) in 62 A.D. We should not, therefore, regard the play as a sequential historical record, rather as a study in the emotional, and more especially, intellectual climate of a period.

Let us then examine individually each of the main intellectual voices in the play. Philo will serve as a point of departure, if only as a way of marking the fact that he is the only one of the major characters whose presence is chronologically inaccurate. Philo Judaeus was born c. 30 B.C. and is believed to have died at around 45—50 A.D. He came from a wealthy family; he writes of himself that he would have found life unthinkable without his slaves, and we know his brother Alexander to have been one of the very richest men in all the ancient world. Here, in *Light Shadows*, he comments to Seneca:

I enjoy being a Roman citizen. You do. The patrician style. We're both millionaires. (*LS*, 2)

Certainly Philo was not without considerable knowledge of the good life, and the life of pleasure as lived in Alexandria. One authority writes of him thus:

In spite of the preoccupation with metaphysics in his writings, he was an habitué of the theaters, the games, and the banquets of Alexandria. He was a critical observer of the athletics of the day . . . He tells of being at chariot races where excitement ran so high that some of the spectators rushed into the course and were killed . . . . At the theatre, too, he has "often" noticed how differently music affects different people . . . When he attended banquets he had to watch himself carefully "take reason along," as he expresses it, or, as frequently happened, he would become a helpless slave to the pleasures of food and drink. With what satisfaction he recalls the banquets he attended where he did *not* thus lose control of himself.[1]

Much of this is implicitly present in the breezy manner of Philo's exchange with Seneca which opens the play; indeed Warner incorporates a phrase from Philo which we have just seen Goodenough quoting:

| SENECA | Milk? Or wine from the Emperor's vineyard? |
| PHILO | I'm not too old . . . |
| SENECA | Can you still absorb alcohol as you used to? |
| PHILO | Ah! My dinner-parties. I have to take reason along with me now when I go to banquets. But you! Still drinking nothing but running water? No wine? Do you still sleep on those planks? Avoid oysters? |
| SENECA | And mushrooms. |
| PHILO | After our late 'divine' Emperor's death, who doesn't! |

(LS, 1)

(This last allusion is to the death of Claudius who, according to most accounts, died by eating poisoned mushrooms administered by Nero's mother Agrippina. Oysters were another favourite vehicle for poison.) As a philosopher, Philo's life-work was devoted to achieving a fusion of all that he most admired in the Greek philosophical tradition with that other tradition of the Torah which he studied as an orthodox Jew. Philo's commentaries on the Pentateuch offer a distinctly Platonist interpretation of the Jewish faith. In several treatises his ethical philosophy comes very close to that of the Stoics. *On the Virtuous Being also Free* and *On Providence* are particularly interesting from this point of view. It is not surprising, then, that here in *Light Shadows* he should, very early in the play, state some of the grounds he has for agreeing with Seneca (though the agreement is not allowed to pass without a characteristic pun):

| PHILO | You've often written 'Death's no disgrace'. We believe the same; but for different reasons. If we die, we are martyrs, we go to the Eternal Light, our Father in Heaven — like the sun in the sky, the source of all life. |
| SENECA | The shades. Yes. It's better to face death than go against your conscience.  (*LS*, 4) |

Seneca, naturally enough, cannot accept the Judaistic notion of God:

But what you Jews believe about a Father-figure is for children

(LS, 4)

but he certainly recognizes his own philosophical tradition in much of what Philo says:

PHILO           Well, you and I have this in common; we both love the teaching of Socrates. 'The body is the prison-house of the soul.' Yet that remark would stir me up trouble in Jerusalem with the Sadducees! Plato and Moses were really saying much the same thing.

SENECA      You startle me! Almost a Roman!

PHILO           What do you mean? I *am* a Roman citizen.

                                                                     (*LS*, 4)

Philo's thought was fundamentally mystical in character. He was steeped in the Platonic dialogues and it is therefore fitting that Warner should make him allude to the *Phaedrus* on at least two occasions. Having witnessed the brutal murder of Poppaea by Nero, Philo observes that

The charioteer has lost control of the white horse.  (*LS*, 53) [2]

One of his descriptions of Paul:

His body seems like the shell of an oyster, to protect a soul laid bare  (*LS*, 36)

is derived from the same source.[3] His mystical expression, though, never deserts the Judaic tradition; Philo himself always claimed that his work was purely Jewish. He believed that Plato's metaphysical ideas and related elements in Greek mysticism were taken by the Greeks from Moses and so were ultimately Jewish in any case. For Philo God is always the goal of the contemplative's search, and it is a God always conceived of in personal terms, however much the language of Platonism may influence him. His main confession of faith here in *Light Shadows* is very much in line with the kind of ideas to be found in his *On the Creation of the World*:

God exists and rules the world. He is present in all things, like a father's features in the faces of his children. He cares. The goal of all our striving is to leave behind our folly, to purify ourselves until, lifted in contemplation, we receive the eternal vision and become united with the source of all being.  (*LS*, 27)

Not surprisingly the idealist Philo gets short shrift at the hands of Poppaea and Petronius. They mock him repeatedly. Petronius calls him a "sentimental old windbag" (*LS*, 17) for his alleged views on kindness to animals (presumably a reference to his treatise *Alexander, or*

*On the Question Whether Dumb Animals Have the Power of Reason*).
More importantly Philo can be seen as representing, within the play's
intellectual polyphony, that confluence of Hellenism and Judaism
which was associated particularly with Alexandria, Philo's home city.
Philo's intellectual distinction, and the mystical cast of his interpretation of Judaism, are in interesting contrast with the less 'brilliant', more
orthodox, Judaism of Josephus.

Thackeray was surely right to suggest that Josephus had only a
limited acquaintance with the work of Philo — "the deeper philosophy
of Philo being beyond his grasp"[4]. Warner is probably fanciful in
making Josephus claim that

> Philo is our greatest philosopher. I read him as a child and he
> changed my life! (*LS*, 17)

We do, though, know that the historical Josephus did indeed make a
visit to Rome in A.D. 64, and for the reason given by Warner (*LS*, 12).
His acquaintance with Poppaea (to whom he actually applies the epithet
"god-fearing"[5]) and Aliturius, the favourite Jewish actor, also has a
historical basis. As a writer Josephus' work is frequently somewhat
tendentious and excessively rhetorical in manner. Warner presents him
as an eager, but naive, accumulator of information:

> I write all the facts I can learn about our race in this notebook.
> (*LS*, 10)

He himself admits that as a historian he "rambles" and "sticks everything in" (*LS*, 35). To Philo he is a "young gossip" (*LS*, 12). Josephus,
in his naivety, is quite willing to believe that Poppaea's 'conversion' to
Judaism has some sort of religious meaning:

> The Emperor's wife is a religious woman; a convert to our faith.
> (*LS*, 12)

Even Petronius' outrageous recipes are deemed suitable material for his
notebook; historical discrimination appears not to be his strong suit.
Nor does he ever speak with any passion of his religious faith. His 'confession' of faith, matching that of Philo, lacks the dignity or conviction
of the older man's words. His words are words of information, rather
than of belief:

| NERO | Josephus, what have you to say? |
|---|---|
| JOSEPHUS | Our Jewish religion is divided. The Sadducees say there is no resurrection, no angels, no spirit. But I am a Pharisee, like Paul, and we believe in a resurrection.  (*LS*, 27) |

His orthodox Judaism is evident in his insistence upon the importance of the Mosaic Law:

The Law, Paul. That saves!    (*LS*, 28)

At the 'symposium' he is given his chance to offer his 'conception of love'. It is as a traditionalist that he speaks:

My love is of my people, and her customs: of her history and her antiquities, of her wars and achievements . . . we also love the blood that runs in the veins of our race, the blood that sets us apart from other races, and that of which it is a symbol, the teachings of our Jewish Law. Moses himself gave us this commandment, that we should teach our children from their earliest awakening, and he taught that the future felicity of us all depended on our Law being engraved on their minds.  (*LS*, 45)

For all this talk he responds with great facility to Nero's offer of the appointment of Governor of Galilee, despite Nero's offer being expressed in terms which display an offensive misunderstanding of all that Josephus has claimed to stand for. His acceptance of the appointment is a selfish betrayal of his people, as its reception makes clear:

| NERO | If you are prepared to come all this way for a wall and a shipload of priests, you must care, and be prepared to take trouble. Take care and trouble for me, now, and keep them quiet. I don't like the news from the East. |
|---|---|
| JOSEPHUS | What can an individual do against the might of Rome? What can a little nation do against an all-powerful State? What can the Jews do against the Roman world? Rome *is* the world, and has subdued the mightiest nations on earth. There is nowhere else to go. We are not Stoics. We love our ways and our traditions. Allow us those and I will promise you our peace. |
| NERO | Yes, but can you enforce it? |

JOSEPHUS        I am the servant of Rome. As Governor, Rome will
                come first.

                *Applause from all save the Jews present.*  (*LS*, 47)

Josephus' ready act of betrayal contrasts with the behaviour of Epicharis,
narrated by Lucan (to Josephus, significantly) in Scene 3, as well as
with the manner of Seneca's and even Petronius' deaths; above all, of
course, it stands in sharp contrast to the fortitude and faith of Paul.
Josephus may have shared with Paul the experience of shipwreck:

> you and I have been on ships that sank in gales in the Adriatic
> on our ways to Rome    (*LS*, 28)

but the play's epigraph could certainly never be applied to the Josephus
we see here. Galilean Judaism is seen as distinctly limited, though limitations of the tradition itself are here inseparable from the individual
limitations of this particular practitioner of the tradition.

Petronius, of course, represents a radically different social and
philosophical tradition; indeed, he could hardly be more different
from Josephus. Warner's interpretation of Petronius sees him as strongly
influenced by Epicurean thinking, though not without a certain Cynic
tone to his behaviour. Warner makes him quote Epicurus:

> My Emperor; some lines of verse, if you will allow me. My version
> of Epicurus.
>
> > About God there is nothing to fear.
> > When life ends let death come without care.
> > Life's pleasures are yours for the taking,
> > So endure grief without your heart breaking.
> > . . . .
>
> I agree with Seneca, impassiveness is the aim. But we Epicureans
> know it comes from admiration of beauty, from joy in pleasure,
> freedom of spirit unshadowed by worries about death and despair.
> It's the only healthy philosophy, because it cultivates happiness.

                                                    (*LS*, 30–1)

Warner's Petronius has an almost Wildean manner to him. His first
entrance is a delightful piece of paradox and wit which manages to be
simultaneously deprecatory of both himself and his master (*LS*, 14).
His concern for the carefully posed presentation of self is neatly
captured:

SENECA          More sleep and less bed would do you a power of
                good, Petronius. Your style's grown stale.

PETRONIUS       Come now, dear old fool. One week of early nights
                would ruin the haggard complexion! My image,
                please!   (*LS*, 14)

He has, at all times, a certain shrewdness which makes clear his own
sense of the absurdity of his position. His cynical shrewdness does,
though, constitute another kind of limitation on his understanding.
Having seen Nero, in Scene 7, overwhelmed by Paul's words, he
comments:

What a clash of fantasies! Our divine Emperor has forgiven you
Jews for the wrong reasons. Whether you look on it as an endearing
mannerism or a confounded nuisance, he judges on whim.

(*LS*, 34)

Since Paul's speech has, in part, been concerned with the divine capacity for forgiveness, there is a knowing impudence about the use of
the phrase "our divine Emperor". He can see that Nero's attraction to
Paul is based entirely upon a failure to understand Paul, that it is no
more than a fantasy. What he can't understand is that Paul's own words
represent something more than a fantasy. Faith on the scale of Paul's
faith is beyond Petronius' imaginative range. His speech which opens
the symposium of Scene 10 is a piece of sustained and impudent
paradox during which one suspects that the tongue only very briefly
leaves the cheek. His concluding remark: "My dish is served" (*LS*, 44)
suggests that the whole speech is to be taken no more seriously than
his menu (fit to rival those of Eumolpus), which Josephus writes down
so solemnly (*LS*, 15). Warner's Petronius has an attractive unwillingness
to take either himself or his contemporaries very seriously. His mockery
plays equally upon all. Oscar Raith has argued at length for Petronius'
Epicureanism. H. D. Rankin's qualification of this view corresponds
more closely with Warner's interpretation:

Epicureanism seems to fit the attitude of disengagement which
he put forward as a mask, and his death was more Epicurean than
anything else . . . His *ignavia* could be either Epicurean or Cynic:
his *neglegentia sui* and his delight in saying outrageous, self-
incriminating things suggest (superficially) the attitudes of a Cynic
. . . In fact, there is no reason to regard him as a serious philosopher
at all . . . He was more artist than philosopher.[7]

Warner's Petronius (nowhere is his authorship of the *Satyricon* alluded to) is very much the social artist, the *arbiter elegantiae excellentissimus*. Though emotionally detached from the people around him, he seems thoroughly involved when seeing himself as the artist disposing the life of the court. His characteristic irony is not absent, but he seems to mean what he says when he addresses to Seneca his claim for the attention of posterity:

> Oh dear, old schoolmaster. My skills will make me more famous than your poets. My shaping taste at the court of our god will be seen by history as a diamond sparkling on the finger of time. A way there, for the goddess Poppaea! (*LS*, 16)

The supreme moment of Petronius' artistry comes at his death. Having acquired what Rankin calls the "protective colouring"[8] of the mannerisms of the Neronian court, Petronius used those very mannerisms as a means of mocking that court in the manner of his death. In his death the mockery was turned on both

> the pleasures and philosophies of the society in which he had chosen to live, and bitterly ridiculed its arch-representative, Nero.[9]

Warner's brief account is put in the mouth of Tigellinus, Petronius' inveterate rival:

> Petronius! He cut his veins, bound them up again, beat his slaves, wrote out a list of Nero's sexual habits and sent them round to him under seal. Then came to dinner, and died during the dessert.
>
> (*LS*, 58)

The account derives from Tacitus; though somewhat briefer than its source, it makes clear the artistic strategy of Petronius' death. It offers a virtual parody of that kind of enforced suicide which, as A. D. Nock writes, had become "the Stoic form of martyrdom *par excellence*"[10] in the first century A.D. To cut one's veins was in the best Stoic tradition — but then to bind them up and come to dinner! To chatter and beat one's slaves, rather than discoursing philosophically upon the immortality of the soul! Where the Stoic behaved so as to gain a reputation for fortitude, Petronius seems to have behaved so as to ensure that he kept up his 'image' of triviality. Tested, he maintained his integrity, unlike the figure of Josephus whom we have just considered. As a final touch, Petronius' 'will' was not the fulsome flattery of Nero customary upon such occasions. Yet, in a final paradox, the list of Nero's sexual perversions *might* be construed as a kind of praise when received from a cynically inclined Epicurean! Nero, the Roman actor, receives a last prompt from his faithful stage-manager.

In Lucan we meet another figure whose attitude towards Nero is ambiguous, though sustained with less complex and conscious irony than that of Petronius. Warner's Lucan is at times impetuous and immature — adjectives which might reasonably be applied to some of his surviving verse, but which would certainly not be apt for Petronius. Lucan's behaviour is that of a young man. Warner puts in his mouth sentiments from his *Pharsalia*. His early angry outburst:

> May Rome be cursed! The Medes and Arabs are content to be slaves. They've never known anything else. Once, we had democratically elected officers. The centuries are out of control, driven by blind chance   (*LS*, 12)

for example, derives from a powerful passage in Book 7 of the *Pharsalia*:

> felices Arabes Medique Eoaque tellus,
> quam sub perpetuis tenuerunt fata tyrannis.
> ex populis qui regna ferunt sors ultima nostra est,
> quos servire pudet. sunt nobis nulla profecto
> numina: cum caeco rapiantur saecula casu,
> mentimur regnare Iovem.[11]

His final words of the play, though, take the form of a quotation from Seneca:

| NERO | No word for me? |
|---|---|
| LUCAN | Only this. 'However many men you kill, Nero, you can never kill your successor.' |
| NERO | Lucan, you too are condemned.   (*LS*, 51) |

Coming as it does immediately on the heels of Lucan's moving account of Seneca's death this quotation is a brave gesture of defiance. Nero's response is revealing, as is Petronius' playful (but eminently serious) attempt to tease the tyrant out of his blood-lust:

| NERO | Lucan, you too are condemned. You know why. (*Brightening suddenly*) I feel better now! There's nothing like getting rid of your old teacher! I loved you. I trusted you. You betrayed me. I will not soil the arena with the poetry in your veins. You are a Stoic who has lost his faith. You may choose the way you die. |
|---|---|

| | |
|---|---|
| TIGELLINUS | (*Seizing Lucan*) He has a knife! |
| PETRONIUS | Who would not rather have his property dis-ordered than his curls? Nero, not the death sentence! His poems immortalize you! |
| NERO | Ambiguously.   (*LS*, 51) |

Nero's savagery does not blind him to the political propaganda inherent in the kinds of martyrdoms it produces. Lucan's hasty production of a knife — whether to take his own life or Nero's, or both — presents us with yet another of the play's variations on the theme of personal responses to extreme pressure. The gesture lacks either the ritual dignity of Seneca's death, or the ironic artistry of Petronius' final hours. Naturally, it falls far short of Paul's simple and absolute forti-tude. It does, though, confirm precisely that sense of the young man influenced by Stoicism, but too eager for action, too readily moved to passion, to be able to be a Stoic — the sense, in short, that is created in Scene 2 in his first appearance in the play. His passion there, in the face of adversity, startles and disappoints Seneca:

| | |
|---|---|
| LUCAN | Uncle, I must talk to you! . . . Father's taken, Piso's condemned! The praetorian guard with that despicable prefect Tigellinus is interrogating Subrius Flavius now! |
| SENECA | (*Shocked*) Why weep? Cause and effect draw all things in their course. Why pray?   (*LS*, 8) |

Lucan was almost of an age with Nero, and the two were originally friends. Indeed in A.D. 59 Nero recalled him from Athens and made him quaestor and augur, as he recounts in Scene 2 of *Light Shadows* (*LS*, 8–9). Some accounts suggest that his subsequent estrangement from Nero was due to his increasing sympathy with Stoicism, but Warner's presentation of him leans more towards the interpretation offered by Ahl,[12] who attributes it to the outspoken nature of Lucan's comments in the lost *De Incendio Urbis*. Warner's Lucan himself offers this explanation:

> Nero turned against me. He disliked my poem on the Great Fire. Banned me reading my poetry; has stopped my professional life in the law-courts. I'm two years younger than he is. Only twenty-five. I write, must publish! He does. And he used to love my poems.
>
> (*LS*, 9)

There is a hint here too of Nero's jealousy of a better poet. This explanation is stressed by both Tacitus and (even more forcefully) Suetonius, in his unsympathetic brief life of Lucan. Certainly, here in *Light Shadows* Petronius sees dispraise of Lucan's poetry as a means of currying favour with Nero (*LS*, 43). Warner's Lucan, though, is not the largely apolitical figure of Suetonius. He is eager to act against Nero:

> SENECA      We are walled in by birth and death, and Nero controls half the architecture.
>
> LUCAN      Now can we act? Seneca, please! (*Seneca raises a warning hand*).    (*LS*, 34)

His poetry is seen as having a very specific political relevance to the contemporary situation. Scholars and critics continue to argue about the apotheosis of Nero in Book One of the *Pharsalia*: is it, or is it not, to be taken ironically?[14] Warner's Lucan is quite explicit about its nature and purpose:

> If he asks once more for the panegyric I wrote, I'll give it him in all its sarcasm.    (*LS*, 37)

As we have seen, Nero is not blind to the ambiguity of Lucan's lines (*LS*, 51). Lucan makes his feelings clear in another effective piece of stage business. Nero's entry, self-proclaiming his divinity, is greeted by the inevitable paid applause and by cries of "Kyrios Caesar!" from Poppaea, Seneca, Petronius, Tigellinus, Philo and Josephus; Lucan's silence is noticeable and noticed. Nero comments, making a term of affection carry a chilling quality of threat:

> Lucan, dear boy, your voice is not raised! Every act is political, even as all politics is an act. I am the Lord thy god.    (*LS*, 22)

Nero's menaces combine the political and the literary:

> My court is a court of poets; isn't it, Lucan? Some of them silent.
> (*LS*, 23)

A philosophical voice which remains to be considered is that of Seneca. Seneca remains an intriguing and puzzling figure; his relationship with Nero retains some unresolved ambiguities. Banished to Corsica in A.D. 41 by Caligula, he was recalled at the instigation of Agrippina in A.D. 49, and appointed Nero's tutor; upon Nero's succession, Burrus and Seneca acted as the new ruler's main advisers.

Agrippina's murder in A.D. 59 signalled the beginning of the decline of Seneca's influence, and the death of Burrus in A.D. 62 prompted the philosopher to seek the safer life of retirement. Always sickly, and given to austerity (yet he accumulated enormous estates), his role as philosopher behind the throne had evident Platonic overtones. Yet his doctrines can hardly be said to have controlled Nero for very long; Nero was hardly the ideal pupil for a philosopher who dedicated to him an important essay entitled *On Clemency*! The Seneca whose thinking we know from the plays and the philosophical essays returns repeatedly to the problem of achieving some kind of reconciliation between the demands of personal morality and the necessities of political activity. His writings dwell on both the evils of tyranny and the virtue of those who resist it. He clearly sought at least to moderate Nero's brutality, and doubtless felt that by staying at his side he could at least exert some influence for good. Pandering to Nero's desires to be actor and singer, racer of chariots, might at least serve to distract him from more violent pursuits. Eventually, and most notably after the murder of Agrippina and the rise of Tigellinus, he was forced to the conclusion that such moderating influence could no longer be exerted — "the cub is now a lion" (*LS*, 1) — and the life of retirement seemed a more sensible choice. Of course he could not, ultimately, be allowed to make such a choice. His enforced suicide was an inevitable consequence. Much of his surviving literary work dates from the brief interval of retirement. The *Epistulae* are restrained in their stoicism; no violent claims are made, the tone is that of a man moderately, but with determination, making himself ready to meet calmly any misfortunes being prepared for him. In expression Seneca's style is characterised by the prevailing brevity and epigrammatic quality of his sentences. Aubrey quotes Kettall's splendid observation that

Seneca writes, as a Boare does pisse, *scilicet* by jirkes.[15]

In both content and manner Warner's Seneca captures a good deal of his original:

A wise man does not provoke those in power. The mast breaks, the reed bends. (*LS*, 3)

God is fate, necessity, Nature. If we follow the world, with detachment, with tranquility of soul, we follow God. (*LS*, 28)

His arguments come close to offering an explicit elucidation of the play's title:

If good exists . . . then we can only know it by the simultaneous presence of evil.  (*LS*, 5)

Shadows can only exist in the presence of light, and light necessarily produces shadows. Each is a certain proof of the existence of the other. Legend (and forgery) had it that Seneca was in correspondence with Paul. Certainly, an assertion such as his

In all adversities we are more than conquerors   (*LS*, 27)

comes very close to Agappy's specifically Christian notion that

My defeats I should count as victories.   (*ME*, 44; *R*, 240)

Scene 7 of *Light Shadows* shows us Paul and Seneca coming as near to one another as they are able, but it also makes clear how wide the remaining gap necessarily is:

| | |
|---|---|
| SENECA | In all adversities we are more than conquerors. |
| PAUL | But only through Christ that loved us. |
| SENECA | There, Nero, we part company . . . |
| | Do you agree that the free man withdraws from the passions — joy, hate, excitement and desire — and so becomes true master of himself? |
| PAUL | We lack that power without God's grace; and rightly used, the passions are the gifts of God. |
| SENECA | Rightly used? |
| PAUL | We all sin, and need an external Saviour. |
| SENECA | God is fate, necessity, Nature. If we follow the world, with detachment, with tranquillity of soul, we follow God. |
| PAUL | Yes, we must overcome our nature, but we can only do so with Grace. On our own we can do nothing.  (*LS*, 27—8) |

Here is the philosophical and theological core of the play. Seneca's vision halts at precisely that point where Paul's takes its strength from belief in, and experience of, a personal God capable of extending His grace to a suffering humanity. The notion of divine personality is quite alien to Seneca's patterns of thought (*LS*, 4—5). In that difference lies a measure of the difference between the 'martyrdoms' of Seneca and Paul. Lucan's account of Seneca's death makes clear its 'Socratic' overtones (*LS*, 50—1). His death, though, is largely a matter of escape. Seneca hurries to death

> Longing to leap into eternal light
> And leave this night of aching flesh behind,
> He took some hemlock from a hiding-place
> And made libation, both to Socrates,
> And Jupiter who sets all prisoners free.   (*LS*, 51)

There is no suggestion that by his death Nero is at all likely to learn anything, least of all any kind of respect for Seneca or his ideals. Scene 13, on the other hand, shows us a Nero who has lost the initiative to Paul, a Paul who makes specific allusion to the 'props' of Socratic and Stoic martyrdom:

> NERO      Why are you, of all men, the only person I have
>           ever met who is totally unafraid of his own death?
> PAUL      My life is already poured out as a libation. I need
>           no hemlock. But our petty libations are returned
>           beyond our imaginings in Christ's own blood.
>
>                                                    (*LS*, 59)

Seneca, like Petronius and Lucan, had good reason to see the danger represented by Tigellinus. It was he who had taken over Seneca's role as counsellor to the Emperor. His philistinism made him an obvious enemy of Lucan's. His lavishness in the organisation of revelry established a rivalry between Petronius and Tigellinus. To Lucan he is "that damned Tigellinus" (*LS*, 9). Petronius dismisses him as "that second-hand horse-dealer" (*LS*, 15) and it is he too who takes great pleasure in recounting a story which Warner has adapted from Tacitus:

> Do you remember, Empress? When he was breaking the legs of Octavia's maid, she said that Tigellinus's mouth was less clean than any part of her mistress's anatomy.   (*LS*, 20)

Violence is Tigellinus' philosophy, if by philosophy we mean a system whereby a man shapes the conduct of his life. Faced with Paul's Christianity he can only endeavour to flog it out of him (*LS*, 29). Paul's "mighty poem" (*LS*, 49) on love is succeeded by Tigellinus' presentation of the head of Octavia. This simultaneously constitutes his contribution to the love-debate ("This is my speech" (*LS*, 49)) and serves as a characteristically toadying gesture designed to bolster his own insecure position. He brings the head because of what he has overheard in Scene 5. When it fails to please Nero he can only complain:

Where's your old sense of fun?      (*LS*, 49)

After Scene 13 has shown us Nero kneeling before Paul, it is only
fitting that Tigellinus should become candle-bearer to Paul, that all
unaware of the significance of what he is doing he should become an
executioner who guarantees the eternal life of his victim (*LS*, 61).

Poppaea follows in the succession of Warner's sensual women as
obviously as Tigellinus succeeds Shango. Lucan's is the first description we are given of her:

> Married, and a son by Crispinus. Has been sleeping with Otho, the
> man Nero appointed to guard her . . . It was Poppaea who nagged
> him into killing his mother.  (*LS*, 10)

Before long we see her prompting another murder:

> Agrippina? She's well rid of. She wanted him to stay with Octavia.
> Petronius! Bring me her head.  (*LS*, 18)

Petronius may treat the request as a joke (though it was scarcely
intended as one) but the overhearing Tigellinus is perfectly ready to
ensure that the request is performed. She deals out death at the very
time that she is pregnant. We are not very far here from the kind of
symbolic role filled by Epigyne in *Lying Figures*. Neither pregnancy, of
course, is allowed to produce new life. Her callousness is at its height
when Tigellinus presents her with the gift and she has the moral impudence to invoke the child in her womb as some sort of justification:

| NERO | Poppaea, did you order this? |
|---|---|
| POPPAEA | You wished it. |
| NERO | Did you order this? |
| POPPAEA | Do you want the child you and I have created, the baby now kicking me, to come into a world where Nero's ex-wife sneers? Look at her. She looks better dead.  (*LS*, 49) |

The brutality of her death may stun, but it is a perfect symbol for the
destructive barrenness of this pair.[16]

The deed is certainly thoroughly characteristic of its perpetrator,
Nero. Warner's Nero is interestingly presented as a figure who is simultaneously corrupter and corrupted. The play's first mention of him
comes from Philo:

I hear Emperor Nero has been bathing in the source of the Marcian
aqueduct, filthying its holy waters.  (*LS*, 1)

It may be water that is polluted here, but it is blood that is Nero's
natural element. It is in the antithesis between milk and blood that the
antithesis between Paul and Nero finds symbolic expression (*cf. LS*,
1, 6, 7, 21, 45, 59). The difference is expressed cryptically, but powerfully, by Philo:

Nero's world is that of Hagar, but Paul's that of Sarah.  (*LS*, 53)

Philo's writings return on a number of occasions to his allegorical
interpretation of Abraham's relations with Hagar and Sarah.[17] His
interpretation is part of an argument (though in Philo's work it is more
often an assumption than a real argument) as to the true reality of the
immaterial and the limited reality of the material. Studies such as
grammar, rhetoric and dialectic are limited by the observations of the
senses. They do not correspond to the highest requirements and capaci-
ties of the human soul. Abraham's first relations were with his concubine
Hagar, and those relations produced Ishmael, the Sophist or pedagogue.
Those relations represent allegorically such scholarship, such learning,
as fails to transcend the material. However, both Ishmael and Hagar
have to be dismissed from the presence of the fully developed Abraham
and Sarah. Sarah, in this interpretation, becomes Philo's version of
heavenly Sophia or Wisdom. Sarah, as Sophia, is seen as embodying
the heavenly light. The burden of Philo's remark thus becomes clear.
　　Nero is confined to the world of Hagar, the world of the material,
the world of the shadows in the Platonic cave. He is unable to see
beyond the material. Our first sight of Nero is as

*a Greek tragic actor, high on cothurni, holding mask.*　　(*LS*, 21)

The relevance of another meaning of the word 'shadow' is thus established. Like Massinger's Domitian, Warner's Nero is a Roman Actor.
His chosen role is as God:

I have absolute power, over all races, and languages, and nations . . .
The Roman Empire is the world, and I am its god.  (*LS*, 21)

The limitations of his vision are both cause and function of his mega-
lomania. As God figure he necessarily imagines himself a creator, a
poet whose creations have a cosmic significance:

my new poem far outshines any that has been written since the creation of the world. It brings joy!     (*LS*, 23)

The poem we are offered is, in fact, Warner's rewriting of a speech actually delivered in Greece in A.D. 67. The original survives on an inscription from Acraephia in Boeotia. Even more fully than its original Warner's version illustrates Nero's complacent inability to perceive the meaning of the very values he claims to admire:

Listen! This is addressed to the Greeks, my beloved race, the heirs of Sophocles and Pericles.

> O men of Hellas! Hold a gift from me
> Unparalleled in magnanimity
> Beyond your faltering hopes. Ask! You shall find
> No gift beyond the greatness of my mind.
> Freedom is granted, and all taxes cease
> For Greeks in Achaea and the Peloponnese.
> Even your happiest era could not dream
> A Roman Emperor and a Philhellene
> Would one day rise to set your people free,
> Bringing back Saturn's golden age in me!
> Caesars exempted cities. I alone
> Protect an entire province as my own.     (*LS*, 23)

The reader may like to compare this with its original:

Men of Hellas, I give you an unlooked for gift — if indeed anything may not be hoped for from one of my greatness of mind — a gift so great, you were incapable of asking for it. All Greeks inhabiting Achaea and the land called till now the Peloponnese receive freedom and immunity from taxes, something which not all of you enjoyed even in your happiest days; for you were subject to strangers or to each other. I wish I were giving this gift when Hellas was still flourishing so that more people might enjoy the benefit, and I blame time itself for spending in advance the greatness of my gift. But I am bestowing this benefaction on you not out of pity but out of good will, in recompense to your gods whose care for me both on land and on sea I have never found wanting, and who are affording me an opportunity to bestow so great a benefaction; for other rulers have granted freedom to cities, but Nero alone to an entire province.[18]

The pattern of a man unable to penetrate to the substance which casts the shadow is repeated elsewhere. In Scene 7 he is overwhelmed by the power of Paul's beautifully expressed convictions, but the scene closes with a speech from Nero which, while praising Paul, demonstrates spectacularly that Nero has altogether failed to see the point. Paul's words act only as a kind of prompt producing Nero's ludicrous appearance as the shepherd-king:

> I'm the first shepherd-boy king to be expert on the water-organ.
>
> (*LS*, 41)

The dilettante has found a new role which may amuse him for a while at least. One more shadow serves to distract him from the light. It is clear that he sees all life, certainly all religious life, as a form of theatre. When Josephus complains of Agrippa's banquet hall built for amused observation of Jewish religious rites, Nero's sympathy is expressed in terms which serve only to trivialise the whole issue, and to betray his repeated failure to understand:

> I hate to be watched when I'm rehearsing.   (*LS*, 46)

So thoroughly is Nero preoccupied by shadows that finally, in Scene 13, he is quite incapable of seeing the light which Paul offers him. The whole movement of that scene makes it clear that the real power resides with Paul. It is only *a* candle, not *the* candle which Nero and Tigellinus can extinguish.

Seneca has earlier observed that "without an antagonist, virtue withers" (*LS*, 19); given the theological perspective provided by Paul, Tigellinus and Nero readily fall into place as parts of the divine scheme which ensures that the play's conclusion will repeat the truth stumbled upon by Nero earlier in commenting upon Tigellinus' torture of Paul:

> Tigellinus, you have strengthened not broken him    (*LS*, 33)

Paul has prepared the ground as early as Scene 7:

> You see me here before you, scourged, and in chains; yet I am free . . . As the loveliest of all our poets, the Psalmist, sang, 'For thy sake are we killed all the day long. We are accounted as sheep for the slaughter.' *(LS*, 31–2)

The words given to Paul in *Light Shadows* are largely translations and adaptations of Biblical originals. Warner appears to have made his own translations, and my own knowledge of Biblical Greek is far too slight for me to be able to comment on their accuracy. One or two passages offer, though, particularly interesting instances of adaptation, inviting comment. In Scene 7 Paul's conversation with Nero borrows extensively from Chapter 17 of *Acts*:

> As I wandered round Athens, I came across an altar dedicated 'To the Unknown God'. The God I proclaim is the one you already worship . . . The God who made the world cannot, of course, be confined to a building, however splendid. He created the human race who built the temples. And why did he create the human race? So that we might look for him and find him again. The temples are outward emblems of our childish attempts. But he is not far from any of us. As the poet Epimenides wrote before Athens became great, 'In him we live and move and have our being'. And as your Stoic poet Cleanthes also wrote, long after Athens had fallen, 'The children of God are we all.'    (*LS*, 26)

In the Biblical original Paul does not specify the sources of his quotations: in the Authorised Version the relevant verse reads:

> For in him we live, and move, and have our being; as certain also of your own poets have said, For we are also his offspring.
> (*Acts*, 17:28)

The scholarly tone of Warner's version is a neat touch; Paul, after all, is addressing a Philhellene Emperor who aggressively asserts his own poetic skills. Elsewhere Paul recounts his ability to establish an identity with those he addresses: weak like the weak, a strict Jew with the Jews, and so on (*LS*, 31–2); here Warner shows him doing the very same thing. On the whole it must be said that Warner copes well with the problem of adapting Paul's epistolary style to the necessarily more 'conversational' idiom of drama. Naturally such set pieces as Nero's 'Symposium' present less of a problem. Paul's hymn to love (*LS*, 48) is, of course, adapted from chapter 13 of the *First Epistle to the Corinthians*. Elsewhere his explanation of the doctrine of resurrection, to the uncomprehending Nero (*LS*, 60), is an adaptation of chapter 15 of the same epistle. What Nero calls his "trumpet-blast out of the Eastern province" (*LS*, 32) adapts chapter 8, verses 31–39, of the *Epistle to the Romans*. Warner's treatment of this passage is interesting. The adaptation here omits one verse: verse 37 in the Authorised Version. The 'missing' verse reads:

Nay, in all these things we are more than conquerors through him that loved us.

Warner omits the verse from Paul's "trumpet-blast" for the simple reason that he has already made even more dramatically effective use of it, earlier in the same scene (scene 7). The verse, in effect, is split between Seneca and Paul:

SENECA      In all adversities we are more than conquerors.
PAUL        But only through Christ that loved us.  (*LS*, 27)

There, in microcosm, is a whole philosophical thesis. The Stoic approaches what is, in the most literal of all senses, a crucial truth, but it is only Paul, the Christian, who can make complete the statement of the truth.

Elsewhere Paul's words adapt passages from *Acts* (9:1–17) in the narration of his experience on the road to Damascus (*LS*, 28–9); from *Galatians* (3:28–9) in explaining how all who accept the love of Christ are made heirs of Abraham (*LS*, 54), and from a number of the other Pauline epistles at other points in the play. Warner's Paul is, above all, an apostle of love. He is the most eloquent spokesman for that conception of love which not only gives the title to one of Warner's plays, but which lies at the very centre of his dramatic work. Love tested and found wanting, love which is strengthened by suffering, love which offers no betrayal, love which redeems – these are the characteristically Warnerian themes. In Paul's conception of love resides that essential optimism of plays which may well appear bleakly pessimistic. The epigraph chosen for *Light Shadows* adds a particular gloss on this central preoccupation of Warner's plays.

The title page of *Light Shadows* bears as its epigraph the following words:

tossed in the welter, you still had vision.

The words are taken from Porphyry's *Life of Plotinus*, where they are part of the verse oracle delivered to Amelius after the death of Plotinus. The oracle takes the form, in fact, of an address to Plotinus and describes a journey across the sea of life, ending in instant transfiguration. The oracle thus invoked by Warner's epigraph has so much relevance to the play's vision of Paul that it must be quoted at some length:

Celestial! Man at first but now nearing the diviner ranks! the bonds of human necessity are loosed for you and, strong of heart, you beat your eager way from out the roaring tumult of the fleshly life to the shores of that wave-washed coast free from the thronging of the guilty, thence to take the grateful path of the sinless soul:

Where glows the splendour of God, where Right is throned in the stainless place, far from the wrong that mocks at law.

Oft-times as you strove to rise above the bitter waves of this blood-drenched life, above the sickening whirl, toiling in the midmost of the rushing flood and the unimaginable turmoil, oft-times, from the Ever-Blessed, there was shown to you the Term still close at hand:

Oft-times, when your mind thrust out awry and was like to be rapt down unsanctioned paths, the Immortals themselves prevented, guiding you on the straightgoing way to the celestial spheres, pouring down before you a dense shaft of light that your eyes might see from amid the mournful gloom.

Sleep never closed those eyes: high above the heavy murk of the mist you held them; tossed in the welter, you still had vision; still you saw sights many and fair not granted to all that labour in wisdom's quest.

But now that you have cast the screen aside, quitted the tomb that held your lofty soul, you enter at once the heavenly consort:

Where fragrant breezes play, where all is unison and winning tenderness and guileless joy, and the place is lavish of the nectarstreams the unfailing Gods bestow, with the blandishments of the Loves, and delicious airs, and tranquil sky:

Where Minos and Rhadamanthus dwell, great brethren of the golden race of mighty Zeus; where dwell the just Aeacus, and Plato, consecrated power, and stately Pythagoras and all else that form the Choir of Immortal Love, there where the heart is ever lifted in joyous festival.

O Blessed One, you have fought your many fights; now, crowned with unfading life, your days are with the Ever-Holy.[19]

The sea-storms in which St. Paul has been tossed are not, of course, merely matters of Mediterranean tempests. The waters are, as they so often are in neo-Platonism, the 'waters of emotion and passion'.[20] They are, indeed, the waves of this "blood-drinking life" — a phrase which offers a precise definition of the limits of Nero's 'spiritual' vision. Told by Paul that

our petty libations are returned beyond our imaginings in Christ's own blood   (*LS*, 59) he can only wonder whether Paul refers to "the ritual drinking of blood" (*LS*, 59).

If Plotinus is released from the "tomb", Paul is similarly released from "that tormented body" which is "God's Temple" (*LS*, 55). The shaft of light vouchsafed to Plotinus is the very same shaft of light that Quark and Ensoff perceive and celebrate in their respective plays.

As *Light Shadows* moves towards its inevitable conclusion, it is indeed true that Paul has "fought . . . many fights" and that he is now "crowned with unfading life". For all that Nero is too much a creature of the shadows to be able to apprehend the light which Paul bears, he does, however little he understands the significance of the moment, kneel before Paul and receive his blessing. Paul approaches his death with a certainty and joy that are far more than merely Senecan. He will accept no stoic suicide:

> I will not take the life God has given me.   (*LS*, 61)

This is a death, not of stoic resignation, but a death which is a triumph of love. Yeats, like all neo-Platonists, was familiar with Porphyry's life of Plotinus. His poem 'The Delphic Oracle Upon Plotinus' is based directly upon it. That poem offers a vision of heaven where

> Scattered on the level grass
> Or winding through the grove
> Plato there and Minos pass,
> There stately Pythagoras
> And all the choir of love.

*Light Shadows* is an unmistakable affirmation of the belief that St. Paul takes his place as a peculiarly pre-eminent member of that same choir. The dramatic process by which he establishes his claim to such a place is characteristically Warnerian in its play of light and shade. This is only the latest in a series of plays which are fundamentally religious in nature, and of which we might use some words spoken by the Chorus in another play written for Canterbury:

> For all things exist only as seen by Thee, only as known by Thee, all things exist
> Only in Thy light, and Thy glory is declared even in that which denies Thee; the darkness declares the glory of light.[21]

## Notes

1   E. R. Goodenough, *An Introduction to Philo Judaeus*, 1940, pp. 8—9.
2   *Phaedrus*, 246a, *ff.*
3   *Phaedrus*, 250c.
4   H. St John Thackeray, *Josephus: The Man and the Historian*, reprinted 1967, p. 94.
5   *Jewish Antiquities*, XX, p. 195.
6   O. Raith, *Petronius ein Epikureer*, Diss. Erlangen, 1963.
7   H. D. Rankin, *Petronius the Artist. Essays on the Satyricon and its Author*, The Hague, 1971, p. 4.
8   *Ibid.*, p. 80.
9   *Ibid.*, p. 81.
10  A. D. Nock, *Conversion*, Oxford, 1933, p. 197.
11  *Pharsalia*, 7, 442—7.
12  F. M. Ahl, 'Lucan's *De Incendio Urbis*, *Epistulae ex Campania* and Nero's Ban', *Transactions of the American Philological Association*, 102, (1971), 1—27; *Lucan: An Introduction*, Ithaca, 1976.
13  Petronius' comments echo a passage in *The Satyricon* (118).
14  See the discussion in Ahl's *Lucan: An Introduction*, pp. 477 *ff.*, and his bibliography on this topic.
15  John Aubrey, *Brief Lives*, ed. O. L. Dick, 1949, p. 186.
16  Tacitus attributes the fatal kick to "a chance fit of anger" on Nero's part, and makes surprisingly little of the incident.
17  See Goodenough, *op. cit.*, pp. 179 *ff.*
18  Quoted from B. H. Warmington, *Nero, Reality and Legend*. 1969, pp. 117—8.
19  Plotinus, *The Ethical Treatises*, transl. S. MacKenna, 1926, Vol. I, pp. 22—3.
20  F. A. C. Wilson, *W. B. Yeats and Tradition*, 1958, p. 199.
21  T. S. Eliot, *Murder in the Cathedral*, Part II, final chorus.

# Index of Works and Characters

Main entries are indicated by figures in italics. The names of individual characters are not indexed where they occur within the pages referred to by the main entry under the title of the play in which they appear.

# General Index

230